Protecting Privacy in China

Hao Wàng

Protecting Privacy in China

A Research on China's Privacy Standards and the Possibility of Establishing the Right to Privacy and the Information Privacy Protection Legislation in Modern China

Springer

Dr. Hao Wang
Renmin University of China
Law School
Zhongguancun Street, No 56
100872 Beijing
China
whsgdsb@gmail.com

ISBN 978-3-642-21749-4 e-ISBN 978-3-642-21750-0
DOI 10.1007/978-3-642-21750-0
Springer Heidelberg Dordrecht London New York

Library of Congress Control Number: 2011935347

Printed on acid-free paper

Springer is part of Springer Science+Business Media (www.springer.com)

Preface

Today, privacy is one of the most hotly debated topics worldwide. However, the development of privacy protection in the People's Republic of China is at least 30 years behind that of Western countries. At present, in China, there are no comprehensive legal principles protecting privacy interests. Most importantly, due to the fact that there is no working definition of privacy in China, the general population of China does not know what the concept of privacy is.

The main aim of this book is to consider how to effectively protect privacy in China. The book thus examines privacy standards in both traditional and modern Chinese society. Moreover, in order to consider how the Chinese laws ought to protect the privacy of the individual, this book also involves a study of other developed countries experiences. This is because, compared to China's privacy protection, there is a high level of privacy protection in certain Western developed countries. Some real advances have not been reflected in Chinese laws, such as the effective protection of privacy interests through information-handling practices.

Based on the Chinese traditions and overseas principles for privacy protection, I realize that two prerequisites of protecting privacy are necessary. First, it is necessary for China, which is moving toward greater democracy, to create the general right to privacy under the Chinese legal system. The creation of the right to privacy will be beneficial to both individual and public. Second, if China wishes to participate fully in the global information community and achieve benefits, we must be prepared to establish an effective privacy protection regime. I believe that the question of how to reasonably deal with privacy issues will be the most significant debate in the Chinese juristic domain in the near future. Therefore, it is hoped that this book will provide an inspiration, or a precedent, for further studies in relation to the protection of privacy in China.

This book is designed to meet the needs of a range of people. Those who study or want to understand Chinese Privacy Law or Industrial Relations streams in Chinese Law will benefit from the book's concise presentation of material. The book also has sufficient detail on key points and a convenient layout that enables it to be a study partner for students of law.

I have been fortunate during the preparation of this book to have received the help and encouragement of many people. First, I owe the greatest thanks to Professor Peter Gillies and Mr John Selby for their valuable support and guidance. Second, I would like to thank Associate Professor Hope Ashiabor, who encouraged me constantly during my study. In addition, many other colleagues in Law School of Macquarie University, including Ms Jiang Xiaoyi and Mr Zhao Xiaobo, have assisted me greatly during this study.

Hao Wang

Contents

Abbreviations

ALRC	Australian Law Reform Commission
APEC	Asia-Pacific Economic Cooperation
BSA	Broadcasting Standards Authority
CNP	Chinese Nationalist Party
CPC	Communist Party of China
ECHR	European Convention on Human Rights
EU	European Union
GPCL	General Principles of the Civil Law of the People's Republic of China
GPS	Global Positioning System
ICCPR	International Covenant on Civil and Political Rights
IPPs	Australian Information Privacy Principles (Cth)
NPC	National People's Congress
NPPs	Australian National Privacy Principles (Cth)
NSW	New South Wales
OECD	Organization for Economic Cooperation and Development
OECD Guidelines	OECD Guidelines on the Protection of Privacy and Transborder Flows of Personal Data
PBC	People's Bank of China
PC	Personal Computer
PRC	People's Republic of China
The EU Directive 95/46/EC	Directive 95/46/EC of the European Parliament and of the Council on the protection of individuals with regard to the processing of personal data and on the free movement of such data
UDHR	Universal Declaration of Human Rights
UK	United Kingdom
US	United States of America
VLRC	Victoria Law Reform Commission

Chapter 1
Privacy

1.1 Introduction

In 1890, the Harvard Law Review published an article by Samuel D Warren and Louis D Brandeis entitled "The Right to Privacy."[1] In that article, Warren and Brandeis pointed out that "the principle which protects personal writings and any other productions of the intellect of or the emotions is the right to privacy..."[2] Since that time, the issue of privacy has commanded public attention around the world.

At present, although there are several skeptical and critical accounts of privacy, most legal theorists and sociologists believe that privacy is a valuable concept.[3] For some, privacy is a concept of "to be let alone"[4]; for others, privacy is "control over when and by whom the various parts of us can be sensed by others"[5] or "the condition of not having undocumented personal knowledge about one possessed by others"[6]; for still others, privacy is "the claim of individuals, groups, or institutions to determine for themselves when, how, and to what extent information about them is communicated to others."[7] However, until now, there has been no unified definition or analysis of the meaning of the term.

This chapter examines the wide array of definitions of privacy and tries to explore a working definition in China. Moreover, the values of privacy and the relationship between privacy protection and technology will be explored, respectively.

---

[1] Warren and Brandeis (1890).

[2] Warren and Brandeis (1890), p. 213.

[3] DeCew (2006).

[4] Warren and Brandeis (1890), p. 193.

[5] Parker (1974), p. 281.

[6] Parent (1983b), p. 269.

[7] Westin (1967), p. 7.

H. Wang, *Protecting Privacy in China*,

DOI 10.1007/978-3-642-21750-0_1,

1.2 The Definition of Privacy

1.2.1 Different Views on the Meaning of Privacy

The first popular definition of privacy is that privacy consists of being let alone. In fact, this definition is too broad. Although almost every loss of privacy may result from our not being left alone, there are still some cases of not being left alone which are not losses of privacy.[8] On the contrary, there are many ways to let a person alone, however, which have done nothing with his or her privacy. For example, suppose X knows some personal information about Y, and X repeatedly insults Y by using Y's personal information. In this example, based on the definition, Y may be let alone, but he or she can do nothing with his or her privacy. Therefore, it is clear that "privacy" in the sense of "to be let alone" today could refer to only a small and rather unimportant area of an individual's life.

The second popular definition equates the essence of privacy with the notion of "autonomy". Initially, in his landmark work, Alan Westin argues that:

> In democratic societies there is a fundamental belief in the uniqueness of the individual, in his basic dignity and worth as a creature of God and a human being, and in the need to maintain social processes that safeguard his sacred individuality. Psychologists and sociologists have linked the development and maintenance of this sense of individuality to the human need for autonomy – the desire to avoid being manipulated or dominated wholly by others.[9]

Moreover, Vincent J Samar believed that autonomy was the "core of privacy" and it was the "ultimate question in developing a jurisprudential theory of privacy protection."[10] He pointed out that "because democratic government in the Western sense values autonomy as a fundamental end, it must value privacy as a fundamental right."[11]

On the other hand, this view of privacy is also unsatisfactory to some extent. In West, it has been held that an individual is autonomous if he or she can ask himself or herself the question that what sort of person he or she wants to be, how he or she wants to live, and whether he or she can then live in this way.[12] Therefore, autonomy is concerned with establishing the right of the individual to express his or her personality regardless of the place or circumstances in which he or she chooses to do so.[13] By contrast, privacy conceals an individual, or information about them, from society. As Beate Rèossler points out that "in substantial terms, the connection between privacy and autonomy exists, therefore, because it is only through such

[8] Parker (1974), p. 276.
[9] Westin (1967), p. 33.
[10] Mason (2006), p. 61.
[11] Mason (2006), p. 61.
[12] Rèossler (2005), p. 17.
[13] Mason (2006), p. 62.

"space" marked out by the borderline between privacy and public that the design, development and exercise of (certain aspects of) autonomy become possible."[14] Therefore, in fact, autonomy is broader, and "suggesting an outward as well as an inward sense of self"; while privacy is narrow, and "suggesting an inward sense of self only."[15] It is thus wrong to treat privacy and autonomy as synonymous.

The third popular definition is that privacy involves control over significant personal matters. As mentioned earlier, Westin defines privacy as the ability to "determine for themselves when, how, and to what extent information about them is communicated to others."[16] Similarly, Raymond Wacks seeks to locate the problems of privacy at the level of personal information.[17] This kind of definition of privacy is very common, and even dominates the literature in certain aspects. Elizabeth Beardsley, Charles Fried, Richard Wasserstrom, Irwin Altman, Ernest Van Den Haag, Richard Parker, and others all adopt it, or have a definition close to it.[18]

For the author, the definitions of privacy as "control over something" are clearly too broad to some extent. For example, a student's examination results or performance in the class may reveal that he or she did not study. Obviously, this student loses control over his or her personal information, but we cannot say that his or her privacy has been invaded. Senator Brett Mason provides another example. Assume a person is unconscious or is unable to disclose personal information, then he or she has lost control of his or her personal information, but that does not necessarily mean he or she has lost their privacy.[19] Therefore, the loss of control over significant personal information is not the necessary element of loss of privacy. As Mason concludes "control over information is an overly board and ultimately unworkable definition of privacy's core."[20]

In addition, it should be noted that a number of commentators have argued that "privacy and intimacy" or "privacy and restricted access" are deeply related. With respect to "privacy and intimacy," Charles Fried, for example, argues that "privacy is not just one possible means among others to insure some other value, but that it is necessarily related to ends and relations of the most fundamental sort: respect, love, friendship and trust."[21] With respect to "privacy and restricted access," Sissela Bok, for example, argues that claims to privacy are claims to control access to one's personal domain, and defines privacy as the condition of being protected from unwanted access by others, and either physical access, personal information, or

---

[14] Rèossler (2005), p. 73.

[15] Mason (2006), pp. 61–62.

[16] Westin (1967), p. 7.

[17] Wacks (1989), p. 21.

[18] Parent (1983a), pp. 326–328.

[19] Mason (2006), p. 54.

[20] Mason (2006), p. 55.

[21] Fried (1968), p. 477.

attention.[22] However, the major problem with these definitions is that most legal theorists and sociologists tried to distinguish privacy from other concepts, such as "intimacy" or "control accesses." It is thus difficult to form a legal right based on the vague that is "central to the development of the individual persona."[23] As a result, all these theorists have failed to uphold privacy as a useful legal concept.

1.2.2 Difficulties in Defining Privacy

The preceding discussion illustrates that the definition of privacy occupies a particularly difficult position in Western legal studies. There are a number of possible reasons. To begin with, it has been argued that many attempts at defining privacy are unsophisticated.[24] That is because most definitions that mentioned earlier have attempted to distinguish privacy from related concepts, such as "intimacy," "autonomy", or "control accesses" by stating necessary and sufficient conditions that set privacy apart.[25] A further difficulty is that the definitions of privacy vary widely according to context and environment.[26] Privacy is a collection of related personal interests and expectations, rather than a single coherent concept.[27] When you ask a selection of people what privacy is, it is inevitable that you will get totally different answers. These answers depend on who these people are, where they come from, and even depend on their different religions. As a result, the author believes that there was little hope of arriving at an all-purpose definition in our modern society.

Referring to the difficulties of defining privacy, the ALRC emphasizes that "the very term 'privacy' is one fraught with difficulty" and "the concept is an elusive one."[28] In addition, Professor Daniel J Solove notes that:

> Privacy, however, is a concept in disarray. Nobody can articulate what it means. Currently, privacy is a sweeping concept, encompassing (among other things) freedom of thought, control over one's body, solitude in one's home, control over personal information, freedom from surveillance, protection of one's reputation, and protection from searches and interrogations.[29]

Similarly, Mason argues that:

> 'Privacy' has no vital core conern that would provide the foundations for a definable legal interest nor principled bureaucratic decision making. Neither the control an individual has over information about himself/herself, the protection of personal information, nor the

[22] Bok (1984), pp. 10–11.
[23] Mason (2006), p. 64.
[24] Lindsay (2005), p. 136.
[25] Lindsay (2005), pp. 136–137.
[26] Romano (2002), p. 346.
[27] McCartney (2006), p. 130.
[28] Australian Law Reform Commission (1983), p. 10.
[29] Solove (2008), p. 1.

concepts of autonomy, intimacy or personhood provide an adequate explanation for our common understanding of privacy. . ..Privacy represents a political or ideological claim. It is a justification or a rallying cry for political debate—just like 'freedom' or 'equality'.[30]

The Victoria Law Reform Commission (the VLRC) has also pointed out that there are at least four immediate problems or questions with basing any law of privacy on individual experience:

The first is the difficulty of extrapolating general privacy criteria based solely on the experience of the individual. . .The second question raised by basing a law of privacy on individual experience is a question that would be raised in any approach, given the fundamental link between privacy and human existence. . . The third problem is that although privacy itself can be defined as involving a boundary and its transgression, and privacy invasion is identifiable via the individual's experience of this transgression, this does not assist in identifying the social values involved in privacy. . . The fourth, related, problem is that placing the individual's experience at the centre of the definition raises the question of the relationship between individuals' rights and society's interests.[31]

Based on these statements, it is thus clear that privacy is one of the most significant concepts in our modern society, yet this concept is also the most elusive.

On the other hand, the fact is that almost everyone agrees privacy has instrumental value, and this is the most common and significant justification.[32] Freedom from disturbance or intrusion is still the substantial meaning of privacy. An appropriate definition can propose appropriate powers to Chinese governments or courts to investigate privacy issues and grant remedies for victim. By contrast, an unrealistic concept will be incompatible with contemporary Chinese society. That is because an unqualified definition of privacy will inevitably cause that some particular privacy interests cannot be protected adequately in China. Therefore, if the concept were not defined explicitly, an invasion of privacy interests will occur and certain legitimate claims might be ignored in China. As a consequence, explicit criteria are required.

1.2.3 Towards a Working Definition of Privacy in China

With regard to defining privacy, Professor Wacks suggests that the ambiguity of the concept of privacy "stems largely from difficulties in respect of its (1) status; (2) features; and (3) coherence."[33] Likewise, Professor Ruth Gavison points out that:

"Privacy" is a term used with many meanings. For my purposes, two types of questions about privacy are important. The first relates to the status of the term: is privacy a situation, a right, a claim, a form of control, a value? The second relates to the characteristics of privacy: is it related to information, to autonomy, to personal identity, to physical access?[34]

[30] Mason (2006), pp. 79–80.

[31] Victoria Law Reform Commission (2002), pp. 5–6.

[32] Bynum and Rogerson (2004), p. 252.

[33] Wacks (1989), pp. 13–14.

[34] Gavison (1980), p. 424.

Dealing first with the status of the term "privacy" in a Chinese context, Professor Zhang Xinbao states that "privacy is a legal right, by which citizens' residences, inner world, financial situations, social relations, sexual life, and past and current matters of purely personal nature they do not wish to divulge to the outside world are protected from any intrusion by others."[35] Similarly, Wang Liming, civil law professor, defines privacy as a right "enjoyed by a person, under which he can protect all personal information, private activities and private areas which belong only to the person and have no relation to public interest."[36] The author agrees that privacy is a right. That is because both the *Universal Declaration of Human Rights*[37] and the *International Covenant on Civil and Political Rights*[38] accord privacy the status of a human right. However, the preceding discussion on different views of the meaning of privacy has clearly illustrated that privacy consists of a number of related individual interests that individuals have in keeping the personal sphere free from interference from others.[39] Privacy thus can be deemed as an existing category of different interests within the human's society. In order words, it is a right and this right to privacy is underpinned by a series of independent individual interests.

In order to distinguish different interests of privacy, the declaration of the Nordic Conference of Jurists on the Right to Respect for Privacy defines a series of different privacy interests. As the declaration states:

> The right of privacy is the right to be let alone to live one's own life with the minimum degree of interference. In expanded form, this means: The right of the individual to lead his own life protected against:
> (a) interference with his private, family and home life;
> (b) interference with his physical or mental integrity or his moral and intellectual freedom;
> (c) attacks on his honor and reputation;
> (d) being placed in a false light;
> (e) the disclosure of irrelevant embarrassing facts relating to his private life;
> (f) the use of his name, identity or likeness;
> (g) spying, prying, watching and besetting;
> (h) interference with his correspondence;
> (i) misuse of his private communications, written or oral;
> (j) disclosure of information given or received by him in circumstances of professional confidence.[40]

This conference also confirmed that there should be "a civil right to guard against intrusion, surreptitious recording, photographs or eavesdropping, and the

---

[35] Zhang (2004), p. 7.

[36] Wang (1994), p. 487.

[37] *Universal Declaration of Human Rights* 1948, art 12.

[38] *International Covenant on Civil and Political Rights* 1966, art 17.

[39] Australian Law Reform Commission (2007), p. 101.

[40] Law Reform Commission of Hong Kong (2004), pp. 12–13.

use of material obtained by unlawful intrusion or which exploits a person's identity, places him in a false light or reveals embarrassing private facts."[41]

Another attempt was made by the Younger Committee in the UK. The Committee identifies that the principal privacy interests are "(1) the freedom from intrusion upon oneself, one's home, family and relationships; and (2) the right to determine for oneself how and to what extent information about oneself is communicated to others."[42] For the author the best examples of privacy interests are illustrated by the ALRC. The ALRC identified four categories of privacy interests, which are:

1. The interest in controlling entry to the "personal place", or "territorial privacy;"
2. The interest in freedom from interference with one's person and "personal space," privacy of the person;'
3. The interest of the person in controlling the information held by others about him "information privacy;" and
4. The interest in freedom from surveillance and from interception of one's communications, or "communications and surveillance privacy."[43]

It should be clear that privacy protection is in the interest of both the individual and the society.[44] Privacy is not only an individual interest, but it is also in the public interest to protect the interests of individuals against injury to their emotions and mental suffering.[45] It is thus wrong to put privacy against other public interests. Privacy involves establishing a balance between individual and public. As Fred H Cate points out that privacy values are in tension with themselves and with other values, and this tension is inevitable.[46] Therefore, when China defines different privacy interests, it is important to bear in mind that privacy interests will inevitably compete, collide, and coexist with other existing values in China, such as freedom of expression, freedom of the press, law enforcement, protection of the revenue, and the effective operation of government. Privacy is significant, but it is not everything. Absolute privacy would mean a total withdrawal of an individual from our society. This will be undesirable for most Chinese people.

A working definition of privacy should also meet the following two criteria in China. First, individuals should understand all (or at least most) of the aspects of their personal information, which are being addressed. In other words, individuals should know when privacy is, or is not, gained or lost. Otherwise, the definition of privacy will be inaccurate. Second, the definition of privacy must be applicable to Chinese social and legal practices. Social and legal practices include the use and testing of the definition by Chinese courts, lawyers, and other governmental agencies.

---

[41] Law Reform Commission of Hong Kong (2004), p. 13.

[42] Law Reform Commission of Hong Kong (2004), p. 13.

[43] Australian Law Reform Commission (1983), p. 21; see also Law Reform Commission of Hong Kong (2004), p. 14.

[44] Law Reform Commission of Hong Kong (2004), p. 97.

[45] Law Reform Commission of Hong Kong (2004), p. 97.

[46] Cate (1997), p. 102.

Particularly, a definition of privacy should be adequate for use in the legal process. Our definition of privacy must be able to appear in complaints and in court opinions.[47] These two criteria should both be satisfied in an adequate definition of privacy.

It should be noted that there is another opinion that the right to control over one's personal information is an alternative method to easily ensure privacy.[48] That is because if individuals have control over information about themselves, they can give or sell that information to someone else and produce net benefits.[49] As a result, a market in information will be established by protecting individual "property rights" in information.[50] However, it also has been argued that there are at least two problems with applying the notion of property to personal information: first, the negotiation of information is very difficult, because without showing the information to the customers, it is hard to tell them what you are selling; and second, a given piece of information can be duplicated at a cost close to zero, for instance, while a information of a selling house is valuable only to the people who want to own it.[51] Therefore, in fact, claims to "property in personal information" are unjustifiable. By contrast, the ALRC points out that "claims to information privacy are justifiable because they involve claims to better protection of established and highly valued basic interests, such as in 'just' decision making and in freedom from misrepresentation of one's situation."[52] Moreover, the rights of information privacy will provide right to know to the individuals. This will allow the individual to know what information is held about him or her by other individuals and organizations, and to protect his or her personal information against the possibility of unfair decision-making.[53] All these rights cannot be protected under the claims to "property in personal information."

It may be difficult to ensure the concept of privacy in precise terms, but this should not preclude China from examining what privacy interests can be embodied in modern Chinese society. The clearer the definition of privacy is, the more accurate the judgments will be in deciding when to protect privacy. Therefore, based on the Australian experiences, the definition of privacy in this book is that privacy is a right, which consists of a number of individual interests that individuals have in keeping their personal information and personal affairs free from interference from others.[54] By attempting to define more clearly the definition of privacy, the author hopes this brief analysis will be helpful to solve privacy issues in China.

---

[47] Parker (1974), p. 277.

[48] Paul et al. (2000), p. 193.

[49] Paul et al. (2000), p. 193.

[50] Paul et al. (2000), p. 193.

[51] Paul et al. (2000), p. 194.

[52] Australian Law Reform Commission (1983), p. 32.

[53] Australian Law Reform Commission (1983), p. 32.

[54] Australian Law Reform Commission (2007), p. 101.

1.3 The Values of Privacy

There has been considerable argument among social philosophers and social scientists about if privacy is needed and its functions.[55] Some social philosophers and social scientists point out that one of the most important reasons why we value privacy is "privacy allows us to maintain the variety of relationships with other people that we want to have."[56] Some argue that privacy is a basic human need.[57] The most famous evaluation of the significance of privacy is provided by Alan Westin. Westin demonstrates that privacy serves four functions for individuals and groups in democratic nations, which include "personal autonomy," "emotional release," "self-evaluation," and "limited and protected communication," respectively.[58] In Westin's view, first, privacy is able to protect individuals from being manipulated or dominated by others; second, privacy provides the opportunity for various types of emotional release; third, privacy is essential to ensure every individual to exert their individuality on events; and finally, privacy provides opportunities for sharing confidences and intimacies.[59]

Similarly, Ruth Gavison has also demonstrated that the significance of privacy in our modern society. In her well-known article entitled "Privacy and the Limits of Law," she first pointed out that privacy can help people to ensure the "freedom from physical access," that is because of privacy "insulates that individual from distraction and from the inhibitive effects that arise from close physical proximity with another individual."[60] Moreover, she also points out that privacy is able to promote liberty of action, which includes freedom from censure and ridicule, promoting mental health, promoting autonomy, and promoting human relations.[61] In addition to promote and protect individual interests, in Gavison's view, privacy is also essential to democratic government. As Gavison states:

> Privacy is crucial to democracy in providing the opportunity for parties to work out their political positions, and to compromise with opposing factions, before subjecting their positions to public scrutiny. Denying the privacy necessary for these interactions would undermine the democratic process.[62]

Although China is far from being a democratic country now, the *Chinese Constitution* (1982) has promised that the National People's Congress (the NPC) and the local People's Congresses at various levels are constituted through democratic elections; they are responsible to the people and subject to their

---

[55] Australian Law Reform Commission (1983), p. 16.

[56] Rachels (1975), p. 329.

[57] Rosenberg (2004), p. 351.

[58] Westin (1967), pp. 32–39.

[59] Westin (1967), pp. 32–39.

[60] Gavison (1980), pp. 446–447.

[61] Gavison (1980), pp. 448–450.

[62] Gavison (1980), p. 456.

supervision.[63] Therefore, if privacy encourages public participation in political decisions by enabling citizens to form judgments and express preferences on social issues,[64] establishing adequate privacy protection will provide a harmonious environment for China to achieve greater democracy pursuant to the Chinese Constitution. As a consequence, although it is very difficult to define privacy accurately, privacy is still a significant value that underpins other fundamental rights. Chinese citizens' privacy should be free from interference from others.

1.4 Privacy and Technology

Technology has played a significant role in the emergence of privacy law. It has been argued that "new laws emerge in response to changes in technology that have increased the collection, dissemination, and use of personal information."[65] In human society's history, several main waves of technological and social change have promoted the development of our laws.[66]

The appearance of the "muckraking" newspapers and the businesses that used people's names or photographs in advertising without authorization caused the first wave of the development of privacy protection law.[67] In fact, the earliest arguments by Warren and Brandeis for explicit recognition of privacy protection in law were in large part motivated by the development of widely distributed newspapers and multiply printed reproductions of photographs.[68] At that time, Western legal theory allowed the victims to go to court to seek compensation against invaders, and this reflected the fact that the invasion came not from the central government, but from other private citizens seeking business gains through new technology.[69]

The appearance and development of technological devices that permitting electronic snooping upon telephone and other conversations brought on the second wave of the development of privacy protection law worldwide.[70] The public concern about the wiretapping of telephone conversations came to the fore in the 1920s, and other forms of electronic eavesdropping have developed, and public concern over these matters too has slowly developed at that time.[71]

---

[63] *Constitution of the People's Republic of China* 1982, art 3.

[64] Law Reform Commission of Hong Kong (2004), p. 18.

[65] Solove (2006), p. 3

[66] Rubin (1988), p. 7.

[67] Rubin (1988), p. 8.

[68] DeCew (2006).

[69] Rubin (1988), p. 8.

[70] Rubin (1988), p. 20.

[71] Rubin (1988), p. 20.

In fact, the second wave of the development of privacy protection has not finished until now. It has been held that privacy is threatened more than ever by technological advances.[72] As DeCew points out that:

> There are massive databases and Internet records of information about individual financial and credit history, medical records, purchases and telephone calls, for example, and most people do not know what information is stored about them or who has access to it. The ability for others to access and link the databases, with few controls on how they use, share, or exploit the information, makes individual control over information about oneself more difficult than ever before.[73]

Therefore, at present, with the development of new technologies, the lawmakers are focusing on the protection of information privacy and other emerging privacy issues in some certain Western developed countries.

1.5 Conclusion

Today, privacy has become one of the most widely demanded rights worldwide. There is an increasing need in China that privacy should be respected by other people, by groups or organizations, and by Chinese governments. If there was no legal restriction on "search of the person, entry to premises and other property, use of electronic surveillance or other 'bugging' devices, recording, photographing or filming, public disclosures of private facts, interception of correspondence, and so on"[74] in Chinese society, China would be an unpleasant and extremely disagreeable place in which to live.

References

Journal Articles and Books

Bok S (1984) Secret: on the ethics of concealment and revelation. Pantheon, New York
Bynum TW, Rogerson S (eds) (2004) Computer ethics and professional responsibility. New York, Wiley-Blackwell
Cate FH (1997) Privacy in the Information Age. Brookings Institution Press, Washington, DC
Fried C (1968) Privacy. Yale Law J 77:475
Gavison R (1980) Privacy and the limits of law. Yale Law J 89:421
Lindsay D (2005) An exploration of the conceptual basis of privacy and the implications for the future of Australian privacy law. Melb Univ Law Rev 29:131
Mason B (2006) Privacy without principle: the use and abuse of privacy in Australian law and public policy. Australian Scholarly Publishing, Melbourne

[72] DeCew (2006).

[73] DeCew (2006).

[74] Law Reform Commission of Hong Kong (2004), p. 13

McCartney C (2006) Forensic identification and criminal justice: forensic science, justice and risk. Willan Pressing, Cullompton
Parent WA (1983a) A new definition of privacy for the law. Law Philos 2:305
Parent WA (1983b) Privacy, morality and the law. Philos Public Aff 12:269
Parker RB (1974) A definition of privacy. Rutgers Law Rev 27:275
Rachels J (1975) Why privacy is important. Philos Public Aff 4:323
Paul EF, Miller FD Jr, Paul J (eds) (2000) The right to privacy. Cambridge University Press, Cambridge
Rèossler B (2005) The value of privacy. Polity Press, Cambridge (translated by Glasgow R D V)
Romano C (2002) Advance tax rulings and principles of law: towards a European tax rulings system? IBFD, Amsterdam
Rosenberg RS (2004) The social impact of computers. Emerald Group Publishing, San Diego, CA
Rubin MR (1988) Public wrongs: the computer and personal privacy. Ablex Publishing, Norwood, NJ
Wacks R (1989) Personal information. Oxford University Press, Oxford
Wang LM (1994) Restatement of the law of rights of the person (Zhu Guobin trans) [trans of: 人格权法新论]. Jilin People's Press, Changchun
Warren SD, Brandeis LD (1890) The right to privacy. Harvard Law Rev 4:193
Westin AF (1967) Privacy and freedom. Atheneum, New York
Zhang XB (2004) The legal protection of the right to privacy (Zhu Guobin trans) [trans of: 隐私权的法律保护]. The Masses Press, Beijing

Legislation

Constitution of the People's Republic of China 1982 art 3
Universal Declaration of Human Rights, GA Res 217A (III), UN Doc A/Res/810 (1948) art 12
International Covenant on Civil and Political Rights, opened for signature 16 December 1966, 999 UNTS 171, 6 ILM 368, (entered into force 23 March 1976) art 17

Government and Law Reform Reports

Australian Law Reform Commission (1983) Privacy. Report paper No. 22, volume 1
Australian Law Reform Commission (2007) Review of Australian Privacy Law. Discussion Paper 72
Solove DJ (2006) A brief history of information privacy law. GWU Law School Public Law Research Paper No 215, The George Washington University Law School
Solove DJ (2008) Understanding privacy. Public Law and Legal Theory Working Paper No 420, The George Washington University Law School
Law Reform Commission of Hong Kong (2004) Civil liability for invasion of privacy
Victoria Law Reform Commission (2002) Defining privacy. Occasional Paper

Electronic Materials

DeCew JC (2006) Privacy. Stanford encyclopedia of philosophy http://plato.stanford.edu/entries/privacy/. Accessed 18 March 2011

Chapter 2
Recent Developments Threatening Privacy in China

2.1 Introduction

As described in Chap. 1, the definition of privacy in this book is that privacy is a right, which consists of a number of individual interests that individuals have in keeping their personal information and personal affairs free from interference from others.[1] Based on the Australian experiences, these individual privacy interests include: "the interest in controlling entry to the personal place"; "the interest in freedom from interference with one's person and personal space"; "the interest of the person in controlling the information held by others about him"; and "the interest in freedom from surveillance and from interception of one's communications".[2]

However, at present, most of these privacy interests are under threat in China, especially from the following features of current Chinese society: first, in order to consolidate China's socialistic system, in the 30 years of China's reform and opening up, the increasing official and administrative powers allowing more and more individuals or organizations to interfere with other people's private affairs, or to access to other people's personal information or data; second, with the rapid development of Chinese economy, more and more commercial practices attempt to find customers in their personal place or personal space actively; and third, with the rapid development of information technologies and information processing devices such as computers in China, it is now very easy for Chinese people to access, handle, and save personal information than ever before. All these developments place privacy under particular threat in China. Most importantly, they are going to continue.

This chapter examines the three pervasive features of contemporary Chinese society listed above. It should be noted that this chapter is not an analysis of modern

[1] See Sect. 1.2.3 of this book.

[2] Australian Law Reform Commission (1983), p. 37.

H. Wang, *Protecting Privacy in China*,
DOI 10.1007/978-3-642-21750-0_2,

changes of administration and technology in China. The purpose of this chapter is to explore the Chinese privacy implications of these changes.

2.2 Increasing Official Powers

2.2.1 Political Basis for Increasing Official Powers

At the time Deng Xiaoping took over the Chinese leadership, the "Cultural Revolution," which had lasted almost 10 years, had pushed China's economy to the edge of collapse.[3] Based on this situation, the Chinese leaders thus decided to re-build China's economy. In 1978, the Third Plenary Session of the Eleventh Central Committee of the National People's Congress (the Eleventh NPC) was held in Beijing. At the Eleventh NPC, the Chinese leaders declared that large-scale nationwide mass political movements should be stopped and the emphasis of the Party's work should be shifted to socialist modernization.[4] Moreover, during the Eleventh NPC, the Chinese leaders also clearly stated that the law must be used to establish stability and order for economic development.[5] As Deng Xiaoping pointed out in 1978 that:

> There is a lot of legislative work to do, and we do not have enough trained people. Therefore, legal provisions will inevitably be rough to start with, and then be gradually improved upon. Some laws and statutes can be tried out in particular localities and later enacted nationally after experience has been evaluated and improvements have been made. In terms of revision and supplemented, we should not wait for a 'complete set of equipment.' In short, it is better to have some laws than none, and better to have them sooner than later.[6]

As a consequence, under Deng Xiaoping's leadership, in the 30 years of China's reform and opening up, China has witnessed massive and rapid enactment of laws and regulations.[7] With respect to this Chinese social phenomenon, Professor Chen Jianfu points out that this piecemeal and unsystematic development in China's legal system produced a number of laws, which include many individual statutes, decisions, orders, administrative regulations, and rules made under different policy orientations.[8] Some of them authorize intrusive powers to government agencies. Based on these laws, today, Chinese officials have myriad powers of intrusion.

The following sections discuss the privacy issues raised by intrusive powers of Chinese authorities in more detail. It should be noted that I use the general term of

---

[3] Chen (1999), p. 41.
[4] Chen (1999), p. 40.
[5] Chen (1999), p. 40.
[6] Chen (1999), p. 43.
[7] Chen (1999), p. 41.
[8] Chen (1999), p. 43.

"intrusive powers" deliberately because it is broad enough to cover many kinds of powers that may endanger privacy, such as to enter, to search, and to require inspection and examination of information.

2.2.2 *Entry and Search*

2.2.2.1 Revenue Collection

In order to achieve the economic reforms, Chinese government emphasized the importance of tax collection. The *Law of the PRC on Tax Administration* (the Tax Administration Law) thus came into effect from 1 May 2001. However, this law does not pay enough attention to the protection of privacy and personal information. A number of provisions empower the Chinese tax officers to search, enter or inspect. The provisions that are most protective of privacy only requires that the officials of the tax authorities should produce tax inspection identity cards to make tax inspections, and if "an official does not produce any tax inspection identity card or tax inspection notice, the party that is to be inspected have the right to refuse the inspection."[9] However, in many cases, there are no limitations were placed to the exercise of the powers, and sometimes, the Chinese tax officers have full and free access.[10]

Some powers conferred by article 54 of the Tax Administration Law are pertinent in this context. Article 54 states:

Tax authorities have the rights to conduct the following tax inspections:

1. To inspect a taxpayer's accounting books, supporting vouchers for the accounts, statements and the relevant information; to inspect a withholding agent's accounting books, supporting vouchers for the accounts and the relevant information in respect of the amount of taxes withheld and remitted or collected and remitted
2. To inspect a taxpayer's taxable commodities, goods or other properties at the taxpayer's places where production or business operations are conducted and the places where goods are stored; to inspect a withholding agent's operational conditions in respect of the withholding and remittance of taxes or the collection and remittance of taxes
3. To order a taxpayer or withholding agent to provide the documents, evidentiary materials and information relating to the payment of taxes or the amount of taxes withheld and remitted or collected and remitted

---

[9] *Law of the People's Republic of China Concerning the Administration of Tax Collection* 2001, art 59; see also *Rules for the Implementation of the Law of the People's Republic of China Concerning the Administration of Tax Collection* 2002, art 89.

[10] *Law of the People's Republic of China Concerning the Administration of Tax Collection* 2001, arts 54, 56, 58; see also *Rules for the Implementation of the Law of the People's Republic of China Concerning the Administration of Tax Collection* 2002, art 86.

4. To make inquiries of a taxpayer or withholding agent regarding the relevant issues and circumstances relating to the payment of taxes or the amount of taxes withheld and remitted or collected and remitted
5. To inspect supporting documents, vouchers and information relating to the taxable commodities, goods or other properties transported by consignment or sent by post by a taxpayer at railway stations, docks, airports, postal services and the branches thereof

In the *Rules for the Implementation of the Law of the PRC on Tax Administration* (2002), article 86 clearly states that the tax authorities can exercise its power that provided in Clause (1) of article 54 of the Tax Administration Law at the business site of a taxpayer or withholding agent. However, both Laws do not clearly define the legal standards of how to enter the taxpayer's business site. The tax authorities' powers may only be restricted by the requirement that search, enter, or inspect should be for the purposes of the Law. That means a tax authority may have right to search, enter, or inspect taxpayers at all times.

Moreover, in order to achieve the implementation of inspection, article 56 of the Tax Administration Law emphasizes that taxpayers or withholding agents must accept the tax inspections by the tax authorities, provide accurate facts and relevant information, and cannot refuse to cooperate with the authority or conceal any facts. Likewise, article 58 of the Tax Administration Law states that "when investigating a tax case in violation of the law, the tax authority may record, tape-record, video-tape, photograph and reproduce the relevant information and material in respect of the case." These two provisions emphasize the Chinese tax officers' right to ask a party that is to be inspected to provide evidence, documents, or any relating information to a matter that the tax officers are authorized. Therefore, if article 54 of the Tax Administration Law concerns the common rights of the Chinese tax authority, both articles 56 and 58 expressly empower the tax authority to obtain more information and documents.

Compared to the Chinese Tax Administration Law, section 263 Clause (2) of Australian *Income Tax assessment Act 1936* clearly states that:

> An officer is not entitled to enter or remain on or in any building or place under this section if, on being requested by the occupier of the building or place for proof of authority, the officer does not produce an authority in writing signed by the Commissioner stating that the officer is authorized to exercise powers under this section.

It is thus clear that some provisions of the Chinese Tax Administration Law and its Implementing Rules in China need further improvement. As mentioned earlier, the provisions contained in the Chinese Tax Administration Law and its Implementing Rules empower Chinese tax officers into personal place and personal space; however, the most protective provisions of privacy only require that the tax officers should show their inspection identity card when they conduct their powers. This is not enough, obviously. Chinese government should ensure that, when the tax officers entry to premises, they should have the consent of the occupier, or at least, pursuant to a warrant issued by the Chinese Administration of Taxation at a certain level or above. Under some particular situations, other stronger evidence should also be provided by the Chinese tax authorities or other authorities to prove that their conducts are both legal and proper. The inspection identity card should not empower the tax officers to enter all premises or places, and to inspect all documents or information at anytime freely. At the time of strengthening the administration of tax collection in China, privacy interests should not be threatened.

2.2.2.2 The Customs Check Law

The *Regulation of the PRC for Customs Check* (1997) (the Customs Check Regulation) is also notable for the extensive powers of intrusion, and confers these powers to China's Customs officials. The Customs Check Regulation provides that if a customs officer having with him a "Customs Check Certificate",[11] he can exercise the following powers:

1. To consult and copy relevant material
2. To enter the production and operation areas and storage areas of the units being checked to inspect the production and operation situation and the goods related to import and export activities
3. To check inward and outward means of transport and examine inward and outward goods and articles; to detain those entering or leaving the territory in violation of this Law or other relevant laws and regulations
4. To inquire into situations and matters related to import and export activities with the legal representative, the person in charge and other related personnel of the units being checked
5. To inquire about the deposit accounts in commercial banks or other financial institutions of the units being checked with the approval of the Director General of the Customs[12]

"Transport" means various types of vessels, vehicles, aircraft and pack-animals, which enter or leave the territory carrying persons, goods, or articles.[13] In China, the Customs Check Certificates are produced and issued by the General Administration of Customs in a unified way. The Customs Check Certificates can only prove that they are legal administrative officers. In fact, the same situation also happens in some developed Western countries. In West, it has been held that the Customs Check Certificates are "completely general and almost entirely without safeguards."[14] Therefore, it is not enough to prove officers have rights to enter, search, or demand free access to people's private property. However, in China, it appears that the Chinese Customs are empowered at all times to enter any premises and check any goods or transports in China. Furthermore, when Customs officers

---

[11] *Regulations of the People's Republic of China for Customs Check* 1997, art 12.

[12] *Regulations of the People's Republic of China for Customs Check* 1997, art 14.

[13] *Customs Law of the People's Republic of China* 2001, art 100.

[14] Australian Law Reform Commission (1983), p. 76.

enter production, operation or storage areas to make inspections, the legal owner must present their account books, open storage areas, move goods, or untie packages at the request of the Customs.[15] Article 10 of the Customs Check Regulation states "...under special circumstances and with the approval of the Director General of the Customs, the Customs can carry out checks without warrant or prior notice."

Compared to the Customs Check Regulation, the Australian *Customs Act 1901* clearly provides that a search warrant is the premise that the executing officer or a person assisting to conduct their duties.[16] Therefore, there are at least two measures that should be emphasized and accepted by the Chinese Customs: first, the Customs Check Certificate should be necessary in all situations, and the Chinese officer of Customs should be identifiable "either by being in uniform or producing written evidence to establish his identity"[17]; second, when conducting checks, the Chinese Customs should formally notify the legal owners. These two measures should be carried out strictly at the same time.

2.2.2.3 Public Health and Safety

These powers are entitled for different reasons: for example, to guarantee the safety of the lives and property of people and to protect the environment,[18] to safeguard the legitimate rights and interests of Chinese citizens with respect to their exit from and entry into China's territory,[19] and to search premises for infected goods.[20] Most of these statutory powers state that, in the absence of consent, the working personnel should show their certificates when they conduct their duties; however, under the remaining powers, no such certificate is required.

The *Law of the PRC on the Prevention and Treatment of Infectious Diseases* (2004) (the Infectious Diseases Law) is a good example. The Infectious Diseases law requires that health administration departments under the people's governments at or above the country level have the right to enter the units subjected to inspection and the places where the epidemic situation of infectious diseases occurs to make investigation and collect evidence, consult or duplicate relevant materials and collect samples; while the said units must cooperate with them and cannot refuse to do so or create obstacles.[21] This provision ensure that a quarantine

---

[15] *Regulations of the People's Republic of China for Customs Check* 1997, art 19.

[16] *Customs Act* 1901 (Cth), s 199.

[17] Australian Law Reform Commission (1983), p. 72.

[18] *Regulations on the Safety Administration of Dangerous Chemicals* 2002 (China), art 1.

[19] *Law of the People's Republic of China on the Control of the Exit and Entry of Citizens* 1986, art 1.

[20] *Law of the People's Republic of China on Animal Epidemic Prevention* 1998, art 45.

[21] *Law of the People's Republic of China on the Prevention and Treatment of Infectious Diseases* 2004, art 54.

officer may, at any time, enter any premises or place for the purpose of inspecting plants or goods infected with a disease. In fact, Western developed countries' experience has told us that the functions of a quarantine officer also include entering and searching for infected goods, if necessary, by breaking open cupboards, drawers, chests, trunks, boxes, packages or other receptacles, and asking questions and inspecting documents relating to the movement of persons, vehicles or goods.[22] Obviously, if we do not set in stone the protection of individuals' interests, it is possible that this will happen in China. In addition, article 45 of the *Law on Animal Epidemic Prevention* (1997) states that:

> Animal-raising farms, slaughter houses, integrated meat-packing plants and other designated slaughter houses (places) shall raise and deal in animals or manufacture and deal in animal products should place themselves under the supervision and inspection by the institutions for supervision over animal epidemic prevention.

That means when conducting supervision and inspection, the Chinese institutions for supervision over animal epidemic prevention and their officers can enter operation areas or storage areas without warrant or notice.

2.2.2.4 Public Works

These powers are entitled to ensure the inspection for the public service purposes. For example, the Chinese *Electric Power Law* (1995) regulates that when electric power supervisors and inspectors perform their duties, they shall have the right to question power providers and consumers about their implementation of the laws and administrative rules and regulations on electric power, look up relevant documents, and conduct on-the-spot inspections.[23] In order to ensure the effectiveness of article 58, the electric power enterprises and consumers also need to provide assistance to electric power supervisors and inspectors who are performing their duties.[24]

Furthermore, in order to ensure normal progress of postal work, and promote development of postal services, the *Postal Law of the PRC* (1986) grants certain intrusive powers to officers. In particular, the Minister may issue a search warrant to any other agencies, such as Customs, to inspect forcibly. As the Postal Law states that "postal enterprises shall inform the Customs of their business hours in advance, and the Customs shall promptly send officials to supervise on-the-spot checking and examination."[25]

It should be noted that article 4 of the Postal Law states that:

> Freedom and secret of correspondence shall be protected by law. No organization or individual shall infringe upon the freedom and secret of correspondence of other persons

[22] Australian Law Reform Commission (1983), p. 78.

[23] *Electric Power Law of the People's Republic of China* 1995, art 58.

[24] *Electric Power Law of the People's Republic of China* 1995, art 59.

[25] *Postal Law of the People's Republic of China* 1986, art 30.

> for any reason, except when the inspection of correspondence in accordance with legal procedures by the public security organ, the state security organ or the procuratorial organ is necessary for the state's safety or the investigation of criminal offence.

However, the secret of correspondence can only be deemed as privacy of written communication. Privacy of written communication is only one interest of related privacy interests. That is to say the protection of secret of correspondence is too narrow to substitute the legal protection of privacy. Moreover, as mentioned earlier, due to the fact that there is no working definition of privacy in China, the general population of China does not know what the concept of privacy is. Therefore, it can be understood as that there is no explicit restriction attaching to the exercise of the power.

2.2.2.5 Summary

Based on China's national nature and unsystematic legal development, intrusive powers are numerous and widely enforced in China. These include powers to enter any personal places or to inspect and obtain personal information. It is undeniable that most unwarranted powers are entitled to deal with some urgent circumstances. However, this should not be deemed as a justification for China to remove the controls of these powers. In fact, Western developed countries' experiences have already shown that even if the power to issue administrative warrants was limited to the Chinese authorities, it would still cause concern.[26] That is because there is not enough independent scrutiny of whether there is the need for a warrant, or whether a warrant should remain in force for certain periods or circumstances in China.[27] As a consequence, the officials that have the power to issue the warrant may give undue weight to departmental interests, and privacy is a significant factor.[28] The only way to achieve effective protection of privacy in this respect may be that confer the power of issuing warrants to Chinese judicial officials.

2.2.3 Arrest and Detention

In this context, the area selected for discussion is a unique measure called "the Detain for Examination." It should be emphasized that this is not to say this area will pose greater privacy problems than others. However, "the Detain for Examination" typically demonstrates the wide range of intrusive powers conferred by Chinese governments, and privacy is put at serious risk under these powers.

[26] Australian Law Reform Commission (1983), p. 82.
[27] Australian Law Reform Commission (1983), p. 82.
[28] Australian Law Reform Commission (1983), p. 82.

Since the economic opening of China, the Chinese police have faced an increasing crime rate.[29] In part, that is the result of increasing numbers of vagrants and beggars. In order to control these vagrants and beggars in China, on May 12, 1982, the State Council of the PRC enacted the *Measures for Detaining and Sending Back of Vagrants and Beggars in Cities* (the Measures for Vagrants and Beggars). The aims of the Measures for Vagrants and Beggars are to strengthen the public safety of cities, and to assist, educate, and find a home for Vagrants and Beggars.[30] Article 2 of the Measures for Vagrants and Beggars states that people will be detained and sent back if they are "countryside citizens who go begging in cities; city's citizens who go begging in cities; and other vagrants." In 1992, the State Council of the PRC enacted the *Detailed Rules about Measures for Detaining and Sending Back of Vagrants and Beggars in Cities* (the Detailed Rules). The Detailed Rules require that, if someone who is not a local citizen stays in a city for more than three days, they will also be seen as an illegal citizen and will be detained and sent back.[31] Moreover if someone had no identity card, certificate for temporary living or certificate for working, they would be detained and sent back.[32] At the time of widening the range of detentions, the freedom of Chinese citizens has also been limited.

It should be noted that "the Detain for Examination" has never been officially adopted by the NPC or by the NPC Standing Committee,[33] but its wide use by police in Chinese society has already caused serious harm to individuals' rights to both liberty and privacy in China. The author acknowledges that vagrants and beggars may have a bad influence on the development of cities; for example, they may increase the possibility of crime in China. However, before they commit a crime, vagrants and beggars are legal Chinese citizens. No organizations or people have the right to intrude on vagrants' and beggars' legal rights. In the last 30 years, although the Chinese State Council and the Ministry of Public Security issued many measures or directives regulate the use of the Measures for Vagrants and Beggars, such as directives covering the jurisdictional scope, approval authority, time limits, and administration of the practice of the Measures, it has been argued that these measures and directives are "largely inconsistent, unclear, overly broad and open-ended."[34]

In 1996, the NPC amended the *Criminal Procedure Law of the PRC* (1979). The new Criminal Procedure Law does not mention "the Detain for Examination" by name, but effectively places all public security compulsory measures in Chapter VI, including "the Detain for Examination."[35] The new criminal Procedure Law

---

[29] Wong (1996), p. 373.

[30] *Measures for Detaining and Sending Back of Vagrants and Beggars in Cities* (1982) (China), art 1.

[31] *Detailed Rules about Measures for Detaining and Sending Back of Vagrants and Beggars in Cities* 1992 (China).

[32] *Procedures of the People's Republic of China about Shelter for Repatriating*, art 2.

[33] Wong (1996), p. 367.

[34] Wong (1996), p. 368.

[35] *Criminal Procedure Law of the People's Republic of China* 1996, Chapter VI.

confers authority on the public security organizations to initially detain active criminals or major suspects under the following circumstances "(6) if he does not tell his true name and address and his identity is unknown; and (7) if he is strongly suspected of committing crimes from one place to another, repeatedly, or in a gang."[36] With respect to the Chapter VI of the new Criminal Procedure Law, it has been argued that some of these provisions are a major departure from the past legal policy and the administrative practice dealing with "the Detain for Examination."[37] The new Criminal Procedure Law provides clear and explicit guidelines for these compulsory measures, such as procedure for detention, procedure during detention, procedure for release, procedure for arrest, procedure for extension of detention, and the requirement for all investigative detentions to be accompanied by a detention warrant.[38] However, the fact is that these compulsory measures in the new Criminal Procedure Law are subject to a serious incidence of abuse by officials exceeding their investigative and other powers. The wide exercise of those powers will endanger not only privacy rights, but also other legal rights in China.

2.2.4 Evaluation of Official Powers

Careful examination makes it clear that intrusive powers exist widely in China. When authorized officers are empowered to conduct their duties, they may use some methods of control to ensure that they can achieve their desired outcome. These methods may include independent judicial scrutiny of the decision to use the power of entry, inspection, or arrest. The starting points of these methods may be correct, but the process and result of these methods seriously endanger the privacy interests of individuals in China. Someone may suggest that there should be a unit to monitor the conduct of current legislation in China. It has been proved that the monitoring of current legislation in a particular context, however, cannot solve all the problems.[39] For example, the process for officers to apply for an inspection warrant is easy and common in China. In this case, based on unsystematic legal development in China, even if the inspection is improper, the Chinese authorities have enough excuse to interpret that their activities are legal under certain laws. They can even interpret that they are conducting administrative duty rather than judicial duty. The author thus believes that the fundamental issue is that there is a lack of the consistent principles of protecting privacy in China. At present, the privacy issues raised by the official powers in China include: (1) whether all these official powers, which are conferred by Chinese current legislation, are really necessary to achieve their purposes; (2) whether adequate attention has been paid

---

[36] *Criminal Procedure Law of the People's Republic of China* 1996, art 61 (6) and (7).

[37] Wong (1996), p. 387.

[38] *Criminal Procedure Law of the People's Republic of China* 1996, arts 64, 65 and 69.

[39] Australian Law Reform Commission (1983), p. 115.

to the protection of privacy and other legal civil rights when we create or amend laws; and (3) whether the further powers of Chinese officials will result in an unwanted harm of privacy interests and other legal civil rights in Chinese society.

2.3 New Methods of Business Practices in China

A number of new methods of business practices also endanger privacy in China in certain aspects.

2.3.1 Increasing New Marketing Practices

Today, facing the booming economy in China, both international and domestic businesses are beginning to extend their products and activities in the Chinese market. New techniques of direct marketing, advertising, and solicitation by mail or telephone are thus widely practiced for commercial purposes in China. With respect to the direct mail, as the Chinese Post Office reported that, "in 2003, the direct mail increased rapidly, hitting 1.78 billion pieces, up 9.4% over last year, and its proportion to the total letter mail stood at 17.1%, 1.7 percentage points higher than the previous year."[40] Based on the Chinese population, the quantity of direct mail is huge. These numbers continue to increase these years. Furthermore, advertising and solicitation by telephone are also widely used in China. However, it has been argued that "while the technique of direct marketing is tolerated and, indeed, appreciated by many people, it causes great anxiety for others."[41] That is because some people may have an antipathy to receive advertising mails or telephone calls, and other people may have an antipathy to have their names and addresses made available without their consent.[42] The same concern about them is that their personal information is being used by some unknown people. This is thus a dangerous signal that, in order to satisfy the commercial interests of the direct marketers, privacy is being abused in contemporary Chinese society.

2.3.2 Private Security Officers and Investigators

Other important instances of Chinese market practices, which may endanger privacy, are intrusive conduct by private security officers and investigators. In recent years, more and more businesses have been established in China. Many of them

[40] China Post office (2005).

[41] Australian Law Reform Commission (1983), p. 39.

[42] Australian Law Reform Commission (1983), p. 39.

employ security staff to protect their business, such as supermarkets or retail shops. The main duty of these security personnel is to stop shoplifters. Likewise, in order to avoid the problem of insurance fraud, insurance agents usually have the legal right to investigate. At present, there is no regulation to regulate private security officers and private investigator in China. Therefore, the reality is that both security officer and private investigator have unlimited rights to take certain actions. Too many existed cases have shown that the frisk by the security officers in certain situations seems to be reasonable in China. In fact, both private security officers and investigators should not be allowed to have unlimited rights to take any actions they consider to be correct in certain situations.[43] Therefore, some external standards should be established in China, which can impose a balance between those who seek to intrude and those who are the subjects of that intrusion.[44]

2.3.3 New Business Practices Threatening Information Privacy

Many people may believe that the new business practices only endanger the privacy of individuals. In fact, new business practices also threaten information privacy. In the past 10 years, consumer credit facilities had become one of the most important commercial developments in China. Many corporate executives, economists, and global investors believe that there will be a sustained growth and vast opportunities in China's underdeveloped consumer credit markets.[45] Therefore, in the following years, credit facilities will be more and more common in Chinese society.

On the other hand, based on the Western experiences, credit facilities also produce certain fears in people's minds.[46] As the ALRC points out that:

> A modern credit system and the trail left behind by users of credit cards would enable the compilation of detailed personal profiles on individuals. ...An enormous range of information can now be assembled concerning single consumer of a vast range of goods and services. Once stored on computer it may be readily analyzed either on its own or in conjunction with information about other individuals. It may be readily transmitted to other data storage systems and could be used for an infinite variety of purposes over an indefinite period of time.[47]

Although the development of credit facilities is in the infant stage in China, the case of stealing other people's personal information of credit card to achieve illegal purposes has been found in Hai Nan province in China in 2008.[48] It is thus dangerous if we ignore the protection of information privacy in the new business practices.

[43] Australian Law Reform Commission (1983), p. 39.
[44] Australian Law Reform Commission (1983), p. 39.
[45] Stakelbeck (2005).
[46] Australian Law Reform Commission (1983), p. 40.
[47] Australian Law Reform Commission (1983), p. 40.
[48] Hai Nan News (2008).

2.4 New Technology in China

While increasing powers of governmental agencies and the new business practices pose threats to privacy, new development of technology places privacy at risk in China. For example, the wide popularity of computers and the Internet in China has permitted Chinese people to gain and save information more conveniently and easily. The following section explores the dangers to privacy from the new technology in China.

2.4.1 Information Processing Technology

2.4.1.1 Penetration of Computers and Internet in China

Today, the use of personal computers is taking off in China.[49] The total number of personal computers in China was about 12 million in 1999, and had jumped to 130 million in 2007.[50] One expert predicts, based on the population and the development of the economy, that the number of computers in China will double every 28 months.[51] With respect to the future of China's personal computers, Yang Yuanqing, president of Legend Group, China's largest personal computer manufacturer, points out that "the popularity of the personal computer (PC) in China is expected to increase at an annual rate of 25–30% in next 5 years. China's market will keep this growth momentum for 5–10 years."[52] Even so, it has been held that:

> PCs are far from being popular in China as the popularity rate was less than 30 percent in big cities, such as Beijing, Shanghai, and Guangzhou which were believed to have the strongest purchasing power across the country. The figure for the country as a whole was no more than 10 percent. The Chinese market has a huge potential...about 10 million medium-sized and small businesses in China are still using computers individually. Only 2 percent of the country's large and medium-sized enterprises have established their intranet.[53]

In addition, Internet accounts number is about 10 million in China.[54] By the end of 2008, the number of Internet users in the country reached about 253 million, helping China overtakes the United States as the world's biggest Internet market.[55]

---

[49] Mekay (2005). See: Reference "China Replacing the United States as World's Leading Consumer (2005)" http://www.atimes.com/atimes/China/GB18Ad01.html

[50] Mekay (2005). See: Reference "China Replacing the United States as World's Leading Consumer (2005)" http://www.atimes.com/atimes/China/GB18Ad01.html

[51] Mekay (2005). See: Reference "China Replacing the United States as World's Leading Consumer (2005)" http://www.atimes.com/atimes/China/GB18Ad01.html

[52] Tougher Time Loomed for China's PC Market (2001).

[53] China's PC Market Sees Great Potential (2001).

[54] China Statistics and Related Data Information and Links (2007).

[55] China's Information Technology (2008).

Table 2.1 The increase of internet account, the online computers and websites in China

Year	Internet account (million)	Number of online computers (million)	Number of websites
1997	0.62		
June 1999	4		
End of 1999	8.9		
June 2000	10		
End of 2000	16.9		
End of 2001	33.7		
June 2002	45		
End of 2002	59.1		
End of 2003	87	30.00	
End of 2004	94	41.69	430,000
End of 2005	111	49.50	694,200
End of 2006	123		2,600,000

Table 2.1 demonstrates the increase of Internet accounts, the number of online computers, and the number of websites from 1997 to 2006 in China[56]:

The impact of computers for contemporary Chinese society is self-evident. Today, more and more Chinese people realize that the importance of computer. The connection between computers, telecommunications, and other relative new technologies has enlarged the impact of the computer on Chinese society. However, the impact of computerization endangers privacy in certain aspects. It is mainly represented in two areas in modern China: the first is the area of public administration; and the second is the area of the finance industry.

2.4.1.2 Public Administration

The new information technology has had a significant impact on public administration in China. Today, it is impossible for many works to be carried out without the help of computers. For example, the system of collecting and claiming tax, named Chinese Golden Tax system, has been widely used by the Chinese Taxation office.[57] At present, in China, the main technologies in use in public administration include: statistical modeling, information/data retrieval and storage, automated filing systems, and so on.

2.4.1.3 Finance Industry

The new information technology has also had a significant impact on finance industry in China. For example, in banking, since the central computer was installed

[56] China Statistics and Related Data Information and Links (2007).

[57] The Analyse System of Tax Collection (2008).

in the Industrial and Commercial Bank of China, almost all branches, while located in different cities in China, have online information/data connection to the central information bank.[58] All branches can access to customers' records and information easily. Today, more and more finance industries in China rely on computer to undertake their tasks. In fact, Western developed countries' experiences have already shown that the growth of building societies, credit unions, merchant banks, and other financial institutions has been made possible only by the use of computers.[59] At present, in China, the main finance industries include: banking; insurance industry; finance companies; real estate agencies; investment services; other business services; and so on. All these finance industries depend on information.

2.4.2 *New Surveillance Technology*

Surveillance is defined as the systematic investigation or monitoring of the actions or communications of one or more persons.[60] Traditionally, surveillance has been undertaken by physical means, such as guarding prisons.[61] In recent decades, it has been enhanced through image amplification devices such as high-resolution satellite cameras.[62] Most of them are readily available in China today. However, some of them are also privacy invasive. They render current Chinese legal protections seriously inadequate. These devices may include: (1) microphones or listening devices that can be concealed; (2) miniature tape recorders; (3) hidden cameras such as cell phone cameras; (4) hidden monitors that operated by remote control; (5) infrared devices enabling photographs to be taken at night; (6) miniature transmitters; and so on.[63]

Initially, in China, most of these devices are used by the Chinese internal security agencies or in the company's security departments. For example, Chinese police use some of these devices to detect crime. Moreover, these devices can also help companies to minimize the risk of theft, to improve customer service, to assist in staff training, and to ensure that employees comply with legal obligations.[64] On the other hand, the misuse of these devices poses a threat of increased invasion of privacy in China. For example, today mobile phones with cameras are popular. It is easy for someone to take a photo using a mobile phone camera, but it is inappropriate that someone be photographed without their consent. Moreover, a person's

[58] The Introduction of Industrial and Commercial Bank of China (2008).

[59] Australian Law Reform Commission (1983), p. 50.

[60] Clarke (1993).

[61] Clarke (1993).

[62] Clarke (1993).

[63] China Monitor.

[64] Bogonikolos (1999).

location can be pinpointed by reference to the transmission tower used when a call is made or with the assistance of the inbuilt Global Positioning System (GPS), which is a feature of some recent model phones.[65] Therefore, all these surveillance devices that may invade individual privacy should be required to comply with appropriate standards.

2.4.3 Other Areas

The telephone network and related equipment have become more complex than ever before in China. Picture phones and data phones have been used in China for many years. Chinese fixed-line telecom operators, China Telecom, China Netcom and China Tie Tong (formally China Railcom) have already increased their efforts in building wireless LAN networks to provide their customers with fast and easy wireless access to the Internet.[66] It has been held that increased efficiency and sophistication of communications media will also make possible an expansion of existing modes into many situations.[67] Furthermore, other technologies, such as Document Facsimile Transmission, Optical Technology, Satellite Technology, Telex and Interactive Information Services and Cable TV and Telephone-Based Systems, have also been introduced to China and influenced Chinese people's lives.

Although there are likely no harms of introduction of these advanced technologies to China, based on Western experiences of protecting privacy, these technologies may also endangering privacy in China. For example, as the ALRC points out that:

> The privacy issue in the area of cable TV and telephone-based systems arises from the fact that the operators managing these systems will have access to an enormous pool of personal information from subscribers. It could cover: purchase of reading material, novelty items and magazine subscriptions; details about subscriptions to special information data bases; times owners left homes or turned off alarm systems; health conditions involving special alerts; the position taken by viewers on survey questions; home profiles produced from aggregating many individual responses, including purchases of sexually oriented films and services, and contributions to political, religious, social and charitable causes.[68]

It has been argued that the potential dangers of misuse of personal information in interactive services may include (1) the improper commercial use by the system operator; (2) breaches of confidentiality to the third parties; (3) commercial pressure on subscribers to authorize release of their information profile; and (4) investigation or litigation.[69]

---

[65] Fisher (2003).

[66] Contact China (2005).

[67] Australian Law Reform Commission (1983), p. 52.

[68] Australian Law Reform Commission (1983), p. 56.

[69] Australian Law Reform Commission (1983), pp. 56–57.

2.5 Need for Privacy Protection

In some certain developed countries, the development of privacy protection is more than a century. Therefore, the risks of invasion of privacy from the official intrusive powers described in this chapter are not new. It has been argued that "it is almost impossible to obtain an accurate quantification of the extent of unjustified interference with privacy."[70] That is because most invasions of privacy do not attract official notice. Moreover, there are no comprehensive legal principles protecting privacy interests in China. The current Chinese laws can only provide a partial response to invasions of privacy. The determined intruder always escapes detection or be detected only after the individual's privacy has been invaded.[71] It is difficult to say that the Chinese people are being hurt by serious privacy problems that caused by the intrusive powers and the development of technology. But it should be clear that the Chinese contemporary society is losing its privacy little by little. The author thus believes that if we cannot deal with privacy issues appropriately, it will be difficult for Chinese society to maintain liberty and democracy. With the rapid development of Chinese society, there will be more instances of invasion of privacy in China. As a consequence, legislative action is necessary.

The next Chapter of this book explores China's privacy standards and the privacy protection in both ancient and modern China. The purposes of the next chapter are to examine China's privacy standards firstly, and then to consider whether existing statutory privacy protections in modern China are able to effectively solve these privacy issues.

References

Journal Articles and Books

Chen JF (1999) Chinese law: towards an understanding of Chinese law, its nature, and development. Kluwer, The Hague

Wong KC (1996) Police powers and control in the People's Republic of China: the history of ShouShen. Columbia J Asian Law 10:367

Legislation

Criminal Procedure Law of the People's Republic of China 1996

Customs Act 1901 (Cth)

Customs Law of the People's Republic of China 2001

---

[70] Australian Law Reform Commission (1983), p. 59.

[71] Australian Law Reform Commission (1983), p. 59.

Detailed Rules about Measures for Detaining and Sending Back of Vagrants and Beggars in Cities 1992 (China)
Electric Power Law of the People's Republic of China 1995
Law of the People's Republic of China Concerning the Administration of Tax Collection 2001
Law of the People's Republic of China on Animal Epidemic Prevention 1998
Law of the People's Republic of China on the Control of the Exit and Entry of Citizens 1986
Law of the People's Republic of China on the Prevention and Treatment of Infectious Diseases 2004
Measures for Detaining and Sending Back of Vagrants and Beggars in Cities 1982 (China)
Postal Law of the People's Republic of China 1986
Procedures of the People's Republic of China about Shelter for Repatriating
Regulations of the People's Republic of China for Customs Check 1997
Regulations on the Safety Administration of Dangerous Chemicals 2002 (China)
Rules for the Implementation of the Law of the People's Republic of China Concerning the Administration of Tax Collection 2002

Government and Law Reform Reports

Australian Law Reform Commission (1983) Privacy. Report Paper No. 22, Volume 1
Bogonikolos N (1999) Development of surveillance technology and risk of abuse of economic information. Working document for the STOA Panel, European Parliament PE 168.184/Int.St./ part 1/4

Electronic Materials

Annual Report of Public Services (2005) China Post office. http://www.chinapost.gov.cn/. Accessed 7 April 2011
China Monitor (Wang Hao trans) [trans of: 中国监控设备] 中国监控设备网. http://www.cn-jkw.cn/product/product.aspx. Accessed 7 April 2011
China Replacing the United States as World's Leading Consumer (2005) Earth Policy Institute. http://www.earth-policy.org/Updates/Update45.html. Accessed 7 April 2011
China Statistics and Related Data Information and Links (2007) China Today.com. http://www.chinatoday.com/data/data.htm. Accessed 7 April 2011
China's Information Technology (2008) China Today.com. http://www.chinatoday.com/it/it.htm. Accessed 7 April 2011
China's PC Market Sees Great Potential (2001) China.org.cn. http://www.china.org.cn/english/16704.htm. Accessed 7 April 2011
Clarke R (1993) Dataveillance: DELIVERING '1984' Roger Clarke's Web-Site. http://www.rogerclarke.com/DV/PaperPopular.html. Accessed 7 April 2011
Contact China (2005) A Resource Guide for Doing Business in the People's Republic of China (2005) p. 48. http://www.usembassy-china.org.cn/fcs/pdf/contact_china.pdf. Accessed 7 April 2011
Fisher M (2003) Mobile phones with cameras privacy victoria. http://www.privacy.vic.gov.au/dir100/PriWeb.nsf/download/5E60D920487E4F34CA256D9000251656/$FILE/05.03Phonecam_MFcredit9pt.pdf. Accessed 7 April 2011
Hai Nan News (2008) Hackers Stealing Other Peoples Credit Card Number in Hainan Province of China (Wang Hao trans) [trans of: 海南省出现个人信息泄露]. http://www.hi.chinanews.com.cn/hnnew/2008-10-19/128195.html. Accessed 7 April 2011

Stakelbeck FW (2005) Time for a Chinese Equifax. Asia Times http://www.atimes.com/atimes/china_business/gj15cb01.html. Accessed 7 April 2011

The Analyse System of Tax Collection (Wang Hao trans) [trans of: 国税税收监控分析系统] (2008) CCID. http://media.ccidnet.com/art/2615/20060512/551641_1.html. Accessed 7 April 2011

The Introduction of Industrial and Commercial Bank of China (Wang Hao trans) [trans of: 中国工商银行简介] (2008) Industrial and Commercial Bank of China. http://www.icbc.com.cn/ICBC/%E5%B7%A5%E8%A1%8C%E9%A3%8E%E8%B2%8C/%E5%B7%A5%E8%A1%8C%E7%AE%80%E4%BB%8B/. Accessed 7 April 2011

Tougher Time Loomed for China's PC Market (2001) China Education and Research Network. http://www.edu.cn/200111_1531/20060323/t20060323_20399.shtml. Accessed 7 April 2011

Chapter 3
China's Privacy Standards

3.1 Introduction

China has one of the longest periods of civilization as a country in the world. In ancient China, the civil disputes were solved by moral principles of Confucianism, which is called "*Li*" (礼). Therefore, at the time of the emergence of *Li*, privacy had been protected indirectly to some extent. However, there are two sides to every story. *Li* indirectly protected privacy in ancient Chinese society on the one hand, but on the other hand, the existence of *Li* also restrained the development of legal privacy protection at that time. Moreover, the substantial meaning of traditional protection for privacy is quite different from modern society. In consequence, it is difficult to postulate that there was legal protection for privacy in ancient China, though privacy had been indirectly protected by the theory of *Li*.

If the article entitled "The Right to Privacy" by Samuel Warren and Louis Brandeis is seen as a milestone in the evolution of the right to privacy in modern society, the modern concept and protection of privacy emerged almost a century later in the PRC than in some certain Western countries.[1] Before 1988, there were not any books or articles on the right to privacy published in the PRC. The first consideration for the protection of privacy in the PRC was a judicial interpretation by the Supreme People's Court in 1988.[2] Since then, China begins to develop its own protection for privacy. Although the Chinese government attempts to protect privacy legally in recent years, all these activities are concerned primarily with general ideas of privacy. A number of problems are still not addressed, such as the distinction between the right of reputation and the right to privacy, or the conflict

[1] Zhu (1997), p. 208.

[2] The title of this judicial interpretation is *Opinions of the Supreme People's Court on Several Issues concerning the Implementation of the General Principles of the Civil Law of the People's Republic of China* (For Trial Implementation) (1988).

H. Wang, *Protecting Privacy in China*,

DOI 10.1007/978-3-642-21750-0_3,

between the freedom of expression and the right to privacy.[3] This is thus a dangerous signal that the current privacy protection in China is not sufficient in certain aspects.

The purpose of this chapter is to explore privacy standards in both ancient and modern China, and consider whether existing privacy protections in China can effectively solve current privacy issues as discussed in Chap. 2. Further, according to China's national circumstances, it can be inferred that the privacy in China is expected to continue to change in the future. Hence, the author explores the future of privacy in China from the following two aspects, which are the public consciousness of privacy in China and the theoretical basis of privacy in China, respectively. This chapter thus has three main parts. The first part discusses privacy in ancient China, which includes traditional Chinese concepts of privacy, traditional Chinese protections for privacy and their evaluation. The second part examines privacy standards and privacy protection in modern China. This part discusses who will enjoy privacy protection in contemporary China and the features of current Chinese privacy protection. The author also explores the possible theories to explain the insufficient level of privacy protection in modern China. The third part discusses the possible development trend of privacy in contemporary Chinese society. Finally, two suggestions are made.

3.2 Privacy in Ancient China

3.2.1 Traditional Definition of Privacy

The traditional Chinese word for "privacy" is "*yin-si*" (阴私). "*Yin-si*" consists of two Chinese words, which are "*yin*" (阴) and "*si*" (私). "*Yin*" means "hidden from view" (隐藏的，不露在外面的).[4] Usually, this is a word possesses derogatory sense and means illegitimate sexual relationship in Chinese. "*Si*" means "private" or "do not want to disclose in public" (秘密的；不公开的).[5] This word covers both "private" and "privacy".[6] "*Yin-si*" has been defined as an individual's shameful secret that the individual does not want to tell others or be disclosed to the public.[7] Strictly speaking, the meaning of the Chinese word "*yin-si*" only represents one aspect of the modern concept of "privacy."

[3] Chao (2005), p. 646.

[4] Zuoqiu 403 BC – 386 BC, Xi gong 15th year.

[5] Sima 91 BC, vol. 7.

[6] McDougall and Hansson (2002), p. 6.

[7] Han Dictionary.

3.2.2 Traditional Protection for Privacy

Ancient Chinese law emphasized the significance of protecting government powers and social interests rather than protecting individual rights and civil matters.[8] Thus, the law did not divide formally into the criminal law and the civil law in ancient China. The law was constructed on the basis of a monolithic and comprehensive code that contained all types of rules, with criminal law as the backbone of the entire system.[9]

On the other hand, this is not to say that there was no civil protection in ancient China. The ancient Chinese legal system defined the duties and obligations of individuals, and this in turn indirectly protected the rights of the individuals.[10] The civil disputes were solved by the theory of "*Li*." Initially, *Li* (ritual rules, etiquette) had been defined as the norms governing the conduct of royal family members and nobles in China.[11] Books of *Li* were carefully kept in the hands of official historians and the common people had no opportunity to accept the teaching of *Li*.[12] This phenomenon was not eliminated until the emergence of the systematic theory of *Li*. The task of establishing a systematic theory of *Li* was completed by Confucius in the Spring and Autumn periods (770–476BC) and the early days of the Warring States periods (475–221 BC).[13]

The core of theory of *Li* is to cultivate morality. In Confucians' view, both ideal social order and perfect human relation can be achieved on the basis of theory of *Li* (morality). Confucians did believe that lead the people "by virtue and keep them in order by the established morality (*Li*), and they will keep their self-respect and come to you."[14] In addition, Confucius states that "do not do to others as you would not wish done to yourself (己所不欲, 勿施于人)."[15] Based on these two famous statements, obviously, morality has been seen as the most effective means to govern a country and regulate civil matters in the theory of *Li*. Confucius treats all people as equal human beings, and believes that certain essential principles of *Li* should be applicable to all people and to all human relationships.[16] Thus, the theory of *Li* has two major functions: one is as a national code reflecting social change; and the other is to train personal character and encourage moral behavior. In order words, "*Li*" influenced the social and state systems and people's thoughts and behavior in

[8] Wang and Zhang (1997), p. 7.

[9] Wang and Zhang (1997), p. 5.

[10] Ladany (1992), p. 33.

[11] Wang and Zhang (1997), p. 3.

[12] Liu (1998), p. 73.

[13] Liu (1998), p. 89.

[14] Chen (1999), p. 7.

[15] Liu (1998), p. 93.

[16] Liu (1998), p. 90.

ancient China.[17] In this respect, Confucius' theory of "*Li*" had the same function as the Western concept of natural law, and was a set of ethical standards that regulated both social conducts and civil matters in ancient China.[18]

The protection of privacy (*yin-si*) was first stated by the famous Analects of Confucius (论语) in the early days of the Warring States periods. As Confucius did state that "do not watch what is improper; do not listen to what is improper; do not speak improperly and do not act improperly (非礼勿视, 非礼勿听, 非礼勿言, 非礼勿动)."[19] Confucius also stated that "to get and talk from gossip or hearsay is improper (道听而涂说, 德之弃也)."[20] Clearly, these two doctrines clearly restricted individual's behaviors to invade other people's private lives. Furthermore, Confucius did believe that there is a border between family and outsiders, and this border maintains the family space free from interference, reserves a right not to reveal family matters, and allows a closely intimate relationship that is differentiated from outsiders.[21] All these doctrines, to some extent, protected the *yin-si* rights of the individuals at that time. In addition, almost all famous Chinese ancient codes such as the *Tang Code* (唐律疏议 624 AD) and the *Ming Code* (大明律 1397 AD) listed impiety as major crimes. This article prohibited reporting one's grandparents' or parents' crimes to the authorities and cursing them.[22] Although the main object of punishing impiety was to consolidate social relationships based on the five major relationships of *Li*, the crime of impiety indirectly prohibited people reporting their grandparents' or parents' personal information to a third party.

It should be noted that the main aims of these doctrines and provisions were not to protect individual's personal privacy. The protection of privacy (*yin-si*) was only the by-product of implementing these doctrines and provisions. Moreover, breaches of *yin-si* were seen as a minor civil matter in ancient China. Usually, the state's legal system did not intervene in such matters, and minor civil disputes would be settled by society itself using its own mediatory methods at that time.[23] Also, based on the traditional meaning of *yin-si*, most Chinese people believed that matters concerned with *yin-si* was shameful, and they did not want them be disclosed.[24] If the invasion was inevitable, they would rather ignore the invasion. Therefore, there are not any records of *yin-si* disputes recorded in writing in ancient China. In fact, Chinese concept of "*yin-si*" was not an equivalent term for the modern concept of "privacy." As Shin-yi Peng states that "at best, we can say that by emphasizing the family/kinship intimacy, some sort of ambiguous "privacy rights" can be found in

[17] Wang (2000), p. 4.
[18] Liu (1998), p. 90.
[19] Confucius, Yen Yüan 12th (1).
[20] Confucius, Yang Huo 17th (14).
[21] Peng (2003), p. 1039.
[22] Kim (1981), p. 98.
[23] Huang (1996), p. 10.
[24] Chao (2005), p. 647.

terms of maintaining family space free from outside interference."[25] It is thus difficult to conclude that there was legal protection for the right to privacy in ancient China, though privacy had been indirectly protected by *Li*.

3.2.3 Possible Theories to Explain the Insufficient Level of Privacy Protection in Ancient China

The possible reasons why the right to privacy (*yin-si*) was not legally protected in ancient China are identified by the author as follows:

3.2.3.1 Absolute Privilege of the Ruling Class

In ancient Chinese society, the rights enjoyed by a person were accorded in relation to one's social status and one's status in the family system.[26] Citizens had been divided into two main categories: the free people, and the serf-people, in feudal China.[27] The free people are upper class, consisting of literati (or official) and ordinary citizens; and the serf-people consisted of two different types, which include governmental serf and private serf.[28] The serf-people's freedom of movement and residence was determined by their master.[29] Compared to the serf-people, their master's right was absolute. Moreover, in order to establish ideal human relationship, Confucianism identified and stressed the five major relationships (emperor–subject, father–son, husband–wife, elder brother–younger brother, and friend–friend). Family relationship in ancient China consists of "father and son," "husband and wife," and "elder brother and younger brother." In this Chinese autocratic family system, Confucian doctrine laid heavy obligations on the son, wife, and children.[30] Compared to the son, wife and younger brother, the rights of father, husband and elder brother were always absolute. It has been argued that "since individuals are subsumed into these different relationships, there are no expectations of these family members for their privacy right within the household."[31]

It is thus clear that, in feudal China, the status of the master and the father, husband and elder brother had the legally dominant position and absolute privilege

---

[25] Peng (2003), p. 1040.

[26] Kim (1981), p, 96.

[27] Kim (1981), p, 96.

[28] Kim (1981), p, 96.

[29] Kim (1981), p, 96.

[30] Peng (2003), p. 1039.

[31] Peng (2003), p. 1039.

over the status of slave, son, wife, and younger brother.[32] It was inevitable that the civil rights of individuals were largely weakened. Moreover, the ruling class controlled the formation of law at that time. Law was not a concept set by the people but imposed from above, to which the people must conform.[33] Ancient Chinese law is only a political tool concerned for the state and the interests of the ruling class, rather than individual rights. The protection for the right to privacy (*yin-si*), however, would challenge the dominant position of the ruling class and the traditional social order at that time. As a consequence, the ruling class would not protect the right to privacy in ancient China.

3.2.3.2 Traditional Attitude to Civil Disputes

Confucianism, as a set of ethical standards, has influenced Chinese people for thousands years in China. As mentioned earlier, the core of theory of *Li* is to cultivate morality. Therefore, the values that Confucianism cherished are co-operation and collaboration, hierarchy and harmony, peace and stability.[34] However, Confucian doctrine unduly stressed the importance of the functioning and the maintenance of the group. It has been argued that Confucianism is more likely to look within the group membership to obtain social harmony, rather than seeking external agencies in the enforcement of one's rights.[35] Any disputes would disturb the desire for social harmony, and any disturbance of this harmony was unacceptable at that time.[36] Therefore, in ancient China, almost every person tried to avoid any civil disputes. If civil disputes were unavoidable, the Chinese method of dealing with them was conciliation or mediation.[37] It is thus clear that inevitable privacy issues, as with minor civil matters, had been solved by society itself in ancient China, though there are no records to prove if this was the case. In consequence, the traditional attitude toward civil disputes demonstrates that it was impossible to ensure privacy rights in ancient Chinese society.

3.2.3.3 Traditional Sense of "Face"

"Face" is a unique word in Chinese. Besides its original meaning, this term is a literal translation of the Chinese "*mian-zi*" (面子) and "*lian*" (脸).[38] It has been

[32] Kim (1981), p. 97.
[33] Kim (1981), p. 17.
[34] Chen (2002), p. 8.
[35] Chen (2002), p. 8.
[36] Chen (2002), p. 9.
[37] Chen (2002), p. 9.
[38] Ho (1976), p. 867.

argued that *mian-zi* is "a reputation achieved through getting on in life through suuess and ostentation"; while *Lian*, on the other hand, "represents the confidence of society in the integrity of ego's moral character, the loss of which makes it impossible for him to function properly within the community."[39] That is to say, in China, "face" is construed to mean one's social prestige and accumulated morality in the eyes of the community.[40] Losing face is losing honor and self-respect.[41] Therefore, it has been held that the principle of "face" is the Chinese equivalent of "honour."[42] For a Chinese person, maintaining face is very important in Chinese social relations. Someone even postulated that "you would rather die than being humiliated (士可杀, 而不可辱)."[43] As Pye states that "the heavy use of shame as a social control mechanism from the time of early childhood tends to cause feelings of dependency and anxieties about self-esteem, which naturally produces self-consciousness about most social relationships."[44] Based on this social phenomenon, most Chinese people believed that matters concerned with *yin-si* was shameful, they did not want them to be disclosed. The publicity of *yin-si* issues would mean the loss of their "face." Therefore, the concern with face, especially moral face, provided an internal moral constraint that directed individuals' actions.[45] Thus, even if the invasion of their privacy was inevitable, they preferred to ignore the invasion.

This opinion has been tested in a case that happened in the early days of the PRC.

- Two young men, who worked as village security guards at night, were suspicious that a third man had stolen some crops, so they followed him to the gate of his yard. When the two guards entered the house, however, they met only the suspect's wife, who said her husband was not home. They insisted that they had seen her husband stealing and then searched the room; the wife then started to cry and accused the two young men of sexual misconduct. Although the two guards left the house as quickly as possible, she filed a complaint against them until they agreed to pay her 500 *yuan* as a gesture of apology. The investigation of her husband was also dropped.[46]

This is a typical means to solve civil disputes in China. In the traditional Chinese sense, sexual misconduct is usually not explicitly illegal; however, it is often against the traditional codes of ethics. Therefore, this kind of activity is abominable in China. Moreover, the two security guards failed to prove that the suspect had

[39] Ho (1976), pp. 867–868.

[40] Chen (2002), pp. 52–53.

[41] Ladany (1992), p. 23.

[42] Chen (2002), p. 52.

[43] Dai and Dai (eds), ch 41.

[44] Chen (2002), p. 53.

[45] Chen (2002), p. 54.

[46] Yan (2003), p. 126.

stolen any crops. They thus believed that what they did had already damaged their "face." If this dispute was disclosed to others, in their minds, they would lose their "face" totally. As a result, in order to save their face, they chose to pay suspect's wife 500 *yuan* to suppress this dispute. On the other hand, for the both suspect and his wife, the loss of privacy also represented a loss of "face." Similarly, in order to avoid the publicity of this dispute, the suspect's wife was also willing to accept 500 *yuan*. Most Chinese people normally tried to prevent a civil (particularly personal or private) dispute from arising, or tried to solve these problems secretly. As a consequence, the traditional sense of "face" also hindered the development of privacy protection in ancient China.

3.2.4 Summary

As discussed above, the indirect protection of privacy in ancient China was only one of the results of the regulating of social harmony by the ruling class. The theory of "*Li*" indirectly protected privacy in ancient Chinese society on the one hand, and on the other hand, the existence of "*Li*" also restrained the development of the right to privacy at that time. When Chinese people's privacy was invaded, they would rather ignore the invasion if it is bearable.[47] If civil disputes were unavoidable, as mentioned earlier, the Chinese method to deal with them was conciliation or mediation. In other words, inevitable privacy issues, as with minor civil matters, had been solved by society itself in ancient China. All these facts may explore the possible reasons why the right to privacy (*yin-si*) was not legally protected in ancient China.

3.3 Privacy in Modern China

3.3.1 The Development and Changes of Privacy Ideas in Contemporary China

3.3.1.1 The Great Changes of Privacy Ideas in Modern China

It has been 30 years since Xiaoping Deng proposed reform and opening up policy in China in 1978. During these 30 years, China has been undergoing essential changes in every corner of the society. These changes can be reflected in four aspects, which are economic field, ideological field, urbanization, and media, respectively.

[47] Chao (2005), p. 647.

First, China's economy is growing rapidly as a result of reform in economic structure. Socialist market economy system replaces the traditional planned economy system. Under the traditional planned economy system, collective interests dominated because of ownership by the whole people. By contrast, according to the nature of market economy, individual is regarded as an independent subject and individual interests are valued. Moreover, one of the important measures of reform is to define the private ownership economy as an important component of socialist economy. Therefore, pursuing individual economic interests is no longer such a taboo subject in China. As a result, today, individual has been regarded as an independent subject and encouraged to pursue individual interests. In addition, economic growth promotes individual's economic independent. In the past, a part of Chinese people did not or could not find an opportunity to earn money to support themselves but rather depended on the others. For example, based on traditional family system, it was very difficult for women in the past to earn enough money. So most women preferred to stay at home and making money was their husbands' task. Therefore, lack of the individual economic independent impeded this part of Chinese to pursue their personal interests. But today, most Chinese are economic independent and thus dare to pursue their complete individual rights.

Second, with opening to the outside world, Western values have gradually permeated throughout the Chinese people in spite of the predominance of traditional values. Western values advocate individual personality and highly praise the development based on individual characteristics. The freedom and equality thinking of Western values makes Chinese begin to value and struggle for their due interests, which include the right to privacy. At the same time, individual's quality has also been improved with the higher educational level. Besides the popularization of primary and secondary education, China increases the investment and enrolment in higher education. Also, increasing Chinese people and scholars are studying overseas in order to broaden their horizon and enhance their knowledge. Therefore, more and more Chinese people realize that they should respect the other people's individual rights such as right to privacy.

Third, more and more Chinese people are moving from rural areas to urban areas due to urbanization. China is a populous country and the rural population accounted for more than 80% in 1970s.[48] Under the reform, the focus is shifted to the cities. Hence, remarkable disparity in economic development can currently be noticed between rural and urban areas. Facing this situation, lots of people in rural areas choose to find job and lead a better life in the city. There are about 10 million new rural labor forces moving annual to the urban areas, and the urban population increased to 43% in 2005.[49] The urbanization process also creates a necessary condition for the development of privacy in contemporary China. In the past, the majority of Chinese lived in rural areas. Almost all the family members lived in the

[48] Zhang and Jiang (1989).

[49] National Development and Reform Commission of PRC 2007, p. 15.

same place. In that case, people were intimate to each other and hence people tended to care for the others' privacy and at the same time they would like to pour out their hearts or troubles to the others. However, the situation has changed with the urbanization process. More and more people move to cities. People coming from the different parts of China are no longer so close to each other. In consequence, they do not want to share their privacy with the others and the other people are not so interested in their private affairs like before.

Fourth, with the technology advancement, media have played an indispensable role in Chinese social life. The popularization of the Internet in twenty-first century, in particular, has transformed the Chinese people's lifestyle. Advanced technology and popularization of the Internet provide a medium for the changes of privacy ideas. In spite of the conveniences of advanced technology and Internet, both of them bring about many privacy issues in new forms. Especially, the anonymity of online behaviors compounds privacy invasion in China. Therefore, Chinese people begin to claim their interests of privacy.

3.3.1.2 The Impacts on Privacy Ideas

All these essential changes in current China bring about increasing diversity, which has a great effect upon Chinese people's ideas of privacy. Chinese people begin to pay more attention to the privacy and their consciousness of privacy turns out to be diversified. Three major changes have taken place in privacy ideas in modern China.

First, Chinese people begin to realize and value their rights to privacy. In the past, one of the ways to judge the loyalty and intimacy of a person to his or her friend, family, party and country is to check whether he or she confesses anything, including his or her personal information. But now, if an individual does not want his or her personal information to be disclosed publicly, he or she would refuse to answer any questions that may relate to his or her privacy. In addition, in China, with a view to protecting their children, the parents always think that their children should keep no secrets from them. Hence, the Chinese parents always take reading their children's diary or entering their room without permission. In spite of the good intention, the children, particularly in the urban area, protest against their parents' excessive concern with the plea of "I want to live in my own world." Also, some movie stars usually use "this is my privacy" as a reason to avoid any questions raised by journalists that they do not want to answer and to accuse the other persons of intrusively interfering with their personal affairs.

Second, more and more Chinese people begin to respect other people's privacy. For example: if a person in China is found carrying with Hepatitis B Virus (HBV), this information would be disclosed even when he/she is a little child. As a result, this person is likely to suffer discrimination not only in the daily life but also in employment. Most of the employers in China, especially before 2003, usually demand a compulsory health check up before employing the applicants and will refuse to employ the HBV carriers no matter how excellent they are. In this circumstance, it is very difficult for the individuals who are carrying with HBV to find an appropriate job. Nowadays, although the discrimination against the HBV carriers has not been basically eliminated, China has realized the necessity of protecting the privacy of HBV carriers and has managed to prevent the carrier's personal information from being leaked through detailed regulations in 2007. [50]

Third, the definition of privacy per se has been expanded. As mentioned earlier, the privacy in ancient China was confined to "*yin-si*," which possesses derogatory sense and means illegitimate sexual relationship that people do not want to be disclosed. However, based on Western developed countries' experiences, the definition of privacy in modern China has been expanded in certain aspects. It includes all personal information that people do not want others to know and personal living that people do not to be disturbed. Today, China has accepted the new concept of privacy, and does no longer regard privacy as shameful secret.

As a summary, the Chinese ideas of privacy are experiencing great changes. Chinese citizens begin to realize and claim their interests of privacy and have gradually understood that they are free to dispose of their own privacy. As a consequence, more and more people begin to express their concern about the protection of legitimate rights to privacy in contemporary China.

3.3.2 Modern Definition of Privacy in China

With the reforms and opening up, as mentioned earlier, the Chinese ideas of privacy are experiencing great changes. Based on the Western opinions of privacy and the right to privacy, at the time that the *General Principles of the Civil Law of the PRC* (1986) (the GPCL) emerged in China, some famous Chinese scholars began to develop Chinese definitions of privacy and the right to privacy.

For some, the right to privacy is one aspect of the personal rights. As Zhang Xinbao states that "the right to privacy is a legal right, by which citizens" residences, inner world, financial situations, social relations, sexual life, and past and current matters of purely personal nature they do not wish to divulge to the outside world are protected from any intrusion by others'. [51] For others, the right to privacy includes both freedom from disclosure of private life and the protection for personal life. Tong Ru, the leading civil law scholar, states that "the right to privacy, also called the right to private life, is a right of personality under which any interference by others with citizens' secrets and liberty of personal life is prohibited."[52] Professor Yang Lixin believes that "the right to privacy is a right of publicity, enjoyed by natural persons only, under which they can dominate their

---

[50] See *Opinions on Protecting the Working Rights of HBV Carriers* 2007.

[51] Zhang (2004), p. 7.

[52] Tong (1990), p. 487.

personal information, private spaces, and private activities."[53] Still others developed the existing analysis, and summarized a further definition. As Wang Liming, civil law professor, postulates that "the right to privacy is a right of personality, enjoyed by a natural person, under which he can dispose of all personal information, private activities, and private areas which belong only to the person and have no relation to public interest".[54]

3.3.3 *Subjects Enjoying Privacy Protection*

Very few people believe that privacy protection can be enjoyed equally by all citizens. This section discusses the subjects who can enjoy privacy protection in modern China.

3.3.3.1 *Citizens (Natural Persons)*

According to the Chinese law, the citizen (natural persons) and the legal person are the two basic types of civil subjects in China. Article 9 of the GPCL clearly states that "a citizen shall have the capacity for civil rights from birth to death and shall enjoy civil rights and assume civil obligations in accordance with the law." However, there are no definitions of "birth" and "death" in the GPCL.[55]

With reference to "birth," the prevalent view in China believes that the separation of a living infant from the mother's body is the indication of birth.[56] As Wang Guiguo states that "a premature baby becomes a citizen earlier merely because of the accident causing the premature birth. A delayed birth merely delays the infant's right to be recognized as a citizen earlier."[57] The capacity to have civil rights in China thus should start from the time of total separation of a living infant from the maternal body. Accordingly, the right recognized in article 9 of the GPCL is the right of a born human being, rather than a "human being."[58] In addition, it should be noted that neither the GPCL nor the Supreme Court views on the GPCL recognize the interest of the fetus.[59] As a consequence, it is clear that a fetus has neither legal rights nor civil rights under the current Chinese law. Therefore, in China, a Chinese citizen has privacy rights and enjoys legal privacy protection after he or she is born.

[53] Yang (2006), p. 304.

[54] Wang (1994), p. 487.

[55] Wang and Mo (1999), p. 101.

[56] Wang and Mo (1999), p. 101.

[57] Wang and Mo (1999), p. 101.

[58] Wang and Mo (1999), p. 101.

[59] Chen (1999), p. 228.

It should be noted that, some Chinese legal scholars think that if the goal of protection of privacy is to protect dignity and feelings, dead people have no feelings about the disclosure of personal information, so it is not necessary to extend the protection to cover them.[60] However, personal information of the deceased cannot disappear with the dead. As Mark Littman points out that "man is a social animal, no human being can exist for long in total isolation from all others."[61] For example, if our doctors release a patient's medical information after his or death, the decedent's family members or friends will inevitably suffer discrimination to some extent. Hence, we should not ignore the privacy interests of those who are living. In addition, in 2001, the *Interpretation of the Supreme People's Court on Problems regarding the Ascertainment of Compensation Liability for Emotional Damages in Civil Torts* provides legal protection of privacy to deceased person. Article 3 of the Interpretation clearly states that the relatives can sue illegal disclosure or use of the privacy of a deceased person or infringement upon the privacy by other means contrary to the societal public interests or societal morality. The author of this book thus believes that the deceased enjoy privacy protection in China, which is not only to protect the reputation of the deceased, but also to adequately protect the privacy interests of those who are living. In consequence, in theory, a Chinese citizen has privacy rights and enjoys legal privacy protection from birth to death under the contemporary Chinese law.

3.3.3.2 Legal Persons

Another civil subject in China is the "legal person (法人)." The formal concept of legal person was officially introduced into the GPCL in 1986.[62] The legal position of "legal persons" in China is dealt with in Chapter Three of the GPCL. Article 36 of the GPCL states that:

> A legal person shall be an organization that has capacity for civil rights and capacity for civil conduct and independently enjoys civil rights and assumes civil obligations in accordance with the law. A legal person's capacity for civil rights and capacity for civil conduct shall begin when the legal person is established and shall end when the legal person terminates.

In modern Chinese law, a legal person and a natural person are equal in certain aspects, and the legal person does not exercise those rights and undertake those liabilities that can only be executed by a natural person.[63] Two types of legal persons are provided by the GPCL, which are enterprise legal persons

---

[60] Chao (2005), p. 654.

[61] Littman (1970), p. 4.

[62] Wang and Mo (1999), p. 119.

[63] Wang and Mo (1999), p. 119.

(企业法人),[64] and official organs (机关), institutions (事业单位), and social organizations legal persons (社会团体).[65]

At present, the prevalent view in China is that only a natural person has the right to privacy and can enjoy privacy protection.[66] As Liang Huixin and Liao Xinzhong state that "people's perception is the origin of privacy, therefore only natural persons are able to enjoy privacy."[67] They believe that the confidential information of enterprise legal persons and other social organizations are trade secrets, and there is no connection between these confidential information and people's feelings.[68] Similarly, Wang Lizhong and Yang Junxing also emphasize the existence of the right to privacy is based on the emotions of natural persons.[69] They believe that enterprise legal persons or other organizations cannot enjoy the right to privacy on the basis of they do not have feelings or emotions, and the parallel right is that relating to trade secrets, which is a property right.[70] Therefore, at present, enterprise legal persons cannot enjoy privacy protection in China.

Other kinds of legal person in China are official organs, institutions, and social organizations. The GPCL does not clearly define these legal persons. However, Chinese literature interprets them to include those nonprofit-seeking organs, which are funded by the state, such as administrative, educational, health or academic institutions.[71] Accordingly, Chinese scholars believe that such organizations' "public" character should preclude them from involving the law of privacy to protect their secrets.[72] Such organizations should be transparent, open, and accountable to the public. If the right to privacy of such organizations were ensured, the corruption will increase inevitably. It is thus clear that official organ, institution and social organization as legal persons also do not enjoy the right to privacy in China. As a summary, the majority of Chinese scholars believe only born citizens (natural persons) can be the subjects of the right to privacy. Legal persons, however, seemingly have no right to enjoy privacy.

On the other hand, the author holds the objection that enterprise legal persons should enjoy privacy protection in China. As mentioned earlier, most Chinese scholars believe that an enterprise only has trade secrets. From a practical viewpoint, trade secrets can comprise any information that gives a business a competitive edge over competitors.[73] Obviously, the term "trade secret" includes a number

---

[64] *General Principles of the Civil Law of the People's Republic of China* 1986, s 2.

[65] *General Principles of the Civil Law of the People's Republic of China* 1986, s 3.

[66] Chao (2005), p. 652.

[67] Liang and Liao (2003).

[68] Liang and Liao (2003).

[69] Chao (2005), p. 652.

[70] Chao (2005), p. 652.

[71] Chen (1999), p. 234.

[72] Chao (2005), p. 653.

[73] Dorr and Munch (1995), p. 45.

of types of business information. As Hyman Gross states that "any information may become a trade secret if it is of value in a business, is confidential, and is of continuing usefulness."[74] In this regard, trade secret seems similar to privacy. However, it is not excusable for Chinese scholars to simply use the term "trade secret" as a substitute for privacy. Gross also points out that "trade secrets are parts of the business itself, not isolated matters in the course of its conduct . . . A trade secret belongs to a particular business, not to a trade or industry."[75] Usually, there are two criteria of trade secrets:

1. Derives independent economic value, actual or potential, from no being generally known to, and not being readily ascertainable by proper means by, other persons who can obtain economic value from its disclosure or use and
2. Is the subject of efforts that are reasonable under the circumstances to maintain its secrecy[76]

Some information about a business may be publicly known, such as the amount of a bid submitted or the time when an important announcement is to be made; some information may not be publicly known, where it relates only to a single occurrence in the lifetime of the enterprise, such as an accident on one particular occasion.[77] All this information cannot be deemed as trade secrets. The disclosure of such information will be harmful to the enterprise, though legal persons do not have feeling or emotion. For example, an unsuccessful bid may affect the next bid, and a serious accident may influence the production of that enterprise. Therefore, similar to an individual hopes to keep his or her personal information out of public view, an organization also need internal privacy to conduct its affairs without having to keep up a "public face."[78] That is to say enterprise legal persons also need the right to decide when and to what extent their information should be made public. Therefore, legal person's privacy is needed and important if a legal person is to play the role of independent and responsible agent that is assigned to them in democratic societies.[79]

As a consequence, in author's view, privacy information differs from trade secret. Privacy is the ability of an individual or group to keep their lives and personal affairs out of public view. Privacy not only includes secrets but also other nonconfidential information.[80] That is to say not all information of an enterprise is a trade secret; some of it is the privacy of the enterprise legal persons. There are no legislation or legal documents to explain whether enterprise has the

[74] Gross (1976), p. 66.
[75] Gross (1976), p. 66.
[76] Dorr and Munch (1995), p. 45.
[77] Gross (1976), p. 66.
[78] Westin (1967), p. 44.
[79] Westin (1967), p. 42.
[80] Chao (2005), p. 652.

right to privacy or to enjoy privacy protection in China. The author thus holds the opinion that enterprise legal persons are also legal subjects entitled to enjoy legal privacy protection in modern China.

3.3.4 Neutrality of Chinese Privacy Protection

The core of the theory of Confucianism is to cultivate morality. Moreover, it is a tradition that family interests in China have been given a higher place than individual interests.[81] Therefore, in China, extramarital affair was seen as an extremely shameful act, and anyone who discovered extramarital sex had the duty to catch the adulterers on the spot. This can be demonstrated by a Chinese old saying, which is "catching adultery in the act, catching a thief with thievery ... (捉奸见双,捉贼见赃)." This kind of activity is also called "*Zhuojian*" (捉奸) in Chinese.

In ancient China, not only the member of spouses could catch extramarital affair, but also anyone who discovered extramarital sex had the duty to catch the adulterers on the spot. This kind of activity used to be encouraged by the ruling class. Both the adulterer and adulteress could be sentenced to death at that time. In modern China, adultery has been prohibited by the Chinese socialist law. Therefore, in the first 30 years of socialist China, "*Zhuojian*" is no more popular. However, in some rural areas, the influence of Confucianism still exists. In addition, "*Zhuojian*," as an effective means to get evidence of divorce, has been widely accepted by Chinese people. That is because article 46 of the *Marriage Law of the PRC* (2001) clearly states that both "bigamy" and "cohabitation between a person who has a spouse but co-habitats with a third person" are the necessary elements for the innocent party to claim mental damages. As a result, in recent years, there is a revival trend of "*Zhuojian*" in Chinese contemporary society.

Based on this unique social phenomenon in China, some Chinese scholars hold the opinion that not all privacy issues are worth protecting by law.[82] They believe that privacy precluded indecent behavior, insults toward a woman, rape, and sexual relations that are illegal, immoral, or abnormal, and thus "privacy" only includes all private matters that are not in violation of law or morality.[83] Therefore, both the adulterer and adulteress's claim of privacy protection should not be supported by Chinese court. On the other hand, there are a number of scholars hold an opinion that there should be privacy protection for "bigamy or cohabits with a married person."[84] They insist that the extramarital act is a secret between adulterer and the

---

[81] Lü (2005), p. 8.

[82] Chao (2005), p. 656.

[83] Zhu (1997), p. 209.

[84] Qian (2003).

adulteress, and that both parties involved in the adultery may insist this secret state would never be known by the outside.[85]

The question of whether "*Zhuojian*" intrudes the privacy of the adulterer or adulteress thus emerges in China. In fact, this question can be understood as another question that is whether an individual, who commits bigamy or cohabitates with a married person, has right to claim his or her privacy right when the extramarital affair is disclosed. At present, in China, the most popular means to "*Zhuojian*" is to take photos from the parties who involve in adultery. Therefore, the author divides "*Zhuojian*" into two different circumstances:

First, the photographs of the adultery are taken from innocent party's own premise. In practice, the photos are taken from innocent party's premise have been adopted by the Chinese court. In the case of *Luo Ling v Wu*,[86] the court pointed out that Luo did not invade Sun's (defendant's inamorata) right to privacy. That is because Luo took photos in her own house, she thus was not an intruder at that time. She has right to enter her own house anytime. Most importantly, she used these photos as the evidence only in the divorce litigation.

Second, the photographs of the adultery are taken from other places rather than innocent part's own premise. In China, if the photographs of the adultery are taken by the innocent party in a third party's premise or the public area such as park or cinema, it will be deemed as that the parties of the adultery have abandoned their rights to privacy. Moreover, article 70 (3) of the *Several Provisions of the Supreme People's Court on Evidence in Civil Procedure* (2002) clearly states that the doubtless audiovisual materials obtained by legal means with other evidence to support or certified copies of these audiovisual materials should be deemed as effective evidence by the Chinese people' court, if the other party objected to the following evidence provided by a party without the evidence to the contrary that can sufficiently refute. Therefore, the photos or records of the adultery that are taken in other places rather than innocent party's own premise have also been accepted by the Chinese court as effective evidence.

Based on the foregoing analysis, it is clear that if the individual does not disclose the photos of adultery to the public, "*Zhuojian*" in both innocent party's own house and public areas has been permitted in China. In fact, there is no conflict between the right to privacy and "*Zhuojian.*" What has been protected by the law is the legal right of the involvers rather than the action carried out by them. People involved in bigamy or cohabits with a married person can claim their right to privacy to defend any third party, but they cannot use right to privacy as the excuse of their immoral act or to prohibit their spouse's right to know. "*Zhuojian*," as the most frequently used way to confirm the disloyal act of spouse, cannot be tread as an action trespassing individual's right to privacy. It should be noted that, today, few Chinese people want to "*Zhuojian.*" "*Zhuojian*" has become a personal affair, and most

[85] Qian (2003).

[86] Jia (2006), p. 48.

Chinese people believe that the issue of "*Zhuojian*" should be solved between the spouses.

3.3.5 Existing Statutory Protections for Privacy in Modern China

Compared to Western developed countries, modern China addresses privacy issues in the different social, political, and legal contexts. At present, most developed countries are experiencing greater centralization and coordination of government authority, even at the supranational level.[87] For example, from the 1957 Treaty of Rome to the 1992 Treaty on European Union signed in Maastricht, more than 240 European Commission directives have been designed to harmonize law cross Europe.[88] Unlike these developed countries, China mainly relies on the current laws, such as the Constitution and other legislations, to regulate the right to privacy. Therefore, inevitably, the protection of privacy in China is sporadic and fragmented to aim some particular areas. The following section examines the existing protections for privacy in contemporary Chinese legislation in more detail.

3.3.5.1 The Chinese Constitution and Privacy Protection

The *Constitution of 1982* is the most important legislation in the PRC. It is the fundamental law of China and has supreme legal power. Article 5 of the *Constitution of 1982* clearly states that:

> No law or administrative or local rules and regulations shall contravene the constitution. All state organs, the armed forces, all political parties and public organizations and all enterprises and undertakings must abide by the Constitution and the law. All acts in violation of the Constitution and the law must be investigated. No organization or individual is privileged to be beyond the Constitution or the law.

Since the establishment of the PRC in 1949, four Constitutions have been adopted in China, which are the *Constitution of 1954*, the *Constitution of 1975*, the *Constitution of 1978* and the *Constitution of 1982*, respectively.[89] At present, the *Constitution of 1982* is effective. The *Constitution of 1982* consists of the Preamble and four chapters, which are the general principle (Chap. 1), the fundamental rights and duties of citizens (Chap. 2), the structure of the state (Chap. 3) and the national flag, the national emblem and the capital (Chap. 4). The majority of Chinese scholars argue that, as the fundamental law of the PRC, this constitution is

[87] Cate (1997), p. 49.

[88] Cate (1997), p. 49.

[89] Zou (2000), p. 492.

the collective expression of the balance of all political forces, and mainly reflects the will and interests of the dominant class in contemporary China.[90]

Fundamental human rights are generally stated in Chapter two of the Constitution. There are two characters of those rights, which are important to comprehending the legal protection of privacy in China. The first character is that the rights expressed in the *Constitution of 1982* are generally protected only against private parties in China, such as the actions of social organizations or citizens. Almost all these constitutional rights do not mention or extend to unwarranted governmental actions. Only article 36 applies directly to both the government and private parties.[91] All other constitutional rights do not protect citizens against the invasion of official powers. Thus, it is not unusual that the invasion of governmental action always emerges when the government acts toward a private person in China. The second character of Chinese constitutional rights is that they are generally "passive." Someone believes that the Chinese Constitution is "positive" rather than "negative" on the basis of that Chinese citizens' fundamental rights are granted by the Constitution and the Constitution emphasizes their importance.[92] However, the *Constitution of 1982* does not restrain the central government or the local government from taking certain actions. For example, unlawful search of the person of citizens is prohibited, except with the approval or by the decision of a people's procurator, or by the decision of a people's court.[93] That is to say when the governmental rights and the basic citizens' rights collide, the former will always prevail in China. Thus, compared to the governments' powers, the Citizens' rights are "passive" in certain aspects.

These two characters of the Constitution indirectly reflect a unique characteristic of the Chinese legal system, which is, in China, the law is a codified fixture of the Party's fundamental principles and policies.[94] As the Preamble of the *Constitution of 1982* states that:

> It is the fundamental law of the state and has supreme legal authority. The people of all nationalities, all state organs, the armed forces, all political parties and public organizations and all enterprises and undertakings in the country must take the Constitution as the basic norm of conduct, and they have the duty to uphold the dignity of the Constitution and ensure its implementation.

The aim of the Constitution is to consolidate the socialism in China, and defines the basic system and basic tasks of China in legal form. Consequently, in author's view, the *Constitution of 1982* only protects basic citizens' rights against private actions. This Constitution does not force the Chinese government to do anything, and even confers huge powers to the Chinese government.

---

[90] Wang and Mo (1999), p. 25.

[91] *Constitution of the People's Republic of China* (1982), art 36.

[92] Chao (2005), p. 659.

[93] *Constitution of the People's Republic of China* (1982), art 37.

[94] Chen (1999), p. 42.

An assessment of constitutional rights is essential to any discussion of the privacy regulation in socialist China.[95] In fact, there is no clear constitutional protection of privacy right in China. However, article 37, article 38, article 39, and article 40 of the *Constitution of 1982* provide protection for privacy in China indirectly. At present, these articles are the constitutional basis for the legal protection of privacy in China, although these articles do not afford protection for any types of privacy explicitly.

Article 37 of the *Constitution of 1982* protects the freedom of person of citizens of the PRC. Under article 37, freedom of citizens in the PRC is inviolable, unlawful detention or deprivation or restriction of citizens' freedom of the person by any means is prohibited, and unlawful search of the person of citizens is also prohibited. Article 39 prohibits unlawful search of, or intrusion into, a citizen's residence. These two articles emphasize that all prohibitions do not include actions taken with the approval of a people's procurator or by decision of a people's court. Clearly, the protections offered by these two articles only protect privacy of body and privacy of territory. However, these protections are still significant. In author's view, these two articles emphasize the significance of Chinese citizens' feelings. They try to protect Chinese citizens in their thoughts and emotions. At least, the result is that, to some extent, the intrusion of privacy by private actions has been prohibited under both articles 37 and 39 in China.

Article 38 of the *Constitution of 1982* protects the personal dignity of citizens. The article clearly states that "the personal dignity" of citizens in the PRC is inviolable and that insult, libel, false accusation or false incrimination directed against citizens by any means will be prohibited.[96] In fact, in the domain of Chinese jurisdiction, "personal dignity" is a specialized phrase. "Personal dignity" can be understood as the right to name, right to portrait, right to privacy, and so on. This is the general name for "human rights" in China. Thus, this provision is the ultimate source from which legislation on the protection of personal rights emanates. Moreover, privacy of written communication is also protected by article 40 of the *Constitution of 1982*. Article 40 states that:

> The freedom and privacy of correspondence of citizens of the People's Republic of China are protected by law. No organization or individual may, on any ground, infringe upon the freedom and privacy of citizens' correspondence except in cases where, to meet the needs of state security or of investigation into criminal offences, public security or procuratorial organs are permitted to censor correspondence in accordance with procedures prescribed by law.

With respect to privacy protection, the significance of these four articles is self-evident. However, inadequacies of these articles are also obvious. First, all these articles do not provide explicit protection to privacy. This will result that the Chinese constitutional protection of privacy is easy to be confused, and the scope

---

[95] Cate (1997), p. 51.

[96] *Constitution of the People's Republic of China* 1982, art 38.

of its protection is limited. As a result, the protection of privacy by these articles is not satisfactory. Second, these four constitutional rights apply only to actions by private citizens, not public bodies. They will not require the Chinese government to take steps to protect individual privacy. As mentioned earlier, when governmental rights and privacy collide, the former will always prevail in China. As a summary, the constitutional protection for privacy in the PRC is very limited. The Chinese Constitution only established a limited framework for protecting privacy. In order words, privacy has received only limited constitutional protection indirectly. It is thus clear that the Constitution's protection for privacy is inadequate in China.

3.3.5.2 Chinese Civil Law and Privacy Protection

While articles 37, 38, 39, and 40 of the *Constitution of 1982* afford individuals limited protection, the GPCL also protects individuals against privacy intrusions. The GPCL provides three torts, which are (1) article 99 provides that Chinese citizens shall enjoy the right of personal name and the interference with, usurpation of and false representation of personal names shall be prohibited; (2) article 100 provides that Chinese citizens shall enjoy the right of portrait, and the use of a citizen's portrait for commercial purposes without his or her consent shall be prohibited; and (3) article 101 provides that Chinese citizens shall enjoy the right of reputation. The personality of citizens shall be protected by law, and the use of insults, libel or other means to damage the reputation of citizens or legal persons shall be prohibited.[97]

In practice, there has been a degree of confusion in applying these provisions to cases concerning privacy.[98] Thus, the Chinese Supreme People's Court issued two general judicial interpretations regarding the application of the GPCL to privacy in 1988 and 1993, respectively. In the *Opinions on Several Questions concerning the Implementation of the GPCL* (1988), the Chinese People's Supreme Court stated that:

> If anyone propagates the privacy of any other person in writing or orally, or fakes acts to vilify the personality of other person overtly, or damages other person's reputation by ways of insulting and slandering, which result in a certain influence, such act shall be determined as an act infringing the citizen's right of reputation.[99]

[97] *General Principles of the Civil Law of the People's Republic of China* 1986, art 101.

[98] Zhu (1997), pp. 211–212.

[99] *Opinions of the Supreme People's Court on Several Issues concerning the Implementation of the General Principles of the Civil Law of the People's Republic of China* 1988 (For Trial Implementation), answer 140 (1).

In the *Reply to Several Questions on Adjudicating the Cases of the Rights of Reputation* (1993), answers 7 states that "anyone who discloses another person's private information without authorization or, in written or verbal form, damages another person's reputation by publicizing that person's privacy shall be dealt in accordance with damaging the right of reputation of that person." Answer 9 states that:

> Any person who causes damage of the reputation by insulting, libeling or disclosing the privacy of the certain person in the literary work based on real life or, in spite of not identifying the real name or address, has caused damage of the reputation of the certain person in the literary work based on that person or that person's story through any content of insult, libel or privacy disclosure in that literary work shall be deemed as damaging the right of reputation of that person.

Since these two general judicial interpretations have been adopted, some privacy cases have been heard and judged on the basis of the right of reputation in China. Also the *Interpretation of the Supreme People's Court Regarding issues of Ascertaining the Liability of Compensation for Spiritual Damage for Tort* (2001) states that "if someone infringes upon other's privacy or other personality interests and the aggrieved party, taking tort as the cause to get compensation for spiritual damages, brings a suit to a People's Court, the People's Court shall accept it as a law."[100]

On the other hand, some Chinese scholars point out that the right to privacy is not a part of the right to reputation, and they thus believe that to protect privacy as part of the right of reputation will be inadequate on the basis of the significantly differences between these two rights.[101] First, they believe that the subjects of these two rights are not the same.[102] They point out that both the citizens and legal persons can be the subject of the right to reputation, but only citizens can be the subject of the right to privacy.[103] Second, the contents of these two torts are different.[104] They held that fabrication is a characteristic of the invasion of the right to reputation, and that is because in the case of the tort of reputation, the person concerned is often invaded by insult, libel or slander, which causes damage to personal dignity, reputation, and honor.[105] Third, the results of these two rights are different.[106] The results of the defamation case are always negative; by contrast, the results of the privacy case are not always negative.[107] Thus, clearly, the right to reputation cannot provide adequate protection for privacy in China today.

---

[100] *Interpretation of the Supreme People's Court Regarding issues of Ascertaining the Liability of Compensation for Spiritual Damage for Tort* 2001, art 1.

[101] Zhu (1997), p. 212.

[102] Zhu (1997), p. 212.

[103] Zhu (1997), p. 212.

[104] Chao (2005), p. 658.

[105] Chao (2005), p. 658.

[106] Zhu (1997), p. 213.

[107] Zhu (1997), p. 213.

Another two torts do not recognize privacy exactly. Both the right to name (article 99) and the right to portrait (article 100) apply only to unauthorized commercial use of another person's name and portrait. If a person uses another's name or portrait for a purpose other than a commercial purpose, but the consequences of the use cause damage to the good name or reputation of another or legal person, the latter can only sue the former if the action invaded the latter's right of reputation.[108] Similarly, if the unauthorized noncommercial use of a person's name or portrait does not constitute defamation or does not cause damage to the person's reputation, the person whose portrait has been used without authority may not have sufficient grounds to sue the party making such use.[109] As a result, obviously, these two torts are also inadequate to protect privacy.

As a consequence, it is clear that both the GPCL and its interpretation are inadequate for protecting privacy in China. The GPCL is too elementary, thus leaving many uncertainties to privacy protection in China. Chinese courts may assess these unanswered questions when they arise. However, this will inevitably require a long time. The courts will seldom have the opportunity to issue high-level decisions, because the potential plaintiffs are unwilling to spend large amounts of time and money on an uncertain course of action.[110] Moreover, they also fear going to count, due to the fact they may believe they will receive even more unwanted publicity.[111]

3.3.5.3 Other Protections

In addition to the *Constitution of 1982* and the GPCL, there are other laws and regulations regulating privacy in modern China. However, these laws only address "a special industry or economic sector" and some specific issues, and this approach "results in a patchwork of uneven, inconsistent, and often irrational privacy protection" in China.[112]

Financial Transactions

The NPC has enacted a variety of laws to regulate financial transactions. The first of those laws, the *Law of PRC on Commercial Banks* (1995) (the Commercial Bank Law), sets several rights for individuals in connection with their personal information. For example, article 29 of the Commercial Bank Law clearly requires that the

[108] Wang and Mo (1999), p. 162.
[109] Wang and Mo (1999), p. 162.
[110] Lulham (2005), p. 122.
[111] Lulham (2005), p. 122.
[112] Cate (1997), pp. 80–81.

Commercial banks should ensure confidentiality for depositors in handling individual savings deposits and protect their personal privacy. In addition, the Law ensures that Commercial banks' right to refuse any entity or individual "to inquire about, freeze or deduct individual savings accounts, unless it is otherwise prescribed by laws."[113] Moreover, this law restricts the power of the banking regulatory organ. When the banking regulatory organ of the State Council exercises his power to check on and supervise the deposits, loans, settlement, bad debts and other conditions of the commercial banks, the checkers and the supervisors must show their legal certificates.[114] Objectively, in certain aspects, the Commercial Bank Law restricts the content and disclosure of personal information. Although the Commercial Bank Law does not clearly regulate the collection and the use of personal information systematically, this law looks toward a regulatory approach to protecting information privacy in the PRC.

The second statute is the *Announcement of the Securities Association of China on Issuing the Interim Measures for the Management of Bona Fide Information of the Members of the Securities Association of China* (2003). The main aims of this announcement are "to promote the sound development of the securities market, and to standardize the management of bona fide information."[115] The announcement states that the Securities Association of China should not disclose information about state secrets, commercial secrets, and personal privacy.[116] Moreover, if members think there are errors in their basic information, or in the business' operating information, they may correct these errors themselves through the special network system.[117] Thus, this announcement restricts the content and disclosure of personal information.

Other laws provide limited protection for specific privacy interests. For example, the *Insurance Law of the PRC* (1995) requires that "the insurer or re-insurance underwriter should be obliged to keep confidential information about the operations and property of the insured."[118] The *Law of the PRC on the People's Bank* (1995) requires that the governor, deputy governors and other staff of the People's Bank should keep state secrets according to law and have the duty to protect the

[113] *Law of the People's Republic of China on Commercial Banks* 1995, art 29.

[114] *Law of the People's Republic of China on Commercial Banks* 1995, art 62.

[115] *Announcement of the Securities Association of China on Issuing the Interim Measures for the Management of Bona Fide Information of the Members of the Securities Association of China* 2003, art 1.

[116] *Announcement of the Securities Association of China on Issuing the Interim Measures for the Management of Bona Fide Information of the Members of the Securities Association of China* 2003, art 16.

[117] *Announcement of the Securities Association of China on Issuing the Interim Measures for the Management of Bona Fide Information of the Members of the Securities Association of China* 2003, art 18.

[118] *Insurance Law of the People's Republic of China* 1995, art 32.

confidentiality of the banking institutions and the clients in relation to the performance of their functions.[119]

The Workplace

The *Labor Law of the PRC* (1995) prohibits discrimination in "employment, regardless of their ethnic community, race, sex, or religious belief."[120] Moreover, if an employer forces laborers to work by resorting to violence, intimidation or illegal restriction of personal freedom; or humiliate, give corporal punishment, beat, illegally search or detain laborers, the person in charge will be taken by the Chinese public security organ into custody for a maximum of 15 days, or levy a fine, or give a warning, and, if the case is serious enough to constitute a crime, criminal responsibility is recorded.[121] It should be noted that this law does not propose how to collect, use or store personal information, though it may protect personal information by restricting the collection of information. In addition, the *Teacher Law of the PRC* (1993) states that teachers shall perform to concern themselves with all students, love them, respect their dignity and promote their all-round development in such aspects as morality, intelligence and physique; and to stop acts that are harmful to students and other acts that encroach upon students' legitimate rights and interests, criticize and combat the phenomena that impair the sound growth of students.[122]

Archives and Records

In 1987, the Standing Committee of the National People's Congress enacted the *Archives Law of the PRC* (the Archives Law). The purpose of the Archives Law is to strengthen the management, collection and arrangement of archives and the effective protection and use of archives.[123] The Chinese government amended the Archives Law in 1996. After amending, privacy has been indirectly protected. For example, article 19 of the Archives Law clearly states that if archives remain unsuitable for accessibility to the public upon the expiration of thirty years, these archives cannot be open to the public even after more than thirty years. Moreover, the Archives Law emphasizes that units or individuals that have transferred or donated archives to archives centers, or deposited archives with them, shall have priority in the use of such archives and may propose restrictions on the use of parts

---

[119] *Law of the People's Republic of China on the People's Bank of China* 1995, art 15.

[120] *Labour Law of the People's Republic of China* 1995, art 12.

[121] *Labour Law of the People's Republic of China* 1995, art 96.

[122] *Teacher Law of the People's Republic of China* 1993, art 8 (4) and (5).

[123] Archives Law of the People's Republic of China 1987, art 1.

of the archives that are not suitable for accessibility to the public, and the archives centers shall protect the lawful rights and interests of such units or individuals.[124] Also, with respect to collectively owned and individually owned archives, the owners shall have the right to make them public, but they must abide by the relevant state provisions, and may not endanger the security and interests of the state or violate the lawful rights and interests of others.[125]

The *Law on Practicing Doctors of the PRC* (1988) requires that doctors should not divulge the privacy of patient during the course of medical practice.[126] Doctors who violate the law will be warned or have their medical practice suspended for a period between 6 months and 1 year by the health administration departments of the people's governments at or above the county level; moreover, their practicing certificates will be revoked for cases with serious circumstances; and their criminal liabilities will be investigated and prosecuted.[127] Furthermore, the State Council published an administrative order in May 1999, and this order declaring that personal information about HIV/AIDS sufferers be kept secret and that the legal rights and interests of those people and their relatives should not be infringed.[128] Also, article 12 of *Law of the PRC on the Prevention and Treatment of Infectious Diseases* (2004) requires that "disease prevention and control institutions and medical agencies shall not divulge any information or materials relating to personal privacy." All these regulations protect privacy by restricting the types or sources of information that doctors or hospitals may gather.

Procedure of Litigation

The *Criminal Procedure Law of the PRC* (1996) provides a fairly extensive array of privacy rights to the reporter, complainant, and criminal suspect. The Criminal Procedure Law emphasizes that the public security agencies, the People's procurators and the People's courts should keep confidential for reporters, complainants, and informants who do not wish to make their names and acts of reporting, complaining or informing known to the public.[129] Moreover, the Criminal Procedure Law prescribes that the criminal suspect must answer the investigators' questions truthfully, but he or she also has the right to refuse to answer any questions that are irrelevant to the case.[130] In addition, the Criminal Procedure Law clearly states that cases of first instance in a People's Court must be

[124] Archives Law of the People's Republic of China 1987, art 21.

[125] Archives Law of the People's Republic of China 1987, art 22.

[126] *Law on Practicing Doctors of the People's Republic of China* 1988, art 37(10).

[127] *Law on Practicing Doctors of the People's Republic of China* 1988, art 37.

[128] Privacy International 2007.

[129] *Criminal Procedure Law of the People's Republic of China* 1996, art 85.

[130] *Criminal Procedure Law of the People's Republic of China* 1996, art 93.

heard in public, but cases involving State secrets or private affairs of individuals should not be heard in public.[131]

While the Criminal Procedure Law provides protection of privacy, both the *Civil Procedure Law of the PRC* (1991) and the *Administrative Procedure Law of the PRC* (1989) also provide protection to privacy. The Civil Procedure Law provides the right of privacy to citizens when involved in litigation, which is that evidence private affairs of individuals should not be presented in an open court session.[132] Moreover, civil cases in a people's court must be tried in public, "except for those that involve state secrets or the private affairs of individuals, or are otherwise provided by law."[133] Administrative Procedure Law requires that a lawyer "may consult materials pertaining to the case in accordance with relevant provisions, and may also investigate and collect evidence from the organizations and citizens concerned," however, if the information involves state secrets or the private affairs of individuals, he or she must keep it confidential.[134]

Other Legislation

Other provisions are set out in more detailed laws. Three articles of the Chinese Criminal Law (1997) provide further basis for the protection of the right to privacy. Article 245 states that:

> Whoever unlawfully subjects another person to a body search or a search of his residence or unlawfully intrudes into another person's residence shall be sentenced to fixed-term imprisonment of not more than three years or criminal detention, and any judicial officer who abuses his power and commits the crime mentioned in the preceding paragraph shall be given a heavier punishment.

Article 252 states that "whoever conceals, destroys or unlawfully opens another person's letter, thereby infringing upon the citizen's right to freedom of correspondence, if the circumstances are serious, shall be sentenced to fixed-term imprisonment of not more than one year or criminal detention." Furthermore, article 253 states that "any postal worker who opens without authorization or conceals or destroys mail or telegrams shall be sentenced to fixed-term imprisonment of not more than two years or criminal detention." In addition, *Amendment Seven to the Criminal Law of the PRC (Draft)* (2008) proposes to add a provision on protection of privacy, penalizing "personnel of financial, telecommunications, communications, educational, and medical work units and the like who sell or unlawfully provide to

131 *Criminal Procedure Law of the People's Republic of China* 1996, art 152.

132 *Civil Procedure Law of the People's Republic of China* 1991, art 66.

133 *Civil Procedure Law of the People's Republic of China* 1991, art 120.

134 *Administrative Procedure Law of the People's Republic of China* 1989, art 30.

others citizens' individual information that was obtained in carrying out their duties or in the course of providing services."[135]

The *law of PRC on Anti-Money Laundering* (2006) clear states that:

> Any client's identity material or transactional information as acquired in the performance of the duties and functions of anti-money laundering according to law shall be kept confidential. None of the aforesaid information may be provided to any entity or individual in the absence of relevant provisions of law. The clients' identity materials and transactional information as acquired by the administrative department of anti-money laundering or any other department or organ bearing the obligation of anti-money laundering supervision and administration according to law in the process of performing their anti-money laundering functions and duties shall only be used in the administrative anti-money laundering investigation. The clients' identity materials and transactional information as acquired by the judicial organ according to the present Law shall only be used in the criminal litigation on anti-money laundering.[136]

The *Law of the PRC on the Protection of Rights and Interests of Women* (1992) prohibits discrimination against women. This law regulates that Women's freedom of the person shall be inviolable. Under this law, "unlawful detention or deprivation or restriction of women's freedom of the person by other illegal means shall be prohibited; and unlawful body searches of women shall be prohibited."[137] In addition, women's right of portrait has been protected by the law. Article 38 states that "the use of a woman's portrait for profit-making purposes in advertisements, trademarks, window displays, books, magazines, etc., without the consent of the woman in question, shall be prohibited." Moreover, women's rights of reputation and personal dignity also have been protected by this law, and "damage to women's reputation or personal dignity by such means as insult, libel and the giving of publicity to private matters, shall be prohibited."[138] Actually, in certain aspects, this law is protecting information privacy by restricting the collection of information.

Similarly, the *Law of the PRC on the Protection of Minors* (2006) provides that "no organization or individual may disclose the personal secrets of minors."[139] Article 40 of this law proposes that:

> No organization or individual may conceal, destroy or discard mail of any minor. Except when the inspection of mail in accordance with legal procedures by the public security organs or the people's procuratorates is necessary for the investigation of a criminal offence, or when the opening of mail of a minor without capacity is done on his or her behalf by the parents or other guardians, no organization or individual may open mail of any minor.

---

[135] *Standing Committee of the National People's Congress Conducted the First Reading of Amendment Seven to the Criminal Law of the PRC (Draft)* 2008, art 6.

[136] *Anti-Money Laundering Law of the People's Republic of China* 2006, art 5.

[137] *Law of the People's Republic of China on the Protection of Rights and Interests of Women* 1992, art 34.

[138] *Law of the People's Republic of China on the Protection of Rights and Interests of Women* 1992, art 39.

[139] *Law of the People's Republic of China on the Protection of Minors* 2006, art 39.

Also, article 58 states that:

> With regard to cases involving crimes committed by minors, the names, home addresses and photos of such minors as well as other information which can be used to deduce who they are, may not be disclosed, before the judgment, in news reports, films, TV programs and in any other openly circulated publications.

Article 7 of the *Prison Law of the PRC* (1994) states that "human dignity of a prisoner shall not be humiliated, and his personal safety, lawful properties, and rights to defense, petition, complaint and accusation as well as other rights, which have not been deprived of or restricted according to law shall not be violated." Article 14 (3) (4) of this Law emphasizes that the people's police of a prison should not commit "to use torture to coerce a confession, or to use corporal punishment, or to maltreat a prisoner; and to humiliate the human dignity of a prisoner." If the people's police of a prison commit any act that mention above, the offenders will be investigated for criminal responsibility; if the case does not constitute a crime, the offenders shall be given administrative sanctions. Section 6(2) of the *NPC's Decision on Safeguarding Internet Security* clearly states that "intercepting, changing, or deleting other people's e-mail or other data information illegally may constitute a crime."[140]

Clearly, all these provisions only provide a minimum level of protection for the privacy in China. They are not able to effectively solve privacy disputes, although China has already strictly administered the regulations as to privacy in some privacy issues.

3.3.5.4 Evaluation

The protection of privacy in China relies on a variety of regulations, each of which applies only to a specific category. Most protections of privacy in Chinese legislation only prohibit actual disclosure, rather than the collection, use or storage of individuals' personal information. The reality is that some protections of privacy interests in particular areas are only a byproduct of another legislative goal. Furthermore, the above discussion suggests that privacy protection in China has been influenced by other existing values, such as the prevention of crime, freedom of expression, and so on. At present, in China, other existing values are more important than privacy interests. In addition, there is no judicial framework for resolving privacy disputes in China.

As a summary, there are, at least, four defects concerning privacy protection in the current Chinese legislation. First, there is no precise protection of privacy in Chinese constitution. Without other supporting legislation, or a clear concept of what privacy is, the Constitution has not been used to protect privacy in the way it

[140] *National People's Congress Standing Committee Decision on Safeguarding Internet Security* 2000, s 4.

might be.[141] Second, all the Chinese constitutional rights apply only against the actions of individuals or private organizations, not the government. Compared to the Chinese governmental powers, privacy is still subordinate. Third, a number of laws in China recognize privacy protection in different forms. Although the GPCL recognizes some special types of privacy interests, none of these individual rights is able to offer adequate protection for the privacy of personal information. Most Chinese laws or provisions apply only to specific categories of privacy. Finally, there is no Chinese legislation is comprehensive enough to provide adequate privacy protection. In fact, there is no overarching privacy legislation in China, which makes privacy protection weak in many instances.[142]

These loopholes of the protection of privacy in Chinese contemporary legislation reveal that the protection of privacy in China is a "fractured, episodic, record-targeted patchwork of laws."[143] In fact, the understanding of the protection of privacy in China should lie in the understanding of what has *not* been done in Chinese legislation, rather than what has been done. However, the significance of protecting privacy does not lie in Chinese legislation at present. This leaves the majority of privacy issues without adequate legal protection. Thus, the author believes that what is needed in China is that the right to privacy to be ensured, not just some simple amendments or interpretations to cater to new governmental policies. The possibility of creating the right to privacy in the Chinese legal system is discussed in more detail in Chap. 5.

3.3.6 Possible Theories to Explain the Insufficient Level of Privacy Protection in Contemporary China

Based on issues discussed earlier, it is clear that Chinese contemporary legislation is not able to protect privacy effectively. What are the reasons for this social phenomenon? In this part, the author explores the reasons why there is no adequate protection of privacy in modern China. To start with, an examination of the source of Chinese socialist law is necessary. The following section then discusses the legal reality in socialist China. This can help us to explore the internal reasons why current Chinese legislation is not able to protect privacy in China. Subsequently, other matters affecting China's approach to the protection of privacy are also discussed.

---

[141] Chao 2005, p. 660.

[142] Chao 2005, p. 660.

[143] Wakana 2004, p. 157.

3.3.6.1 The Source of Contemporary Chinese Law

Unlike the Chinese Nationalist Party (CNP),[144] which overthrew the Qing Dynasty but allowed the continuation of its legal order, the effect of the establishment of the PRC was not only to end the CNP's political rule, it was also to dismantle the CNP's legal system and to abolish the CNP codes.[145] At that time, as the first socialist country in the world, the Soviet law had evolved more than thirty years. China thus started to study the Soviet legal experience. Vyshinsky's theory is the most famous. According to Vyshinsky's theory,

> Law is a formal, normative expression of the will of the ruling class, as formulated and enforce by the state in the interests of that class. In a socialist state . . . the communist Party, as the representative of the ruling proletariat, should enjoy absolute control over the creation of positive law by the organs of the state. The party should also determine the form and content of these laws according to the requirements of its evolving programme of economic and social development.[146]

After systematic studying of the Soviet experience, Mao Zedong and his fellow jurists accepted Vyshinsky's theory. Therefore, at the early stage of the PRC, Soviet legal theory, in particular the work of the Stalinist jurist and chief prosecutor AY Vyshinsky, had a decisive impact on the construction of Chinese socialist law.[147]

According to the Chinese adaptation of the Soviet legal experience, the Communist Party of China (the CPC) holds absolute authority over the determination of the content of the law, while the function of law is to express, in a positive, normative form, current Party policy.[148] Moreover, law, as a weapon of class struggle, like the army, is used by the ruling class as a visible coercive force to "suppress its class enemies."[149] Shen chunju, who was the first president of the People's Supreme Court, emphasized that socialist China's judicial system must actively serve its political ends.[150] As Professor Chen jianfu states that:

> To start with, the Marxist concept of law as being a tool to remould society and to suppress class enemies, to enforce party policy rather than to protect individual rights, was taking root. Secondly, justice was politicised, such as in the enforcement of 'class justice' in which distinctions were made according to class membership in administering justice. . . Thirdly, extrajudicial organisations and procedures and extralegal measures were often utilised to impose sanctions and to settle disputes.[151]

---

[144] The Chinese Nationalist Party was established in mainland China in 1912. It was organized by Sun Yat-sen after the Xinhai Revolution. It was a major force in Chinese politics for several decades before its retreat to Taiwan in 1949.

[145] Chen (1999), p. 34.

[146] Keller (1994), p. 720.

[147] Keller (1994), p. 720.

[148] Keller (1994), p. 721.

[149] Chen (1973), p. 84.

[150] Chen (1973), p. 88.

[151] Chen (1999), p. 34.

When Deng Xiaoping took over the leadership, the "Cultural Revolution," which had lasted 10 years, had pushed the Chinese economy to the edge of collapse.[152] Thus, in Deng's opinion, Chinese law had to "be used to establish stability and order for economic development."[153] Moreover, Deng insisted that "there is a lot of legislative work to do . . . it is better to have some laws than none, and better to have them sooner than later." [154] Therefore, under Deng's leadership in the 1980s and 1990s, numerous laws and administrative regulations were adopted to encourage foreign investment and domestic economic reform.[155] However, careful deliberation of Deng's speeches on law makes it clear that Deng also insisted that law is only an instrument of Party policy. That is to say, under Deng's leadership, the political system in China did not change. The only change was the aim of party policy, which is from "class struggle" to "economic construction."

In addition, it should be noted that since the establishment of the PRC, the old legal system seems to have been replaced by the socialist legal system. However, legal culture and local norms cannot disappear easily. Especially, the influence of Confucianism still exists in the current Chinese legal culture.

3.3.6.2 Chinese Attitudes to Law

The following paragraphs discuss the Chinese attitudes to law in the first thirty years of socialist China. This can help us to explore the internal reasons why current Chinese legislation is not able to protect privacy in China.

Law Is Only a Supplementary Means to Regulate Social Affairs

Since the establishment of the PRC, the most effective instrument to regulate social affairs has been the CPC.[156] Moreover, governmental powers, the network of all kinds of social relations and the rampant local protectionism often render law a secondary authority.[157] It thus has been argued that the Chinese communist law holds no special sanctity and is often just a mere tool of party policy in China.[158] The Chinese law is generally subordinate to both the CPC's policy and the social norms in practice.[159] As a consequence, it is inevitable that the effectiveness of

[152] Chen (1999), p. 41.
[153] Chen (1999), p. 41.
[154] Chen (1999), p. 43.
[155] Chen (1999), p. 41.
[156] Wang (2000), p. 37.
[157] Wang and Zhang (1997), p. 14.
[158] Chen (1999), p. 41.
[159] Chen (1999), p. 41.

provisions that protect privacy rights has been weakened or substituted by this unique social phenomenon in contemporary China.

Law Is Only a Political Tool

In socialist China, law is only a tool to achieve certain political or economic goals. For example, as mentioned earlier, when Deng attempted to enforce economic reform, he pointed out that "there is a lot of legislative work to do ... law is better than no law, faster is better than slower."[160] As a result, almost all regulation adopted at that time attempted to achieve a socialist market economy. In fact, as Kui Hua Wang points out that:

> He seemed to fail to address the implications of particular laws or fully consider the fact that the laws were ahead of society's attitudes at that time or that the socio-legal infrastructure was not yet in place to implement those laws or that it might be difficult to implement Western codes on a society that was at best in a state of transition from a centrally planned economy to a socialist market society.[161]

Therefore, for the traditional Chinese communists, law is only a tool of party policy, while "Chinese officials and citizens are merely part of a political structure in which the Party's will and policies have long been the most effective law."[162] The aim of Chinese law is to ensure the implementation of policies rather than to protect individual rights, such as the right to privacy, in China. As a consequence, Chinese citizens' personal rights were ignored by the CPC in certain respects, and the right to privacy is no exception.

Mediation Is More Preferred than Litigation

It also has been argued that there is a general dislike or mistrust of the law among Chinese citizens on the basis of the factors such as the influence of Confucian philosophy and knowledge of the bribery of judges.[163] As mentioned earlier, most Chinese people believed matters concerned with *yin-si* was shameful, they did not want them to be disclosed. Thus, for the sake of "face," even if the invasion of their privacy was inevitable, they preferred to ignore the invasion rather than go to court. Mediation, as a traditional Chinese means of solving civil disputes, is still popular in China today. A number of privacy disputes in current China have been solved by society itself through mediation. Hence, obviously, the wide use of mediation restricts the effectiveness of privacy protection in modern China.

---

[160] More details see Sect. 2.2.1.

[161] Wang (2000), p. 39.

[162] Wang (2000), p. 37.

[163] Wang (2000), p. 38.

Criminal Law Is More Important and Effective than Other Laws

According to socialist legal theory, criminal law is the most powerful weapon of the ruling class to conduct class struggle.[164] Hence, criminal law had been deemed as the most important and effective law to "suppress class enemies" and to protect ruling class in the early stage of socialist China. By contrast, the Chinese civil law had been regarded as an important measure to handle people's internal disputes. However, the CPC also emphasized that there is no conflict of basic interest among the Chinese people.[165] This attitude of Chinese civil law demonstrates that the main function of Chinese civil law is to develop socialist society rather than solve internal civil disputes in China. While this misguided concept of Chinese civil law was widely accepted, the significance of privacy protection has inevitably been ignored in China.

3.3.6.3 Understanding of Collective Interests in Socialist China

In addition to the Chinese attitudes to law, the unique status of public property in China also hinders the development of privacy protection. The 1978s reforms and opening up was seen as a watershed in ethical reflection concerning privacy in contemporary China. Before 1978, China had a planned economy. During that period, the whole nation was devoted to pursuing with great enthusiasm for the realization of communist society. In this scenario, collective/public interests were certainly given a highest and exclusive priority. In the socialist theory, socialist collective interests are the result of the Communist revolution, and they are also the foundation for the further development of socialist society and, also, the source of state wealth and strength.[166] Therefore, traditional Chinese communists believed that only by protecting collective interests can prevent the restoration of capitalism. For this reason, article 12 of the *Constitution of 1982* states that the public property and the public interests of the PRC to be sacred and inviolable. As Phillip M Chen states that "the principle that public property and interests are 'sacred and inviolable' is a legal principle peculiar to socialist countries, which are built on the foundation of public ownership."[167] Anyone who dared to pursue individual interests would be criticized by the other people and would even been called an egoist against the trend of social development. In consequence, absolutely selfless thinking was the basic moral standard at that time.

However, at the same time as protecting public property and interest, socialist China ignored the significance of personal property and interest in certain aspects.

[164] Chen (1973), p. 84.
[165] Chen (1973), p. 86.
[166] Chen (1973), p. 123.
[167] Chen (1973), p. 124.

As mentioned earlier, the constitutional protection of private property and personal rights exists only against private parties, such as social organizations or citizens' actions. Almost all these constitutional rights do not extend to unwarranted governmental actions. Although the Chinese government emphasized that individual interests and the social public interest are closely integrated under the Socialist system, the justification is that only by giving full protection to public interest can the individual be secure where his personal interests are concerned.[168] Thus, compared to the collective/public interest, all personal rights and interests are subordinate. It is totally in contrast to the legal principle of Western democracies that private property is sacred and cannot be violated.[169] Inevitably, this socialist feature hinders the development of privacy in China.

It should be noted that this situation has changed since 1978. With the reforms and opening up, China has transformed from a planned economy to a socialist market economy. China has more opportunities of having access to the outside world. Economic development and broad horizon bring about increasing social diversity, which promotes the Chinese people to begin to pay attention to and value individual characteristics and interests. Gradually, the individual interests challenge the predominance of collective interests. In spite of increasing value of individual interests, the long term formed foundation status of collective interests in Chinese moral standard cannot be changed. Consequently, individual interests and collective interests are deemed both important, but the collective interests still comparatively have priority over individual interests.

As a summary, it can be seen that there was no privacy protection before 1978 as the individual interests were overwhelmed by collective interests. Nevertheless, the individual privacy begins to be emphasized as a result of the increasing concern for individual interests after 1978 in spite of the dominance of collective interests.

3.3.6.4 Other Matters Affecting China's Approach

Besides the reasons caused by socialist China itself, there are some other matters affecting China's approach to the protection of privacy. They are the difficulties in defining privacy, the variation and change in cultural values, and the difficulties of detection, respectively.

Difficulties in Defining Privacy

As discussed in Chap. 1, privacy may be one of the most complex human rights to define. A difficulty is that the definitions of privacy vary widely according to

[168] Chen (1973), pp. 126–127.

[169] Chen (1973), p. 124.

context and environment.[170] Privacy is a collection of related personal interests and expectations, rather than a single coherent concept.[171] When you ask a selection of people what privacy is, it is inevitable that you will get totally different answers. These answers depend on who these people are, where they come from, and even depend on their different religions. Professor John Burrows thus states that "privacy is notoriously hard to define."[172] The ALRC even points out that "the instances of invasions are so readily recognizable, but so disparate, that it concluded that there was little hope of arriving at an all-purpose definition."[173] This difficulty of defining privacy also emerged in China. As a consequence, the difficulties in defining privacy may affect China's approach to the protection of privacy in certain respects.

Variation and Change in Cultural Values

In practice, the rapid change of privacy values and the variety of attitudes to privacy affect China's approach to the protection of privacy.

First, the values of privacy are always changing. At the time of the emergence of the right to privacy, privacy had an obviously "class-based character."[174] It focused on the "problem" of access by the lower classes of society to information about the upper classes.[175] By contrast, as mentioned earlier, in modern society, privacy reflects the right of an individual or group to keep their lives and personal affairs out of public view, or to control the flow of information about them. Privacy thus seems to consist less of a class-based, and more of a democratic, character.[176] Furthermore, in 1890, privacy issues mainly focused on how to deal with the disclosure of private affairs in the public forum, particularly in the mass media.[177] In modern society, however, how to effectively control the information (or data) has become the main task.

Second, attitudes to privacy are different. The ALRC provides an example. Some people may wish their health details to be known by other people. They even sell their abnormal medical histories to the mass media for publication to the community at large. In contrast, others wish their health details to remain strictly private and are strongly against use of these details, even by medical researchers.[178]

---

[170] Romano (2002), p. 346.

[171] McCartney (2006), p. 130.

[172] Todd (2005), p. 744.

[173] Australian Law Reform Commission 1983, p. 10.

[174] Bezanson (1992), p. 1139.

[175] Bezanson (1992), p. 1139.

[176] Bezanson (1992), pp. 1139–1140.

[177] Bezanson (1992), p. 1140.

[178] Australian Law Reform Commission 1983, p. 11.

Finally, recognitions of privacy are also different in different society. This is a result of a comparison of the privacy perceptions of several contemporary cultures:

> Germans, [Hall] found marked off their private Lebensraum by closed doors, fences, and strict rules about trespass: German law, for instance, forbids the photographing of strangers in public places without their consent. Americans have open doors and no fences, but mark their social status with 'private' offices and 'private' secretaries. The French pack closely together in public, but rarely invite outsiders to their homes, even if they know them well. And the English, it seems, rely mainly on their reserve: when an Englishman stops talking, that is a signal that he wishes to be left alone.[179]

Thus, a qualified protection for privacy must be able to accommodate all these differences.[180] However, China is a new socialist country with limited legislation. Chinese scholars may begin to consider this feature of privacy, and the courts may deal with these questions when they arise little by little. All this will inevitably require a long time. Consequently, the variation and change in cultural values of privacy also affect China's approach to the protection of privacy.

Difficulties of Detection

The ALRC also points out that, based on the nature of privacy, "there exists considerable difficulty in identifying privacy invasions."[181] This phenomenon also exists in China. For example, at present, devices of surveillance are being widely used in China. However, we cannot speculate the precise details and levels of the use of secret surveillance in most cases. Usually, the difficulties of detecting privacy invasions create two problems: first, it is difficult for us to ensure that there is a need for protection; second, it is difficult for us to provide effective legal sanctions and remedies.[182] Therefore, the author believes these are factors affecting privacy protection in China as well.

3.3.7 *Summary*

Legal development and the existence of law in China under communist rule started with the introduction and domination of a Chinese-style Marxist ideology.[183] There is a fundamental difference between the principle of Chinese socialist law, and the principle of law in states governed by the Rule of Law, in their respective attitudes

[179] Australian Law Reform Commission 1983, p. 11.
[180] Australian Law Reform Commission 1983, p. 12.
[181] Australian Law Reform Commission 1983, p. 12.
[182] Australian Law Reform Commission 1983, p. 12.
[183] Chen (1999), p. 55.

toward individual rights.[184] In Western legal systems, the agencies of the State are required to observe the laws in order to respect individual freedom.[185] By contrast, under the Chinese socialist legal system, the individual is required not only to adhere to the law, but he or she must also collaborate actively in the implementation of socialist law.[186] Thus, the purpose of socialist law is not to protect individual freedom. As a result, all these features of Chinese society and law have determined or partly determined that there is no adequate protection for privacy in China.

3.4 The Possible Development Trend of Privacy in Contemporary Chinese Society

Based on the above analysis and according to China's national circumstances, although there is no adequate privacy protection regime in contemporary China, it can be inferred that the privacy issue in China is expected to continue to change in the future. Hence, the author explores the future of privacy in China from the following two aspects, which are the public consciousness of privacy in China and the theoretical basis of privacy in China, respectively.

3.4.1 The Development Trend of the Public Consciousness of Privacy in Contemporary Chinese Society

The public consciousness of privacy will continue to be enhanced in China. In addition, the scope of privacy interests per se will be further expanded.

First of all, the public consciousness of privacy will be more widespread in future China. The current situation is that Chinese people begin to pay more attention to and value the privacy. As mentioned earlier, this social phenomenon can often be observed in cities as a result of urbanization. The people coming from rural areas are not inclined to share their personal information with the others. At the same time, people also begin to respect and do not interfere with other people's privacy. Although the privacy disputes rarely happen in rural areas nowadays, the idea of valuing and respecting the privacy will gradually be spread from cities to rural areas. In addition to the economic development in rural areas, this is because the people coming from rural areas and working or living in the cities would bring back the idea of respect for privacy, thus gradually influencing the rural residents'

---

[184] Chen (1973), p. 206.

[185] Chen (1973), p. 206.

[186] Chen (1973), p. 206.

consciousness of privacy. As a result, the emergence of the consciousness of the right to privacy in rural areas will be an inevitable trend in the future.

Moreover, it is the long time formed and common thinking in China that there should be no secret within the family. That is to say there should be no privacy interests between husband and wife and those parents are supposed to know everything about their minor children. Currently, a few of Chinese people begin to express their desire of not sharing everything private with their family members. This phenomenon can especially be observed between husband and wife and parents and children. On the other hand, with the increasing economic independence in China, both of the spouses are likely to enjoy more individual freedom in their marriage. Also, as mentioned earlier, relatively mature and well-educated children will require that their parents should respect their privacy and do not excessively interfere with their lives. At the same time, more and more parents are enlightened enough to respect their children's privacy. Therefore, it is apparent that the respect for the right to privacy will become very common within the family in the near future.

In addition, the age group of the people who have awareness of privacy and right to privacy will be extended from young age group to all age groups. At present, it is mainly the young people who begin to value their privacy and claim the right to privacy in China as most of them are well educated and are prone to accept Western values. As these young people gradually grow up and with the social development, the people who advocate the respect for privacy will not be limited to the young age group. Rather, all the people from different age groups are expected to pay attention to the privacy in China.

Second, the scope of privacy interests per se will be further expanded in the future. As introduced above, the privacy today in China has already been expanded and is no longer restricted to "*yin-si*" (a shameful secret). Trend of the expansion is expected to continue in the future as a result of increasing internationalization process of China. China has opened up to Western world and has entered many international organizations. As a populous country with surging economic development, it can be said that China has played an important role in the international community. In this scenario, Western ideas regarding privacy will continue to permeate through China, and gradually influence Chinese consciousness of privacy. Therefore, it is an unavoidable trend that the more and more Chinese people will be affected by Western values. All the personal information, for example, personal address, income, height, the educational background and so on, is likely to be included in privacy interests in the future.

3.4.2 The Development Trend of the Theoretical Basis of Privacy in Contemporary Chinese Society

The emergence and development of privacy in China also need theoretical support. The theoretical basis of the privacy will be influenced by Western values and is expected to be infused into more attention to individual rights and interests in the future.

In China, the current theoretical research on privacy generally belongs to ethics. This is mainly because privacy deals with the ethical relationship between people. At present, the traditional Chinese ethics still dominates the moral evaluation of and moral thinking about people's social activities. As mentioned earlier, based on the theory of *Li*, the traditional Chinese ethics can be demonstrated as "family standard" and "morals standard," respectively. The "family standard" refers to taking the family as a core and starting point of social activities. Family is the basis of society and the society is made up of each family. Within a family, a person is first regarded as a family member rather than an individual. Therefore, individual rights do not exist within a family and individual interests should be subordinate to family interests. In this connection, the "family standard" is similar to "collective standard." All the social activities should be with the purpose of promoting collective interests rather than individual interests. The "morals standard" means that the ethics is the basic factor to maintain the social order. China always cherishes harmony and people's activities should be regulated by ethics. In this scenario, people should do what they are supposed to do according to moral standard, such as that child must obey parents, wife must obey husband, and subject must obey emperor. Otherwise, they will be criticized by the whole society. Although nowadays Chinese people begin to pay attention to individual interests, the dominance of traditional Chinese ethics remains as this moral thinking has been existed in China for thousands of years.

As more and more privacy issues are emerging, Chinese scholars in ethics, on the one hand, want to build up ethical theoretical basis for privacy and privacy rights; on the other hand, collective interests remain to be the supreme moral standard of evaluating people's activities. Hence, the current ethical research based on collective interests cannot be sufficient to provide theoretical support for the development of privacy in China. Facing this situation, the Chinese scholars in ethics may consult Western ideas regarding privacy, which advocate privacy and privacy interests on the basis of individual interests. Western ethical research regards individual rather than collective as a starting point of social development and thus fully recognizes privacy and right to privacy. Accordingly, Western values place emphasis on individual rights and claim to promote individual development through social development.

It can be concluded that the ethical research in China is likely to make some large adjustment to meet the new demands of privacy development in the future. The scholars may emphasize individual development and individual interests and may advocate privacy and right to privacy from both individual and collective perspectives. Consequently, this new moral thinking and moral evaluation will have a great effect upon traditional values while the traditional values will continue to dominate the ethics in China for quite a long time.

3.5 Conclusion

Based on the foregoing analysis, it is clear that privacy issues have become more and more important than ever before in Chinese contemporary society. Chinese citizens need privacy. As Chao points out that "it is a concept that, though less developed, is not alien to Chinese society and culture."[187] On the other hand, based on discussions in this chapter, we must acknowledge that the reality is that the current Chinese legislation cannot solve privacy issues effectively. Two suggestions are thus made here: First, as mentioned earlier, what is needed in China is that the right to privacy to be ensured, not just some simple amendments or interpretations to cater to new governmental policies. Another suggestion is to create Chinese personal information privacy protection legislation. In other words, specific personal privacy protection laws and official agencies should be set up in China. The benefit of the latter would be not only adequate information privacy protection, but also economic benefit for China. Regardless of what happens elsewhere, the author really hopes that, at least, in Chinese society in the early twenty-first century, we should recognize that there is such a thing as privacy, that it is generally something we value, and that we think it should be legally protected in some way.

References

Journal Articles and Books

Bezanson RP (1992) The right to privacy revisited: privacy, news, and social change (1890–1990). Calif Law Rev 80:1133

Bourn C, Benyon J (eds) (1983) Data protection: perspectives on information privacy. University of Leicester, Leicester

Chao JC (2005) Protecting the right to privacy in China. Vict Univ Wellin Law Rev 36:645

Cate FH (1997) Privacy in the information age. Brooking Institution Press, Washington, DC

Chen GB (2002a) Law without lawyers, justice without courts: on traditional Chinese mediation. Ashgate Publishing, Aldershot

Chen PM (1973) Law and justice: the legal system in China 2400 BC to 1960 AD. Dunellen Publishing Corporation, New York

Chen JF (1999) Chinese law: towards an understanding of Chinese law, its nature, and development. Kluwer, The Hague

Chen GB (2002b) Law without lawyers, justice without courts: on traditional Chinese mediation. Ashgate Publishing, Aldershot

Confucius, Yüan Y 12th The analects of Confucius (Wang Hao trans) [trans of: 论语, 颜渊十二]

Dai D, Dai S (eds) Ru Xing of the book of rites (Wang Hao trans) [trans of: 礼记, 儒行四十一]

Dorr RC, Munch CH (1995) Protecting trade secrets, patents, copyrights, and trademarks. Wiley, New York

[187] Chao (2005), p. 664.

Gross H (1976) Privacy: its legal protection. Oceania Publications, Dobbs Ferry, NY
Ho DY-f (1976) On the concept of face. Am J Sociol 81:867
Huang PCC (1996) Civil justice in China: representation and practice in the Qing. Stanford University Press, Stanford, CA
Keller P (1994) Sources of order in Chinese law. Am J Comp Law 42:711
Kim HI (1981) Fundamental legal concepts of China and the West: a comparative study. Kennikat Press, New York
Ladany L (1992) Law and legality in China: the testament of a China-watcher. University of Hawaii Press, Honolulu, HI
Littman M (1970) A report by justice: privacy and the law. The Eastern Press, London
Liu Y (1998) Origins of Chinese law: penal and administrative law in its early development. Oxford University Press, Oxford
Lulham S (2005) What is, and what should be, the extent of New Zealand's new tort of breach of privacy? Canterbury Law Rev 11:91
Lü Y (2005) Privacy and data privacy issues in contemporary China. Ethics Inf Technol 7:7
McCartney C (2006) Forensic identification and criminal justice: forensic science, justice and risk. Willan Pressing, Cullompton
McDougall BS, Hansson A (2002) Chinese concepts of privacy. Brill, Leiden
Peng S (2003) Privacy and the construction of legal meaning in Taiwan. International Lawyer 37:1037
Romano C (2002) Advance tax rulings and principles of law: towards a European tax rulings system? IBFD, Amsterdam
Sima Q (91 BC) The biography of Hsiang Yu of the historical records (Wang Hao trans) [trans of: 史记卷七, 项羽本纪]
Todd S (ed) (2005) The law of torts in New Zealand. Thomson Brookers, Wellington
Tong R (ed) (1990) Chinese civil law (Zhu Guobin trans) [trans of: 中国民法]. The Press of Laws, Beijing
Wakana JM (2004) The future of online privacy: a proposal for International legislation. Loyola Los Angel Int Comp Law Review 26:151
Wang LM (1994) Restatement of the law of rights of the person (Zhu Guobin trans) [trans of: 人格权法新论]. Jilin People's Press, Changchun
Wang CG, Zhang XC (eds) (1997) Introduction to Chinese law. Sweet & Maxwell Asia, Hong Kong
Wang GG, Mo J (eds) (1999) Chinese law. Kluwer, The Hague
Wang KH (2000) Chinese commercial law. Oxford University Press, Oxford
Westin AF (1967) Privacy and freedom. Atheneum, New York
Yang LX (2006) The law of personality rights (Wang Hao trans) [trans of: 人格权法论]. Court Press, Beijing
Yan YX (2003) Private life under socialism: love, intimacy, and family change in a Chinese village 1949–1999. Stanford University Press, Stanford, CA
Zhang WX, Jiang XR (1989) The transformation of the agricultural population and the urbanisation process in China. Int J Soc Econ 16:40
Zhang XB (2004) The legal protection of the right to privacy (Zhu Guobin trans) [trans of: 隐私权的法律保护]. The Masses Press, Beijing
Zhu GB (1997) The right to privacy: an emerging right in Chinese Law. Stat Law Rev 18:208
Zou KY (2000) Towards rule of law in China: experiences in the last two decades. China Report 36:491
Zuoqiu M (403 BC – 386 BC) Xi Gong of the chronicle of Zuo (Wang Hao trans) [trans of: 左传], Xi gong (15th year) [trans of: 僖公十五年].

Legislation

Administrative Procedure Law of the People's Republic of China 1989
Announcement of the Securities Association of China on Issuing the Interim Measures for the Management of Bona Fide Information of the Members of the Securities Association of China 2003
Anti-Money Laundering Law of the People's Republic of China 2006
Archives Law of the People's Republic of China 1987
Civil Procedure Law of the People's Republic of China 1991
Constitution of the People's Republic of China 1982
Criminal Procedure Law of the People's Republic of China 1996
General Principles of the Civil Law of the People's Republic of China 1986
Insurance Law of the People's Republic of China 1995
Interpretation of the Supreme People's Court Regarding issues of Ascertaining the Liability of Compensation for Spiritual Damage for Tort 2001
Labour Law of the People's Republic of China 1995
Law of the People's Republic of China on Commercial Banks 1995
Law of the People's Republic of China on the People's Bank of China 1995
Law of the People's Republic of China on the Protection of Minors 2006
Law of the People's Republic of China on the Protection of Rights and Interests of Women 1992
Law on Practicing Doctors of the People's Republic of China 1988
National People's Congress Standing Committee Decision on Safeguarding Internet Security 2000
Opinions of the Supreme People's Court on Several Issues concerning the Implementation of the General Principles of the Civil Law of the People's Republic of China 1988 (For Trial Implementation)
Standing Committee of the National People's Congress Conducted the First Reading of Amendment Seven to the Criminal Law of the PRC (Draft) 2008
Teacher Law of the People's Republic of China 1993

Government and Law Reform Reports

Australian Law Reform Commission (1983) Privacy. Report paper No. 22 volume 1
Opinions on Protecting the Working Rights of HBV Carriers 2007, Ministry of Labour and Social Security and the Ministry of Health, People's Republic of China (Wang Hao trans) [trans of: 中国劳动保障部, 卫生部关于维护乙肝表面抗原携带者就业权利的意见]

Electronic Materials

China's National Climate Change Programme (2007) National Development and Reform Commission of People's Republic of China. http://www.ccchina.gov.cn/WebSite/CCChina/UpFile/File188.pdf. Accessed 8 April 2011
Han Dictionary (Wang Hao trans) [trans of: 汉典]. http://www.zdic.net/cd/ci/6/ZdicE9Zdic98ZdicB4264096.htm. Accessed 8 April 2011
Liang H, Liao X (2003) The essence of privacy and the concept of the right to privacy (Wang Hao trans) [trans of: 隐私的本质与隐私权的概念] 中外民商裁判网 http://www.zwmscp.com/list.asp?unid=4139. Accessed 8 April 2011

Jia M (2006) Red book of divorce (Wang Hao trans) [trans of: 离婚红宝书]. http://www.iamlawyer.com/redbook/redbook.doc. Accessed 8 April 2011

People's Republic of China (2007) Privacy International. http://www.privacyinternational.org/article.shtml?cmd[347]=x-347-559508. Accessed 8 April 2011

Yewei Q (2003) The research of several difficult problems when practicing judicature of harm damages on divorcement (Wang Hao trans) [trans of: 离婚损害赔偿制度中举证难问题研究]. http://scholar.ilib.cn/A-czszxb200302036.html. Accessed 8 April 2011

Chapter 4
The Legal Protection of Privacy in International Practices: Potential as Models for a Chinese Privacy Protection Regime

4.1 Introduction

There have been a number of legislative activities by Western legislatures researching to control and create standards for protection of privacy in the past 30 years. At the international level, initiatives have been taken in relation to the privacy aspects of changes in information-handling practices, spurred on by new technological developments.[1] At the national level, there also have been activities in some certain Western developed countries regarding privacy protection in the past 30 years. In a number of developed Western countries, the protection of privacy interests has been connected with information or data protection, which deems privacy as the management of personal information.[2] For example, the Australian *Privacy Act 1988* (Cth) regarding privacy of personal information; similarly, the UK's *Data Protection Act 1998*, came fully into force in March 2000, is to regulate how to obtain, record, use or disclose the personal data that contained in the data.

On the other hand, this is not to say that Western privacy protection is being effectively implemented to a high standard universally. However, compared to China's protection of privacy, there is a high level of privacy protection in some certain Western developed countries. There have been real advances that are not yet reflected in Chinese laws, such as effective protection of privacy interests through information-handling practices. Therefore, it is time for China to study other countries' experiences first and then consider how our laws ought to protect the privacy interests of the individual.

In this chapter, privacy protection in International Human Rights Instruments will be studied first. Then, privacy protection in some major Western developed countries will be examined. Finally, the author explores what China can learn from

---

[1] Australian Law Reform Commission 1983, p. 263.

[2] Privacy International 2007.

H. Wang, *Protecting Privacy in China*,
DOI 10.1007/978-3-642-21750-0_4,

other jurisdictions. The author hopes that the following considerations can provide inspiration for Chinese privacy protection in the near future.

4.2 International Standards

4.2.1 International Human Rights Instruments

4.2.1.1 The Charter of the United Nations

The Charter of the United Nations was signed on 26 June 1945 and came into force on 24 October 1945.[3] The Charter states that one of the main aims of the United Nations is "to achieve international co-operation in solving international problems of an economic, social, cultural, or humanitarian character, and in promoting and encouraging respect for human rights and for fundamental freedoms for all without distinction as to race, sex, language, or religion."[4] Therefore, the Charter of the United Nations of 1945 is designed "to reaffirm faith in fundamental human rights, in the dignity and worth of the human person, in the equal rights of men and women and of nations large and small."[5]

Article 55 (c) of the Charter provides that the United Nations should promote "universal respect for, and observance of, human rights and fundamental freedoms for all without distinction as to race, sex, language, or religion"[6]; while article 56 states that "all Members pledge themselves to take joint and separate action in co-operation with the Organization for the achievement of the purposes set forth in Article 55."[7] Therefore, the Charter of the United Nations has been seen as the foundation of modern international instruments on human rights. Today, most international instruments on human rights are established on the basis of the Charter. These international instruments include the Universal Declaration of Human Rights (1948), the European Convention on Human Rights (1950), the International Convention on Civil and Political Rights (1966), the American Declaration of the Rights and Duties of Man (1948), and the American Convention on Human Rights (1969). In order to explore the international standards of privacy protection, it is necessary to examine the privacy provisions of these treaties in turn.

[3] *Charter of the United Nations*, Introduction.

[4] *Charter of the United Nations*, art 1(3).

[5] *Charter of the United Nations*, Preamble.

[6] *Charter of the United Nations*, art 55(c).

[7] *Charter of the United Nations*, art 56.

4.2.1.2 The Universal Declaration of Human Rights

The General Assembly of the United Nations adopted the Universal Declaration of Human Rights (the UDHR) in 1948 at Paris. With respect to privacy protection, article 12 of the UDHR states that "no one shall be subjected to arbitrary interference with his privacy, family, home, or correspondence, nor to attacks upon his honour and reputation. Everyone has the right to the protection of law against such interference or attacks." It has been argued that the scope of the individual privacy has been extended to include the kinship "zone" of the family since this article emerges.[8]

4.2.1.3 The European Convention on Human Rights

Privacy has been dealt with in article 8 of the European Convention on Human Rights (the ECHR). Article 8 states that:

> (1) Everyone has the right to respect for his private and family life, his home and his correspondence.
> (2) There shall be no interference by a public authority with the exercise of this right except such as is in accordance with the law and is necessary in a democratic society in the interests of national security, public safety or the economic well-being of the country, for the prevention of disorder or crime, for the protection of health or morals, or for the protection of the rights and freedoms of others.

Some scholars postulated that certain encroachments on an individual's privacy may be deemed not to constitute an interference with respect for private life and, accordingly, not protected by the provisions of article 8.[9] However, careful deliberation makes it clear that article 8 protects different interests which together may be regarded as constituting the "right to privacy" for the following reasons: First, the notion of "private life" in article 8 is very broad. It thus can be understood as that article 8 ensures individuals to practice their private lives as they choose without interference from third parties.[10] According to "private life" in article 8, Western legal authority has identified the following elements that include:

(1) Protection of the individual's physical and mental inviolability and a person's moral and intellectual freedom;
(2) Protection against attacks on an individual's honour or reputation and assimilated torts;
(3) Protection of an individual's name, identity or likeness against unauthorised use;
(4) Protection of the individual against being spied on, watched or harassed; and
(5) Protection against disclosure of information covered by the duty of professional secrecy.[11]

---

[8] Michael (1994), p. 19.

[9] Heffernan et al. (1994), p. 153.

[10] Heffernan et al. (1994), p. 153.

[11] Merrills and Robertson (2001), p. 138.

Second, the scope of "correspondence" that contained in article 8 is also broad. In fact, "correspondence" can be comprehended as letters, emails, faxes, telephone calls, and any other means of communication. Therefore, article 8 of the ECHR also includes the right to keep information about one's personal life outside the public sphere in certain circumstances. The author thus believes privacy interests have been protected by article 8 of the ECHR per se.

4.2.1.4 The International Convention on Civil and Political Rights

The main purposes of the International Convention on Civil and Political Rights (the ICCPR) are to comply with the principles proclaimed in the Charter of the United Nations, to recognize that all rights derive from the inherent dignity of the human person, and to consider the obligation of States under the Charter of the United Nations to promote universal respect for human rights and freedoms.[12] Therefore, the right to privacy is guaranteed by article 17 of the ICCPR, which states that "(1) no one shall be subjected to arbitrary or unlawful interference with his privacy, family, home or correspondence, nor to unlawful attacks on his honor and reputation; (2) everyone has the right to the protection of the law against such interference or attacks." In fact, article 17 of the ICCPR used the similar words to those used in the Universal Declaration.

4.2.1.5 The American Declaration of the Rights and Duties of Man

At the ninth Inter-American Conference at Bogotá in 1948, the American States undertook a review of their methods of cooperation and reorganized the whole system.[13] The "Charter of Bogotá" adopted on this occasion provided the new constitutional instrument that was needed and thereby established the Organisation of American States.[14] One of basic texts adopted at Bogotá was the American Declaration of the Rights and Duties of Man (1948). This Declaration of 1948 signed by the 21 countries who formed the Organization of American States in Bogota.[15] The American Declaration of 1948 emphasizes that:

> All men are born free and equal, in dignity and in rights, and, being endowed by nature with reason and conscience, they should conduct themselves as brothers one to another.
>
> The fulfillment of duty by each individual is a prerequisite to the rights of all. Rights and duties are interrelated in every social and political activity of man. While rights exalt individual liberty, duties express the dignity of that liberty.[16]

---

[12] *International Convention on Civil and Political Rights*, art 17.

[13] Robertson (1968), pp. 347–348.

[14] Robertson (1968), pp. 347–348.

[15] Human Obligations 2005.

[16] *American Declaration of the Rights and Duties of Man* 1992.

Therefore, article V of the American Declaration of 1948 states that "every person has the right to the protection of the law against abusive attacks upon his honour, his reputation, and his private and family life." This is a regional declaration, and has been reinforced by the American Convention on Human Rights of 1969.[17]

4.2.1.6 The American Convention on Human Rights

The American Convention on Human Rights (the ACHR), also known as "Pact of San Jose de Costa Rica," was drafted at Costa Rica in November 1969 and entered into force in 1979.[18] Canada and the USA are members of the Organization but neither has ratified the Convention.[19] Article 11 of the ACHR states that:

(1) Everyone has the right to have his honor respected and his dignity recognized;
(2) No one may be the object of arbitrary or abusive interference with his private life, his family, his home, or his correspondence, or of unlawful attacks on his honor or reputation; and
(3) Everyone has the right to the protection of the law against such interference or attacks.

It should be noted that these provisions have not yet been applied or interpreted in the way that older equivalents in the ECHR have been.[20]

4.2.2 International Data Protection Law

In addition to the privacy protection afforded by the international human rights instruments, the Privacy Guidelines of the Organisation for Economic Cooperation and Development (the OECD Guidelines); Directive 95/46/EC of the European Parliament and Council on the protection of individuals with regard to the processing and free movement of personal data (the Directive 95/46/EC); and Asia–Pacific Economic Cooperation's Privacy Framework, have also significantly influenced the development of privacy law worldwide. The following paragraphs examine these three frameworks in turn.

4.2.2.1 The OECD Guidelines

The *OECD Guidelines on the Protection of Privacy and Transborder Flows of Personal Data*, adopted on 23 September 1980, represents international consensus on general guidance concerning the collection and management of personal

---

[17] Michael (1994), p. 26.

[18] Mendezl and Mariezcurrena (1999).

[19] Law Reform Commission of Hong Kong 2004, p. 55.

[20] Michael (1994), p. 27.

information.[21] Part Two of the OECD Guidelines creates eight key principles for the personal information protection and states that these basic principles for national application "should be regarded as minimum standards which are capable of being supplemented by additional measures for the protection of privacy and individual liberties."[22]

The first principle is the collection limitation principle that "there should be limits to the collection of personal data, and any such data collected should be obtained by lawful means and with the consent of the data subject, where appropriate."[23] Second is the data quality principle that "collected data should be relevant to a specific purpose, and be accurate, complete, and up-to-date."[24] Third is the purpose specification principle that "the purposes for which personal data are collected should be specified not later than at the time of data collection and the subsequent use limited to the fulfillment of those purposes or such others as are not incompatible with those purposes and as are specified on each occasion of change of purpose."[25] The fourth principle is use limitation principle that "personal data should not be disclosed, made available or otherwise used for purposes other than those specified except: (1) with the consent of the data subject; or (2) by the authority of law."[26] Fifth is the security and safeguards principle that "personal data should be protected by reasonable security safeguards against such risks as loss or unauthorized access, destruction, use, modification, or disclosure of data."[27] The sixth principle is openness principle that "there should be a general policy of openness about developments, practices and policies with respect to personal data."[28] The seventh principle is individual participation principle that an individual should have the right to obtain, confirm, and communicate to their personal data.[29] The last principle is accountability principle that a data controller should be accountable for complying with the principles of the privacy guidelines.[30]

Although the OECD Guidelines are nonbinding on members of the OECD, it has been influential in shaping many national privacy protection laws.[31] For example, Australian *Privacy Act 1988* (Cth) contains a set of 11 Information Privacy Principles (IPPs) and a set of 10 National Privacy Principles (NPPs) on the basis of the OECD Guidelines. New Zealand enacted *Privacy Act 1993* to regulate

[21] *OECD Guidelines on the Protection of Privacy and Transborder Flows of Personal Data.*

[22] *Guidelines on the Protection of Privacy and Transborder Flows of Personal Data*, para 6.

[23] *Guidelines on the Protection of Privacy and Transborder Flows of Personal Data*, para 7.

[24] *Guidelines on the Protection of Privacy and Transborder Flows of Personal Data*, para 8.

[25] *Guidelines on the Protection of Privacy and Transborder Flows of Personal Data*, para 9.

[26] *Guidelines on the Protection of Privacy and Transborder Flows of Personal Data*, para 10.

[27] *Guidelines on the Protection of Privacy and Transborder Flows of Personal Data*, para 11.

[28] *Guidelines on the Protection of Privacy and Transborder Flows of Personal Data*, para 12.

[29] *Guidelines on the Protection of Privacy and Transborder Flows of Personal Data*, para 13.

[30] *Guidelines on the Protection of Privacy and Transborder Flows of Personal Data*, para 14.

[31] Australian Law Reform Commission 2006, p. 126.

personal information collection and use in both the public and private sectors. It adopts 12 privacy protection principles based on the OECD Guidelines.[32] In Japan, a 1988 act, which regulates electronic personal information maintained by the Japanese government, adopts many principles of the OECD Guidelines, including the collection limitation principle, the purpose specification principle, and the openness principle.[33]

4.2.2.2 The EU Directive (95/46/EC)

One of the most significant pieces of EU legislation is the EU Directive 95/46/EC, which provides a framework for data protection. The EU Directive 95/46/EC was created in the early 1990s and formally adopted in 1995.[34] The purpose of the EU Directive 95/46/EC is to "protect the fundamental rights and freedoms of natural persons, and in particular their right to privacy with respect to the processing of personal data."[35] The principles set out in the EU Directive 95/46/EC are that:

1. Legitimacy: personal data may only be processed for limited purposes
2. Finality: personal data may only be collected for specified, explicit and legitimate purposes and may not be further processed in a way incompatible with those purposes
3. Transparency: the data subject must be given information regarding data processing relating to him
4. Proportionality: personal data must be adequate, relevant, and not excessive in relation to the purposes for which they are collected and further processed
5. Confidentiality and security: technical and organizational measures to ensure confidentiality and security must be taken with regard to the processing of personal data and
6. Control: supervision of processing by Data Protection Authorities must be ensured[36]

The EU Directive 95/46/EC is a form of EU law that the Member States must comply with. It has been held that the directive has a "direct effect" on individuals, which is because "it grants them rights that can be upheld by the national courts in their respective countries if their governments have not implemented the directive by the set deadline."[37] As Professor Solove points out that the EU Directive 95/46/

---

[32] *Privacy Act 1993* (NZ), s 6.

[33] World Privacy Forum 2006.

[34] Solove and Rotenberg (2003), p. 714.

[35] *Directive 95/46/EC*, art 1.

[36] Hendrickx (2002), p. 4.

[37] Solove and Rotenberg (2003), p. 715.

EC "grants rights rather than creates obligations, and they are enforceable by individuals rather than by public authorities."[38]

For China, the most important provision of the EU Directive 95/46/EC is Article 25. This article proposes that the transfer to a third country of personal data, whether are undergoing processing or are intended for processing and whether the source is public or private sector, should be permitted only when the third country in question ensures an adequate level of protection.[39] Moreover, the EU Commission has been given the power by the EU Council and the EU Parliament to find whether a third country ensures an adequate level of protection by reason of its domestic law or of the international commitments it has entered into.[40] If China hopes to take part in the global information community and achieve its benefits fully, China must set up an effective and adequate privacy protection regime. Otherwise, both privacy protection and information transfers will be damaged in the near future. As a consequence, it requires China to enact information privacy protection legislation that provides an adequate level of protection to Chinese citizens' information privacy so that Chinese businesses could maintain commercial relations with EU businesses.

4.2.2.3 APEC Privacy Framework

APEC is the premier forum for facilitating economic growth, cooperation, trade and investment in the Asia–Pacific region.[41] APEC has 21 members.[42] In order to conduct business in a global economy, APEC adopted the Privacy Framework at their November 2004 meeting in Santiago, Chile. The APEC Privacy Framework promotes a flexible approach to information privacy protection for APEC Member Economies, while avoiding the creation of unnecessary barriers to information flows.[43]

The APEC Privacy Framework consists of a Preamble and Scope in parts I and II, nine APEC privacy protection principles in Part III, and Implementation in Part IV.[44] The commentary (10) in Part II explicitly states that "the APEC Privacy Framework applies to persons or organizations in the public and private sectors who control the collection, holding, processing, use, transfer or disclosure of personal

---

[38] Solove and Rotenberg (2003), p. 715.

[39] *Directive 95/46/EC*, art 25 (1).

[40] *Directive 95/46/EC*, art 25 (6).

[41] Asia–Pacific Economic Cooperation 2009.

[42] APEC's 21 Members include: Australia; Brunei Darussalam; Canada; Chile; People's Republic of China; Hong Kong, China; Indonesia; Japan; Republic of Korea; Malaysia; Mexico; New Zealand; Papua New Guinea; Peru; The Republic of the Philippines; The Russian Federation; Singapore; Chinese Taipei; Thailand; United States of America; Viet Nam.

[43] *APEC Privacy Framework* 2009.

[44] APEC Privacy Framework 2005.

information." The nine privacy protection principles of the APEC Privacy Framework are: preventing harm; notice; collection limitation; uses of personal information; choice; integrity of personal information; security safeguards; access and correction; and accountability, respectively.[45] However, it has been argued that these privacy principles do not include the OECD principles concerning "purpose specification" or "openness."[46] As Professor Greenleaf concludes that the Framework does not include any stronger principles contained in any of the region's privacy legislation developed since 1980.[47] Therefore, at present, the prevalent views of the APEC Privacy Framework are that it:

(1) is unlikely to provide an adequate level of protection as required by the European Data Protection Directive;
(2) is likely to result in inconsistent implementation by APEC member states and a confused hotchpotch of national data protection laws, regulations or rules;
(3) is likely to be policed by a very weak regulatory regime;
(4) is likely to allow member states to adopt divergent policies on important privacy aspects with the result that the Framework is unlikely to provide a sound, long-term, basis for the international trade in personal data; and
(5) contains principles and procedures which could be implemented in a way that results in an unacceptable or minimal level of protection for personal data.[48]

As Dr Pounder points out that the "APEC Privacy Framework is intended to provide a legal basis for facilitating international transfers of personal data and at the same time providing a minimum standard of privacy protection."[49] Greenleaf concludes that "the APEC Framework is thus considerably weaker than any other international privacy instrument in terms of its implementation requirements, even the OECD Guidelines required legislative implementation."[50]

On the other hand, it should be noted that the APEC Framework does not prevent Members from adopting privacy rights that are stronger than the Framework's Principles.[51] Hence, in fact, the APEC Privacy Framework has no explicitly harmful effects on countries that already have privacy legislation.[52]

4.2.2.4 Summary

The developments of information technology are universal. It thus causes privacy concerns in China. As a developing country that wants to follow the steps of advanced technology, China must ensure its domestic laws are cognizant of the

[45] *APEC Privacy Framework* 2005, para 14–26.
[46] Greenleaf (2005).
[47] Greenleaf (2005).
[48] Pounder (2007).
[49] Pounder (2007).
[50] Greenleaf (2005).
[51] Greenleaf (2005).
[52] Greenleaf (2005).

principles incorporated in these international instruments. In order words, China's domestic laws must be able to be compatible with these agreements. The best example is that China's businesses that run in Europe or trade with Europe will be influenced by the EU Directive 95/46/EC inevitably. According to the EU Directive 95/46/EC, these businesses must show that their practices of exchanging personal information with Europe meet the standards of the EU Directive 95/46/EC. Otherwise, as mentioned earlier, both privacy protection and information transfers will be damaged and the adverse economic consequences will be inevitable in China in the near future. As a consequence, China should move rapidly towards the adoption of appropriate privacy principles as well.

4.3 Legal Protection of Privacy in Some Selected Western Countries

4.3.1 Countries with the Common Law Legal System

4.3.1.1 United Kingdom

Privacy Generally

Initially, in the significant English case of *Entick v Carrington*,[53] which is commonly regarded as an early decision on "privacy," Lord Camden CJ's states that the "eye cannot by the law of England be guilty of trespass."[54] In 1990, in the case of *Kaye v Robertson*, it was held that when a reporter and a photographer gained unauthorized entry to a hospital and interviewed and photographed a very ill man (a celebrity actor) who had incurred brain injury and had just left intensive care, there was no cause of action for breach of privacy.[55] In 1996, Lord Hoffmann emphasized in the House of Lords that "English common law does not know a general right of privacy."[56] Therefore, so far, the right to privacy has not been accepted by the common law in the UK.

On the other hand, this is not to say that there is no legal privacy protection in the UK. It has been held that the protection for the right to privacy is arising from the law of confidence that has been used as far back as 1849 to protect the unauthorized disclosure of personal information in the UK.[57] In order words, in the UK, individuals' privacy interests have been protected by the law of confidence for

[53] *Entick v Carrington* [1765] 95 ER 807.

[54] Lindsay (2005), p. 138.

[55] Todd (2005), p. 751.

[56] Todd (2005), p. 752.

[57] Privacy International: United Kingdom of Great Britain and Northern Ireland 2007.

many years. In addition, there are also some statutory protections to personal privacy in the UK. For example, in 1998, the UK *Human Rights Act* gave the European Convention for the protection of Human Rights and Fundamental Freedoms status in UK domestic law.[58] As mentioned earlier, article 8 of the convention directly protects the interest of privacy. Based on the *Human Rights Act*, in *Douglas v Hello! Ltd*,[59] the court suggested that it is time for the UK courts to treat privacy as an enforceable right.[60] Furthermore, the *Data Protection Act 1998* is also significant for privacy protection in the UK. This Act came into force on 1 March 2000. It implements the EU Directive 95/46/EC. It provides a legal basis and allows for the protection of privacy and personal data in the UK. Other UK statutes protect privacy in different areas. The following section examines these privacy protections afforded by the UK in more detail.

Common Law Privacy Protection

The Law of Confidence

Traditionally, in the UK, the law relating to breach of confidence had developed in order to prevent employees leaking trade secrets to rival companies, and enabled employers to seek an injunction to prevent disclosure of the information, or damages once it had been disclosed.[61] However, the UK courts have applied these principles that developed in the commercial field to protect information in other areas where a confidential relationship operates.[62] Today, the UK courts still prefer to use the breach of confidence principle to protect privacy rights, although it applies only to a narrow set of circumstances. Usually, injunction and damages are main remedies for breach of confidence in the UK.

The origins of the equitable action for breach of confidence date back to 1848, in the case of *Prince Albert v Strange*[63]:

- Prince Albert and Queen Victoria had etchings made of their children for their private use. The defendant managed to purchase copies made without authorization by an employee of the printer. He intended to exhibit and publish them in a catalog for profit. Prince Albert applied for an injunction to prevent this usage. The matter first came before Knight Bruce V-C, who favored the Prince's application. The defendant agreed not to exhibit the etchings but appealed against the injunction not to catalog them.[64]

---

[58] Todd (2005), p. 751.

[59] *Douglas v Hello! Ltd* [2003] EWHC 2629 (CH).

[60] Black (2007).

[61] Sieghart (1988), p. 125.

[62] Sieghart (1988), p. 126.

[63] *Prince Albert v Strange* [1849] EWHC Ch J20.

[64] Moore (2003), p. 31.

With respect to this case, the Lord Chancellor stated that "the property of an author or composer of any work, whether of literature, art, or science, in such a work unpublished and kept for his private use or pleasure, cannot be disputed."[65] In consequence, the decisions of High Court of Chancery is that:

> The maker and owner of etchings which have never been exhibited or published, and of which no impressions have been made except for his private use, but impressions whereof have, by improper and surreptitious means, come into the possession of other parties, is entitled to an injunction, not only to restrain those parties from exhibiting those impressions, and from publishing copies of them, but also to restrain them from publishing a catalogue compiled by themselves, in which an enumeration and descriptive account of those etchings is contained, and that, although there is no violation of any contract, either express or implied, between the owner and the compilers of the catalogue.[66]

Based on this statement, it has thus been held that this case is "the seminal case in the development of the equitable doctrine of confidence."[67]

In *Coco v A.N. Clark (Engineers) Ltd*,[68] the traditional elements of a breach of confidence were established, which are:

(1) The information itself must have the necessary quality of confidence about it.
(2) The information must have been imparted in circumstances importing an obligation of confidence.
(3) There must be an unauthorized use of that information to the detriment of the party communicating it.[69]

According to the first two elements, "the necessary quality of confidence" means that the information must be confidential, and "it must not be something which is public property and public knowledge."[70] For example, George Blake, a former MI5 employee and spy, faced an action for breach of confidence following the publication of his autobiography.[71] Although, in this case, Blake had committed an offence under the *Official Secret Act 1989* and an injunction was granted to prevent Blake to sell his book, the Court of Appeal nevertheless held that "there was no breach of confidence, as the information given in his book was no longer secret."[72] It is thus clear that this element requires that the information must be confidential in nature. "An obligation of confidence" means that the party who disclosed the information must be aware that it was confidential.[73] Usually, a duty of confidence has been imposed by statute in the UK.[74] For instance, doctors have the duty of

---

[65] *Prince Albert v Strange* [1849] EWHC Ch J20.

[66] *Prince Albert v Strange* [1849] EWHC Ch J20.

[67] Moore (2003), p. 31.

[68] *Coco v A.N. Clark (Engineers) Ltd* [1969] RPC 41.

[69] *Coco v A.N. Clark (Engineers) Ltd* [1969] RPC 41.

[70] *Coco v A.N. Clark (Engineers) Ltd* [1969] RPC 41.

[71] Henry (2001), p. 442.

[72] Henry (2001), p. 442.

[73] Moore (2003), p. 33.

[74] Henry (2001), p. 441.

confidentiality to protect patients' medical records under the UK *Data Protection Act 1998*.

Most recently, the law of confidence in the UK has been used to protect intimate information. For example, in the case of *A v B*,[75] Gary Flitcroft, the Blackburn Rovers soccer player, who sought to prevent the Sunday People revealing details of the fact that he had extramartial affairs with two women, one of whom was a lap dancer.[76] The decisions of *A v B* held that the more stable the relationship, the greater the significance attached to information relating to it.[77] In this case, the UK courts finally decided that this soccer player has right to keep his personal information of extramarital affair out of the newspaper. Furthermore, breach of confidence has also been used to protect noncontractual and domestic relationships. For example, in the case of *Creation Records v News Group Newspaper Ltd*,[78] the pop group Oasis was granted an injunction to prevent publication of a photograph taken at a private photo-shoot for the cover of their new album.[79]

It should be noted that, under the common law, even in situations where all other elements are satisfied, the disclosure may still be permitted under public interest. That is to say "information cannot be protected from disclosure if it is in the public domain."[80] For example, in the case of *A-G v Guardian Newspaper Ltd*, Peter Wright wrote and published a book to describe his experiences of being a military intelligence agent of the British security service.[81] The courts held that Peter Wright, as a former military intelligence agent, should have "a lifelong duty of confidence owed to the Crown."[82] However, the book was finally published. That is because the Attorney General was not able to prove that the public interest would be damaged by the publication of the book. In consequence, the courts refused to grant a permanent injunction.

Recent Development

Recently, in order to make the law of confidence more effective to protect privacy interests, the UK courts have been prepared to provide substantial guidance on these issues. In the Campbell case:

- The Mirror newspaper published a prominent article on its front page about the model Naomi Campbell, a celebrated fashion model. The article said that Naomi Campbell, who had always publicly denied that she was a drug user, was in fact

[75] *A v B* (QB 2001) All Eng L Rep 449.

[76] Fry (2006).

[77] Lulham (2005), p. 104.

[78] *Creation Records v News Group Newspaper Ltd* [1997] EMLR 444.

[79] Henry (2001), p. 443.

[80] Henry (2001), p. 442.

[81] *Attorney-General v Guardian Newspaper Ltd* [1990] 1 AC 109.

[82] *Attorney-General v Guardian Newspaper Ltd* [1990] 1 AC 109.

an addict, and frequently attended meetings of Narcotics Anonymous to beat her addiction. Naomi Campbell commenced proceedings against the publisher of the newspaper, claiming damages for breach of confidence. The judge upheld her claim, awarding her £ 2,500 damages, plus £ 1,000 aggravated damages in respect of further articles published by the newspaper.[83]

Although the decisions of the court are made on the basis of breach of confidence, the Lordships use the terminology of "reasonable expectation of privacy" six times. As Lord Nicholls stated in the case that:

> The continuing use of the phrase 'duty of confidence' and the description of the information as 'confidential' is not altogether comfortable. Information about an individual's private life would not, in ordinary usage, be called 'confidential'. The more natural description today is that such information is private. The essence of the tort is better encapsulated now as misuse of private information.[84]

Clearly, the UK court acknowledges that this case "affords respect for one aspect of an individual's privacy."[85] The court held that individual privacy is the value underlying this course of action, and that can be invaded in ways not involving publication of information.[86] It is thus a good signal that the UK courts have focused on the nature of information that has been disclosed, rather than the simple relationship between plaintiff and defendant.

Statutory Protection of Privacy

Statutes have also been identified as a useful form of privacy protection in the UK. The following section concerns the main privacy protections provided by UK statutes.

The Human Rights Act 1998

The aim of the *Human Rights Act 1998* is to give further effect in UK law to the rights contained in the European Convention on Human Rights.[87] The Act came into force on October 2, 2000. Schedule 1 of the Act is concerned with setting out the Convention. Article 8 (1) provides that "everyone has the right to respect for his private and family life, his home and his correspondence." Therefore, obviously, the UK courts have to recognize the privacy interests.

---

[83] *Campbell v MGN Ltd* [2004] UKHL 22.

[84] *Campbell v MGN Ltd* [2004] UKHL 22, [14].

[85] *Campbell v MGN Ltd* [2004] UKHL 22, [15].

[86] *Campbell v MGN Ltd* [2004] UKHL 22, [15].

[87] *Human Rights Act 1998* (UK), preamble.

Data Protection

The Data Protection Act 1998 Initially, a Data Protection Bill, introduced in July 1983, went on to become the *Data Protection Act 1984*.[88] However, there was no compulsory requirement to comply with the Act and its principles.[89] As a result, based on the EU Directive 95/46/EC, the *Data Protection Act 1998* received Royal Assent on July 16, 1998, and came fully into force on March 1, 2000.[90]

The purpose of the *Data Protection Act 1998* is to regulate how to obtain, record, use or disclose the personal data that contained in the data.[91] It thus has been held that the provisions of the Act apply only to personal data.[92] Under the Act, "'personal data' means data which relate to a living individual who can be identified (a) from those data, or (b) from those data and other information which is in the possession of, or is likely to come into the possession of, the data controller."[93] In addition, personal data also includes "any expression of opinion about the individual and any indication of the intentions of the data controller or any other person in respect of the individual."[94]

Schedule 1 of the the Act sets out eight principles with which every data controllers must comply with. These principles include: (1) personal data should only be processed fairly and lawfully; (2) personal data must be obtained only for specified and lawful purposes; (3) the data collected must be adequate, relevant, and not excessive; (4) personal data must be accurate and up to date; (5) the data should not be kept for longer than is necessary for that purpose or those purposes; (6) personal data should only be processed in accordance with the data subject's rights; (7) appropriate technical and organizational measures should be used against any damages to personal data; (8) and personal data shall not be transferred to a country or territory outside the European Economic Area unless that country or territory ensures an adequate level of protection for the rights and freedoms of data subjects in relation to the processing of personal data.[95]

The Act is overseen by the Office of the Information Commissioner, which is an independent agency that maintains the register and enforces the Data Protection and Freedom of Information Acts.[96] Part V of the Act clearly demonstrates how the Commissioner can ensure the data controllers comply with the Act. If the Commissioner believes that a data controller has contravened any of the data protection principles, the Commissioner will serve the data controller "an enforcement

---

[88] Carey (2003), p. 3.

[89] Carey (2003), p. 4.

[90] Carey (2003), p. 6.

[91] *Data Protection Act 1988* (UK), pt I, s 1(2).

[92] Carey (2003), p. 11.

[93] *Data Protection Act 1988* (UK), pt I, s 1(1).

[94] *Data Protection Act 1988* (UK), pt I, s 1(1).

[95] *Data Protection Act 1988* (UK), sch 1, pt I.

[96] Privacy International: United Kingdom of Great Britain and Northern Ireland 2007.

notice," requiring him to refrain from (1) taking after certain time; or (2) processing any personal data.[97] The criterion of the Commissioner to serve an enforcement notice to the data collectors is that "the contravention has caused or is likely to cause any person damage or distress."[98] Failure to comply with a notice is guilty of an offence.[99]

The Telecommunications (Data Protection and Privacy) Regulations 1999 The *Telecommunications (Data Protection and Privacy) Regulations 1999* came into force on 1st March 2000.[100] This Regulation regulates the use of certain traffic and billing data by a telecommunications network provider or a telecommunications service provider.[101] Under the Regulation, the relevant telecommunications service provider will ensure that a subscriber has a simple means to prevent presentation of both subscribers' outgoing and incoming calls.[102]

The Regulation of Investigatory Powers Act 2000 The main purposes of the *Regulation of Investigatory Powers Act* 2000 are to regulate "the interception of communications, the acquisition and disclosure of data relating to communications and the carrying out of surveillance."[103] The Act prohibits listening, storage or other kinds of interception or surveillance of communication system without lawful authority at any place in the UK.[104] A person who is failure to comply with the Act is guilty of an offence, and will be liable to imprisonment for a term up to 2 years or to a fine, or to both.[105]

The Official Secrets Act 1989

The object of the *Official Secrets Act 1989* is to protect official information, mainly related to national security.[106] Under this Act, it is guilty if a member of the security and intelligence services discloses any information, document, or other article relating to security or intelligence without lawful authority.[107] An individual guilty of an offence under any provision of this Act other than will be liable: "(1) on conviction on indictment, to imprisonment for a term not exceeding two years or a

[97] *Data Protection Act 1988* (UK), pt V, s 40(1).

[98] *Data Protection Act 1988* (UK), s 40(2).

[99] *Data Protection Act 1988* (UK), s 47.

[100] *Telecommunications (Data Protection and Privacy) Regulations 1999* (UK), pt I, s 1(1).

[101] *Telecommunications (Data Protection and Privacy) Regulations 1999* (UK), pt II.

[102] *Telecommunications (Data Protection and Privacy) Regulations 1999* (UK), pt III, ss 11, 12.

[103] *Regulation of Investigatory Powers Act* 2000 (UK), preamble.

[104] *Regulation of Investigatory Powers Act* 2000 (UK), pt I, s 1(1).

[105] *Regulation of Investigatory Powers Act* 2000 (UK), s 1(7).

[106] *Official Secrets Act 1989* (UK), preliminary.

[107] *Official Secrets Act 1989* (UK), s 1.

fine or both; (2) on summary conviction, to imprisonment for a term not exceeding six months or a fine not exceeding the statutory maximum or both."[108]

The Rehabilitation of Offenders Act 1974

The purpose of the *Rehabilitation of Offenders Act 1974???* is to enable individuals' criminal convictions should be ignored after a "rehabilitation period." Under the Act, the length of the rehabilitation period depends on the sentence given.[109] For example, if the prison sentences is 6 months or less, rehabilitation period of people who aged 18 or over when convicted will be 7 years, while rehabilitation period of people who aged 17 or under when convicted will be three-and-a-half years.[110] It should be noted that, under the act, custodial sentences of more than two-and-a-half years can never become spent.[111] If a newspaper maliciously publishes information about a person's rehabilitated criminal past, then a defamation case may result.[112]

Other Protections

There are also several other statutes that protect privacy rights in the UK. For example, the *Access to Medical Reports Act 1988*, the *Access to Health Records Act 1990* and *the Health and Social Care Act 2001*, which govern medical records. The *Consumer Credit Act 1974* governs consumer credit information. Other laws with privacy components include *the Police Act 1997*, *the Broadcasting Act 1996* and *the Protection from Harassment Act 1997*.[113] Moreover, the National Health Service recently completed a consultation on privacy as part of a program to computerize all patient records on a central database.[114]

4.3.1.2 The Commonwealth of Australia

Privacy Generally

Australia's legal system reflects its English heritage that the common law legal system composes the basis of jurisprudence. However, until the decision in *Grosse v Purvis*,[115] the common law action for breach of privacy has not been recognized

[108] *Official Secrets Act 1989* (UK), s 10.
[109] *Rehabilitation of Offenders Act 1974* 2001.
[110] *Rehabilitation of Offenders Act* 1974 2001.
[111] *Rehabilitation of Offenders Act 1974* 2001.
[112] Henry (2001), p. 444.
[113] Privacy International: United Kingdom of Great Britain and Northern Ireland 2007.
[114] Privacy International: United Kingdom of Great Britain and Northern Ireland 2007.
[115] *Grosse v Purvis* [2003] QDC 151.

in Australia. Initially, certain privacy interests are protected indirectly through the developments of other common law principles, such as trespass, nuisance, defamation, and breach of confidence in Australia.

In addition to common law, there are some legislation or statutory provisions provide protection to privacy interests in Australia. At the federal level, the most significant legislation of privacy protection is the *Privacy Act 1988* (Cth). At the state level, New South Wales, Victoria, and the Northern Territory have also enacted privacy protection legislation to regulate the handling of personal information in their respective public sectors.[116] Furthermore, many other legislation and industry bodies' codes of practice have also been recognized as privacy safeguards in Australia. For example, the *Commonwealth Telecommunications (Interception and Acess) Act 1979* protects privacy interests by prohibiting the interception of, and other access to, telecommunications; Clause 9 of the *Code of Ethics of the Australian Journalists Association* states that journalists "shall respect private grief and personal privacy and shall have the right to resist compulsion to intrude on them." The following section examines these efforts by Australia in more detail.

Common Law Privacy Protection

The Past

For many years, certain privacy interests have been indirectly protected if other interests of the plaintiff have been violated in Australia. There are some examples of other torts indirectly protecting privacy.

Trespass to Land Trespass to land is a direct physical interference by a person with other person's exclusive possession of land.[117] In Common law countries, it has been held that "land" includes not only the surface of any ground, soil or earth but also any buildings or structures and the air space above the land.[118] In Australia, the tort of trespass to land thus protects individuals' privacy interests by prohibiting those who enter private property for the purpose of attempting to obtain an interview, or to photograph, film or otherwise record the occupants and their activities.[119] It should be noted that not all interferences will be actionable as trespass in Australia. With respect to privacy protection, the tort of trespass serves only to protect an individual in so far as their land is trespassed upon for an unauthorized or unlawful purpose.[120]

[116] Doyle and Bagaric (2005), p. 9.

[117] Trindade et al. (2007), p. 132.

[118] Trindade et al. (2007), p. 132.

[119] Doyle and Bagaric (2005), p. 63.

[120] Henry (2001), p. 27.

Nuisance In the common law, a private nuisance is an unreasonable interference with the use and enjoyment of land, and this tort is applicable in cases of interferences such as noise, smoke, smells, vibration, glare, and so on.[121] With respect to privacy protection, a private nuisance serves only to protect an individual when the interference is substantial and unreasonable, as opposed to merely trivial interference or interference flowing from the reasonable exercise of another person's rights to use of their own or public land.[122] At present, based on the opinion of that the rights of the occupier do not include a freedom from view, the protection of nuisance does not apply to prevent filming and photographing in Australia.[123]

Defamation Defamation is any publication or imputation which tends to injure a person's reputation in the estimation of others by making them think less of that person, usually by bring the person into hatred, contempt or ridicule.[124] Sometimes, in common law countries, a defamation action may lie in respect of the publication of a photograph of, or information about, the plaintiff that carries imputations affecting his or her reputation which cannot be proved true.[125] Therefore, "truth" at common law, also known as justification, is a complete defense to such an action.[126] For example, in *Tolley v JS Fry & Sons*, a well-known amateur golfer had been defamed by the use of his image to advertise a brand of chocolate, the defamatory imputation being that he had authorized the commercial use of his image for money.[127] Tort of defamation thus has protected an interest for privacy in some cases.

Confidentiality Paralleling the UK law, confidential information has also been protected under Australian law. That is to say certain personal information privacy has been protected on several occasions. For example, in the case of *Foster v Mountford and Rigby Ltd*, an interlocutory order was obtained restraining the continued publication of a book which disclosed cultural and religious secrets of the Aboriginal people.[128] It has been held that the potential damage to the plaintiffs far outweighed any perceived public right to information which might afford valuable material for anthropological research.[129] Usually, Australian courts will not grant final or interlocutory injunctions where damages will provide adequate compensation for the continuing breach.[130] Moreover, a number of recognized

---

[121] Trindade et al. (2007), pp. 167–168.

[122] Henry (2001), p. 28.

[123] Henry (2001), p. 28.

[124] Doyle and Bagaric (2005), p. 64.

[125] Todd (2005), p. 746.

[126] Tucker (1992), p. 36.

[127] Doyle and Bagaric (2005), p. 66.

[128] Tucker (1992), p. 30.

[129] Tucker (1992), p. 30.

[130] Henry (Henry 2001), pp. 29–30.

defenses have emerged, in particular that the information is in the public domain and thus no longer confidential, and that it is in the public interest that the information be published.[131]

Evaluation It is undeniable that Australian common law has protected privacy interests in certain areas. However, the limitations of common law protection are still obvious. First, the existence and development of common law protections present "a confused melee of laws" to protect privacy interests.[132] This is mainly because most common law protections just evolve to have the subordinate effect of safeguarding privacy.[133] Second, at present, the common law protections in Australia are not able to cover all situations of intrusive conduct. It has been held that, at least, there are four situations where the law provides no remedy:

> (1) the taking of photographs of a person without their permission, even where the person is on his or her own premises;
> (2) a journalist approaching a person on their premises for an interview;
> (3) conduct which causes offence, distress or embarrassment but which is not an assault, defamatory or trespass;
> (4) revealing private information unless defamatory or in breach of an obligation of confidence, or copyright.[134]

A Tort of Invasion of Privacy

Introduction In Australia, *Victoria Park Racing and Recreation Grounds Co Ltd v Taylor*, more than three quarters of a century ago, has been interpreted as presenting a major obstacle to the development of privacy tort in Australia.[135] In this case, the Australian High Court held that the owner and operator of a racecourse could not prevent another party, situated on adjoining land, from observing and broadcasting particulars of events carried out on the racecourse.[136] In *Australian Broadcasting Corporation v Lenah Game Meats Pty Ltd*, [137] the High Court of Australia discussed a possible tort of invasion of privacy, and concluded that the tort of invasion of privacy "is the missing cause of action for which everyone in the case has so far been searching." However, the court held that:

> The recognition of a tort of invasion of privacy as part of the common law of Australia does not involve acceptance of all, or indeed any of the jurisprudence of the United States which is complicated by the First Amendment. There is good reason for not importing into this country all of the North American law particularly because of the substantial differences in

[131] Todd (2005), p. 747.

[132] Tucker (1992), p. 57.

[133] Tucker (1992), p. 57.

[134] Henry (2001), pp. 29–30.

[135] Doyle and Bagaric (2005), p. 59.

[136] Telford (2003).

[137] *Australian Broadcasting Corporation v Lenah Game Meats Pty Ltd* [2001] HCA 63, [38].

> our political and constitutional history. Any principles for an Australian tort of privacy would need to be worked out on a case by case basis in a distinctly Australian context.[138]

As a result, the High Court of Australia did not rule out the possibility that such a tort might exist in Australia.[139]

Grosse v Purvis: A New Tort The challenge was recently taken up by the Queensland District Court in *Grosse v Purvis*, a case which is involved a civil action for damages arising from the stalking of the plaintiff by the Defendant.[140] In this case:

- The plaintiff was a female shire councilor, heavily involved in the establishment of public facilities on the Sunshine Coast in Queensland, including a TAFE college and a university. For a period of time, the plaintiff had been romantically involved with the defendant, both parties having worked together on various community-related ventures. From 1992 that relationship soured and in April 2002 the plaintiff commenced a proceeding in the District Court of Queensland, seeking damages pursuant to various causes of action including harassment, nuisance, negligence, trespass to person, and the intentional infliction of physical harm to the plaintiff.[141]

Presiding trial judge, Senior Judge Skoien (District Court of Queensland) reviewed the individual judgments of the High Court in *Australian Broadcasting Corporation v Lenah Game Meat Pty Ltd* and concluded that the common law right to privacy should be enforced in Australia.[142] Skoien has formulated the "intrusion" version of a common law privacy tort in terms somewhat similar to those used by members of the High Court in *ABC v Lenah* and by United States decisions and commentators such as Prosser.[143] In his Honor's view the essential elements of the action are:

> (1) a willed act by the defendant,
> (2) which intrudes upon the privacy or seclusion of the plaintiff,
> (3) in a manner which would be considered highly offensive to a reasonable person of ordinary sensibilities, and
> (4) which causes the plaintiff detriment in the form of mental psychological or emotional harm or distress or which prevents or hinders the plaintiff from doing an act which she is lawfully entitled to do.[144]

---

[138] *Australian Broadcasting Corporation v Lenah Game Meats Pty Ltd* [2001] HCA 63, [332].

[139] Todd (2005), p. 751.

[140] Paterson (2005), p. 18.

[141] Telford (2003).

[142] *Grosse v Purvis* [2003] QDC 151, [425].

[143] Greenleaf (2003).

[144] Greenleaf (2003).

Finally, Skoien believed that the plaintiff's claim for damages was successful. These were assessed at a total of $178,000 (compensatory damages $108,000, aggravated compensatory damages $50,000, and exemplary damages $20,000).[145]

In fact, the judgment in this case established that it is possible to sue for breach of privacy in Australian common law.[146] That is because Australia finally has a decision based on a finding of a separate cause of action of a right of privacy.[147]

Statutory Protection of Privacy

Similarly to the UK, certain privacy interests are protected under different statutes in Australia. Two main privacy statutes are the *Privacy Act 1988* (Cth) and the *Telecommunications Act 1979* (Cth) respectively. Furthermore, there are some State and Territory laws dealing with privacy interests in Australia. The author examines the main privacy-specific statutes that operate throughout the country in the following paragraphs.

Commonwealth Jurisdiction

The Privacy Act 1988 (Cth) The Commonwealth Privacy Act, regarding privacy of personal information, was enacted in 1988. Initially, the *Privacy Act 1988* was Australia's attempt to regulate how personal information is collected, transferred, and disposed of in the public sector.[148] In 2001, the Act was amended to cover the private sector. Therefore, today, the main purpose of the Act is that "to establish a single comprehensive national scheme providing, through codes adopted by private sector organizations and National Privacy Principles, for the appropriate collection, holding, use, correction, disclosure and transfer of personal information by those organizations."[149]

Part II of the Act sets out some significant definitions. Part III of the Act defines interferences with privacy. Section 14 of the Act establishes 11 IPPs to protect privacy in public sector. Similar to the privacy principles of the OECD Guidelines, the IPPs require that (1) personal information must be collected for the lawful purpose; (2) individuals should have right to know the purpose of the collection; (3) the collected personal information must be up-to-date and complete; (4) the collected personal information should be kept secure; (5) the record keeper who has possession or control of records that contain personal information hold personal information must make it known that they hold such personal information; (6)

[145] *Grosse v Purvis* [2003] QDC 151, [483].

[146] McKinnon (2005).

[147] Greenleaf (2003).

[148] Kohel (2002), pp. 703–704.

[149] *Privacy Amendment (Private Sector) Act 2000* (Cth), s 3.

individuals should have right to access their personal information; (7) inaccurate records that containing personal information should be corrected; (8) personal information should be checked before being used; (9) the personal information should not be used for other irrelevant purpose; and (10) exemptions.[150] Schedule 3 of the Act sets out a set of NPPs that apply to private sector organizations in Australia. Under the Act, "organization" includes (1) an individual; or (2) a body corporate; or (3) a partnership; or (4) any other unincorporated association; or (5) a trust.[151]

The Australian Privacy Commissioner has been established under the Part IV of the Act. Section 36 of the Act clear states that an individual may complain to the Privacy Commissioner about an act or practice that may be an interference with his or her privacy. The Privacy Commissioner has right to decide whether there is a need to investigate complaints. If so, the individuals have responsibility to tell the truth. Anyone who fails to answer the Commissioner or refuse to be sworn or make an affirmation may be subject to a fine of up to $2,000 or imprisonment for 12 months, or both.[152]

The *Privacy Act 1988* (Cth) effectively entrenched a great many existing practices within both the public and the private sectors.[153] Further, the Act establishes a range of controls over agencies' practices, and has led to a greater degree of openness and confidence among agencies when dealing with personal information.[154] However, the scope of the Privacy Act is still limited. First, the regulatory content differs as between the two sectors.[155] As mentioned earlier, there are 11 IPPs that apply to the Commonwealth (and Australian Capital Territory) government agencies; while there are also 10 NPPs which apply to some parts of the private sector and health service providers.[156] Second, although the Australian Federal Government has recently announced the extension of certain privacy provisions to the private sector, it has been held that the *Privacy Act 1988* (Cth) does not regulate State or local government information gathering, or the similar activities of private firms or individuals.[157] Third, the NPPs in the private sector lack teeth because the regulatory standard they create is weak, and the language is easily manipulated by business organizations.[158] Finally, the Act does not regulate common intrusive practices such as video or optical surveillance or intrusions into household privacy, or limit the effect of direct marketing operations.[159]

---

[150] *Privacy Act 1988* (Cth), s 14.

[151] *Privacy Act 1988* (Cth), s 6c.

[152] *Privacy Act 1988* (Cth), s 64.

[153] Clarke (1998).

[154] Clarke (1998).

[155] Doyle and Bagaric (2005), p. 99.

[156] Doyle and Bagaric (2005), p. 99.

[157] Henry (2001), p. 21.

[158] Kohel (2002), pp. 704–705.

[159] Australian Human Rights and Equal Opportunity Commission 1995, p. 19.

The Telecommunications (Interception and Acess) Act 1979 (Cth) The primary purpose of the *Telecommunications (Interception and Acess) Act 1979* (Cth) is to prohibit the interception of, and other access to, telecommunications.[160] This Act thus safeguards privacy interests by prohibiting the interception of communications over the telecommunications system.[161] The Act prohibits the interception of communications passing over a telecommunications system and prohibits access to stored communications, such as email, SMS, and voicemail messages stored on a carrier's equipment, except where authorized in specified circumstances.[162] The primary exception is to enable law enforcement agencies to lawfully intercept or access telecommunications in specified circumstances pursuant to an interception warrant or a stored communications warrant issued under the Act.[163] A small number of other exceptions are specified for particular purposes including tracing the location of callers in emergencies, and the operation and maintenance of a telecommunications system.[164]

Other Protections Part VIIC of the *Crimes Act 1914* (Cth) provides protection for individuals with old, minor convictions in certain circumstances.[165] The *National Health Act 1953* covers the storage, use, disclosure and retention of individuals' claims information under the Pharmaceutical Benefits Scheme and the Medicare program.[166] In addition, the *Data-Matching Program (Assistance and Tax) Act 1990* regulates data matching between the Tax Office and four assistance agencies to detect overpayments and ineligibility for assistance.[167]

State Privacy Initiative

There are also some State and Territory laws protecting privacy interests in Australia. It has been held that, in Australia, the States with the most comprehensive privacy regimes are New South Wales (NSW) and Victoria.[168]

New South Wales In NSW, the *Privacy and Personal Information Protection Act* (NSW) was enacted in 1998. The purpose of the Act is to provide "the protection of personal information" and "the protection of the privacy of individuals

---

160 *Telecommunications (Interception and Acess) Act 1979* (Cth), long title.

161 Doyle and Bagaric (2005), p. 99.

162 *Telecommunications Interception & Access Laws: Telecommunications (Interception and Acess) Act 1979* (Cth) 2006.

163 *Telecommunications Interception & Access Laws: Telecommunications (Interception and Acess) Act 1979* (Cth) 2006.

164 *Telecommunications Interception & Access Laws: Telecommunications (Interception and Acess) Act 1979* (Cth) 2006.

165 Cromptom (2000).

166 Cromptom (2000).

167 Cromptom (2000).

168 Doyle and Bagaric (2005), p. 100.

generally."[169] This Act covers public sector only and creates the NSW Privacy Commissioner. Similar to the Commonwealth Privacy Act, it also sets down privacy some information protection principles in part two of the Act. Furthermore, the *Health Records and Information Privacy Act* (NSW) was enacted in 2002. The purpose of the Act is to protect "health records and information."[170] With respect to the protection of privacy and personal information, other relevant legislation in NSW includes the *Listening Devices Act 1994* (NSW) and the *Workplace Video Surveillance Act 1998* (NSW).[171]

Victoria In Victoria, the *Information Privacy Act* (Vic) was enacted in 2000. One of the main purposes of the Act is "to establish a regime for the responsible collection and handling of personal information."[172] This Act covers Victorian public sector only and creates the Victorian Privacy Commissioner. Based on the *Privacy Act 1988* (Cth), it sets out 10 information privacy protection principles. Furthermore, the *Health Records Act 2001* (Vic) provides protection to health information, and the *Surveillance Devices Act 1999* (Vic) provides protection to the information that obtained through the use of surveillance devices.

4.3.1.3 New Zealand

Privacy Generally

Similarly to Australia, New Zealand is also a country whose political and legal system reflects its English heritage. Therefore, initially, the New Zealand legal system did not accept the tort of invasion of privacy. Moreover, the *New Zealand Bill of Rights Act 1990* does not explicitly ensure a general right to privacy. Contrarily, section 14 of *Bill of Rights Act 1990* clearly proposes a right of freedom of expression. This section ensures that "everyone has the right to freedom of expression, which includes the freedom to seek, receive, and impart information and opinions of any kind in any form." Also, the media are excluded from the ambit of the *Privacy Act 1993* provided they are engaged in news-gathering activities.[173] As a result, there was no effective protection of privacy in New Zealand for a long time.

On the other hand, recently, a new tort of privacy has been established in New Zealand. Furthermore, New Zealand's statutes also provide some protections for different aspects of privacy. Statutory protection for the privacy mainly exists in the form of the *Privacy Act 1993* and the *Broadcasting Act 1989*, respectively. The

[169] *Privacy and Personal Information Protection Act 1998* (NSW), long title.

[170] *Health Records and Information Privacy Act 2002* (NSW), long title.

[171] Doyle and Bagaric (2005), p. 100.

[172] *Information Privacy Act 2000* (Vic), s 1.

[173] Henry (2001), p. 327.

Privacy Act promotes and protects individual privacy in general and the *Broadcasting Act* protects individuals' privacy interests in the activities of broadcasters. This section examines privacy protection in New Zealand in more detail.

Common Law Privacy Protection

A New Tort of Invasion of Privacy

It has been held that the New Zealand High Court proposed a tort of invasion of privacy for almost 20 years.[174] In the case of *Tucker v News Media Ownership Ltd* in 1985, McGechan J suggested that there should be "a tort covering invasion of privacy at least by public disclosure of private facts" in New Zealand.[175] In the case of *P v D* in 2000, where an injunction was obtained to prevent publication of a newspaper article revealing that P, a well-known professional person, had had treatment at a psychiatric hospital. Nicholson J held that breach of the tort existed and is determined by considering four factors:

(1) that the disclosure of the private facts must be a public disclosure and not a private one;
(2) facts disclosed to the public must be private facts and not public ones;
(3) the matter made public must be one which would be highly offensive to a reasonable person of ordinary sensibilities; and
(4) the nature and extent of legitimate public interest in having the information disclosed.[176]

The most significant case of the High Court, however, was *Hosking v Runting*,[177] which ensured a new tort of invasion of privacy in New Zealand in 2004.

- In this case, the first respondent Mr Runting, a photographer, was commissioned by the second respondent, the publisher of the magazine *New Idea!* to photograph the appellants' 18-month-old twins. He did so, in the street in New Market. The appellants in this proceeding seek to prevent publication of the photographs. They seek to have the Court extend the law to provide them with a remedy.[178]

The New Zealand Court of Appeal unanimously held that the Hoskings must fail because the photos were taken in a public place and showed nothing that could not have been observed by a member of the public on that particular day.[179] On the other hand, the majority of all members of the New Zealand Court of Appeal believed that a tort of invasion of privacy should exist in New Zealand.

---

[174] Todd (2005), p. 754.
[175] Todd (2005), p. 754.
[176] Henry (2001), p. 328.
[177] *Hosking v Runting* [2004] NZCA 34.
[178] *Hosking v Runting* [2004] NZCA 34, [1].
[179] Todd (2005), p. 755.

It should be noted that there were different opinions in the Court of Appeal Gault P, Blanchard J, and Tipping J held that a tort of invasion of privacy should exist in New Zealand.[180] That is because, first, they believed it was artificial to deal with the matter through breach of confidence, and it was thus better to go directly to the heart of the matter; second, they believed the law should keep up with the times, and that judges can develop the law when that is appropriate; and third, they believed that it did not impose an unjustifiable limit on freedom of speech in terms of the *Bill of Rights Act*.[181] Ultimately, in their leading judgment, Gault P and Blanchard J state that there are two fundamental elements a tort of invasion of privacy in New Zealand, which are "(1) The existence of facts in respect of which there is a reasonable expectation of privacy; and (2) Publicity given to those private facts that would be considered highly offensive to an objective reasonable person."[182]

Evaluation

The judgment of *Hosking v Runting* in the New Zealand Court of Appeal is significant for the privacy protection in New Zealand, and has provided an interesting precedent for overseas jurisdictions to contemplate.[183] As Evans points out that "it has established – at a high judicial level – that a separate tort of invasion of privacy does indeed form part of the landscape of the common law on this side of the Ditch and has given some indications about what that tort looks like."[184]

The advantages of a new tort of privacy are self-evident. Compared to previous common law protection, which holds that the interest of privacy can be recognized only if another interest of the plaintiff has also been violated, the tort of invasion of privacy is more precise and transparent. In addition, in both the *Independent News Auckland Ltd* case and the *Bradley* case, New Zealand's high court relied on US texts, it thus has been held that the US jurisprudence on privacy will be applicable in New Zealand.[185] Therefore, with respect to common law privacy protection, New Zealand judges seem to go further than other parts of the Commonwealth.

On the other hand, the new tort of privacy in New Zealand still needs much cautious refinement, and it is likely to be some time before a systematic guideline emerges.[186] Also, the New Zealand courts may be unwilling to allow this new tort to encroach on traditional areas of law, which have been carefully formulated to balance the various interests involved.[187] In consequence, in fact, the development of a tort of invasion of privacy in New Zealand is still in its infancy.

---

[180] Todd (2005), p. 755.

[181] Todd (2005), p. 755.

[182] Todd (2005), p. 755.

[183] Evans (2004).

[184] Evans (2004).

[185] Henry (2001), p. 328.

[186] Todd (1997), p. 968.

[187] Todd (1997), p. 968.

Statutory Protection of Privacy

The Privacy Act 1993

The aim of the *Privacy Act 1993* is to promote and protect individual privacy in New Zealand in general accordance with the OECD Guidelines Concerning the Protection of Privacy and Trans-border Flows of Personal Data.[188] Therefore, to some extent, this Act is a data protection law. The New Zealand Privacy Act covers both public and private sectors. Similar to the NPPs in the *Australian Privacy Act 1988*, the Act sets out twelve information privacy principles. These principles cover: (1) purpose of collection of personal information; (2) source of personal information; (3) collection of information from subject; (4) manner of collection of personal information; (5) storage and security of personal information; (6) access to personal information; (7) correction of personal information; (8) accuracy, etc., of personal information to be checked before use; (9) agency not to keep personal information for longer than necessary; (10) limits on use of personal information; (11) limits on disclosure of personal information; (12) and unique identifiers.[189] These principles guide the way that how individuals' information is to be collected, used, and stored. These 12 principles are expressed in general terms, but all are subject to exceptions, some of which are explained in the Act explicitly.[190] It has been held that these principles are technology neutral, with the expectation that they will operate in a number of contexts and not be superseded by new technologies.[191]

Section 12 of the Act establishes a National Privacy Commissioner. Complaints should be made to the Privacy Commissioner first. After investigating, the commissioner should decide whether there has been an invasion of privacy. If the Privacy Commissioner finds the complaint justified, he or she may act as a conciliator to secure a settlement between the parties, or an assurance against repetition of the infringing conduct.[192] It should be noted that the decision of the Privacy Commissioner should base on whether there is a breach of one of the twelve information privacy principles that mentioned above. In other words, information privacy principles are enforceable in the first instance by complaint to a Privacy Commissioner.[193] If the Privacy Commissioner fails to secure such a settlement or assurance, the commissioner may refer the matter to the Proceedings Commissioner of the Human Rights Commission to decide if proceedings should be instituted in the Complaints Review Tribunal.[194] The Tribunal may carry out one or more of the following orders:

---

[188] *Privacy Act 1993* (NZ), title.

[189] *Privacy Act 1993* (NZ), s 6.

[190] Todd (1997), p. 970.

[191] Privacy Guide: New Zealand (2003).

[192] Todd (1997), p. 971.

[193] Todd (1997), p. 970.

[194] Todd (1997), p. 971.

(1) A declaration that the action of the defendant is an interference with the privacy of an individual;
(2) An order restraining the defendant from continuing or repeating the interference, or from engaging in, or causing or permitting others to engage in, conduct of the same kind as that constituting the interference, or conduct of any similar kind specified in the order;
(3) An award of damages to the complainant in accordance with section 88 of this Act;
(4) An order that the defendant perform any acts specified in the order with a view to remedying the interference, or redressing any loss or damage suffered by the aggrieved individual as a result of the interference, or both;
(5) Such other relief as the Tribunal thinks fit.[195]

Decisions of the Complaints Review Tribunal may be appealed through the general court system with the first level of appeal to the High Court.[196] All individuals have been protected under the Privacy Act whether nationals or citizens of foreign countries.[197]

The New Zealand *Privacy Act 1993* gives protection to individuals against those who collect and store information about them. It has been held that the rationale of this Act is similar to other countries' privacy legislation, but it is wider in its coverage.[198] For instance, as mentioned earlier, the *Privacy Act 1993* covers both public and private sectors, while the Privacy Act of the United States extends only to public sector agencies; the New Zealand *Privacy Act 1993* covers all personal information, while the English legislation extends only to electronically stored data.[199] Moreover, the New Zealand *Privacy Act 1993* does not preclude the development of a common law tort of invasion of privacy in New Zealand, although the Act does not create tortuous rights and duties.[200]

The Broadcasting Act 1989

The main object of the *Broadcasting Act 1989* is to provide for the maintenance of program standards in broadcasting in New Zealand.[201] The Act establishes the Broadcasting Standards Authority (BSA), which is now the major regulator of media-related privacy in New Zealand, to practice jurisdiction under this Act.

Section 4(1)(c) of the Act requires every broadcaster should be "responsible for maintaining in its programs and their presentation, standards which are consistent with the privacy of the individual." In 1992, the BSA formally formulated five principles to protect privacy. However, in 1996, the BSA realized that these

---

[195] *Privacy Act 1993* (NZ), s 85.
[196] Henry (2001), p. 328.
[197] Henry (2001), p. 329.
[198] Todd (1997), p. 970.
[199] Todd (1997), p. 970.
[200] Todd (2005), p. 750.
[201] *Broadcasting Act 1989* (NZ), title.

principles were not able to cover all situations. They thus added two principles. There are now seven privacy principles applied by the BSA in New Zealand. The BSA's Privacy Principles of 1992, incorporating the two 1996 Principles, are as follows:

a) The protection of privacy includes legal protection against the public disclosure of private facts where the facts disclosed are highly offensive and objectionable to a reasonable person of ordinary sensibilities.
b) The protection of privacy also protects against the public disclosure of some kinds of public facts.
c) There is a separate ground for a complaint, in addition to a complaint for the public disclosure of private and public facts, in factual situations involving the intentional interference (in the nature of prying) with an individual's interest in solitude or seclusion.
d) The intrusion must be offensive to the ordinary person but an individual's interest in solitude or seclusion does not provide the basis for a privacy action for an individual to complain about being observed or followed or photographed in a public place.
e) The protection of privacy also protects against the disclosure of private facts to abuse, denigrate or ridicule personally an identifiable person.
f) The protection of privacy includes the protection against the disclosure by the broadcaster, without consent, of the name and/or address and/or telephone number of an identifiable person.
g) An individual who consents to the invasion of his or her privacy cannot later succeed in a claim for breach of privacy.[202]

Moreover, the BSA has also emphasized that "(1) these principles are not necessarily the only privacy principles that the Authority will apply; (2) the principles may well require elaboration and refinement when applied to a complaint; and (3) the specific facts of each complaint are especially important when privacy is an issue."[203] Section 13(1) of the Act provides compensatory damages and an award of costs to the complaint. Besides to prohibit advertising for up to 24 h, the broadcaster may pay to the complaint a sum not exceeding $5,000 as compensation, if the complaint privacy has been infringed.

It should be mentioned that the enforcement of this standard is not (at least initially) by way of court proceedings, but by way of complaint under procedures formulated by the Broadcasting Act.[204] That is to say any decisions of the BSA are not binding on the courts. However, it has been held that the jurisprudence built up by the BSA still provides "many useful illustrations of the various manifestations of privacy."[205] At least, based on this Act, New Zealand's common law has established that the filming of an individual's activities or private life on private property may invade privacy where there is no consent.[206]

[202] McBride (2000).

[203] Privacy Principles 2006.

[204] Todd (1997), p. 971.

[205] Todd (2005), p. 750.

[206] *TV3 Network Services Ltd v Broadcasting Standards Authority* [1995] 2 NZLR 720.

4.3.1.4 The United States of America

Privacy Generally

Similar to other common law countries, the US Constitution does not explicitly ensure the right to privacy. However, based on several provisions in the Bill of Rights, the US Supreme Court has pointed out that there is a limited constitutional right of privacy in the USA.[207] They are:

(1) the right to privacy from government surveillance into an area where a person has a 'reasonable expectation of privacy';
(2) in matters relating to marriage, procreation, contraception, sexual activity, family relationships, child rearing, and education;
(3) the right of anonymity; and
(4) the right of political groups to prevent disclosure of their members' names to government agencies.[208]

Moreover, the tort of invasion of privacy had been established in 1905. Today, in the USA, 48 states have recognized the tort of invasion of privacy in their laws. The following section sets out a brief overview of United States law on privacy.

The Public Sector

Constitutional Protections

Although the US Constitution does not clearly ensure the right to privacy, there are several provisions provide protection for privacy interests under the Constitution and these provisions have been explained as providing a right to privacy in the US.[209]

The First Amendment to the US Constitution states that "congress shall make no law respecting an establishment of religion, or prohibiting the free exercise thereof; or abridging the freedom of speech, or of the press; or the right of the people peaceably to assemble, and to petition the Government for a redress of grievances." According to this Amendment, it has been held that it protects the right to speak anonymously, and its freedom of association clause protects individuals from being compelled to disclose the groups to which they belong or contribute.[210] The Third Amendment states that "no soldier shall, in time of peace be quartered in any house, without the consent of the Owner, nor in time of war, but in a manner to be prescribed by law." According to this Amendment, it has been held that this Amendment protects the privacy of the home by preventing the government from

---

[207] Privacy International: United States of America 2007.

[208] Privacy International: United States of America 2007.

[209] Solove and Rotenberg (2003), p. 20.

[210] Solove and Rotenberg (2003), p. 20.

requiring soldiers to reside in people's homes.[211] Furthermore, the Fourth Amendment to the US Constitution provides that people have the right "to be secure in their persons, houses, papers, and effects, against unreasonable searches and seizures. . . ."[212] In addition, the interests of privacy are also protected by the Fifth Amendment to some extent. First, this Amendment protects privacy by restricting the ability of the government to force individuals to divulge certain information about themselves[213]; second, this Amendment prohibits the government from taking private property for public use without both due process of law and just compensation.[214]

Statutes

The Privacy Act The US Congress enacted a federal Privacy Act in 1974. The Act protects privacy by creating some rights in personal data. For example, the Act requires that each agency that maintains a system of records should (1) permit individual to access and review his or her record; (2) permit the individual to request amendment of a record pertaining to him or her; (3) permit the individual who disagrees with the refusal of the agency to amend his record to request a review of such refusal; and so on.[215] Also, the Act obligates agencies to: (1) maintain in its records only such information about an individual as is relevant and necessary to accomplish a purpose of the agency; (2) collect information to the greatest extent practicable directly from the subject individual when the information may result in adverse determinations about an individual's rights, benefits, and privileges; (3) inform each individual whom it asks to supply information; (4) maintain all records which are used by the agency in making any determination about any individual with such accuracy, relevance, timeliness, and completeness as is reasonably necessary to assure fairness to the individual in the determination; (5) make reasonable efforts to serve notice on an individual when any record on such individual is made available to any person under compulsory legal process when such process becomes a matter of public record; (6) establish rules of conduct for persons involved in the design, development, operation, or maintenance of any system of records, or in maintaining any record (7) establish appropriate administrative, technical and physical safeguards to insure the security and confidentiality of records.[216]

Moreover, twelve exemptions have been proposed in 552(a) b of the Act. For example, the Act does not apply to statistics for the purposes of the Census Bureau and the Bureau of Labor Statistics; it does not restrict disclosures of congressional

[211] Solove and Rotenberg (2003), p. 20.

[212] Solove and Rotenberg (2003), p. 20.

[213] Solove and Rotenberg (2003), p. 21.

[214] Cate (1997), p. 72.

[215] *Privacy Act of 1974* (US), 552a (d).

[216] *Privacy Act of 1974* (US), 552a (e).

investigations; it does not apply to the National Archives and Records Administration as a record which has sufficient historical or other value to warrant its continued preservation by the United States Government; it also does not apply to the law enforcement activities; and so on.[217]

Other Protections Other statutes and regulations protect the interests of privacy from government intrusion or misuse. For example, the *Computer Matching and Privacy Protection Act of 1988* amended the *Privacy Act of 1974* by adding certain protections for the subjects of records, whose records are used in automated matching programs.[218] As amended by *the Computer Matching and Privacy Protection Act of 1988*, the *Privacy Act of 1974* requires Federal agencies involved in computer matching programs to:

(1) Negotiate written agreements with the other agency or agencies participating in the matching programs;
(2) Obtain the relevant Data Integrity Boards' approval of the match agreements;
(3) Furnish detailed reports about matching programs to Congress and OMB;
(4) Notify applicants and beneficiaries that their records are subject to matching; and
(5) Verify match findings before reducing, suspending, terminating, or denying an individual's benefits or payments.[219]

Another privacy-related legislation is the *Drivers Privacy Protection Act of 1994*. This Act restricts the state's ability to disclose or otherwise make available to any person or entity personal information about any individual obtained by the department in connection with a motor vehicle record.[220] The Act defines "motor vehicle record" as "any record that pertains to a motor vehicle operator's permit, motor vehicle title, motor vehicle registration, or identification card issued by a department of motor vehicles."[221] "Personal information" is defined under the Act as any "information that identifies an individual's photograph, social security number, driver identification number, name, address, telephone number, and medical or disability information, but not including information on vehicular accidents, driving violations, and driver's status."[222]

The Private Sector

Federal Statutes

Financial Transaction The USA has enacted a number of laws to provide the protection of personal information in financial transactions. One of these laws is the

[217] *Privacy Act of 1974* (US), 552a (b).

[218] Computer Matching and Privacy Protection Act 2005.

[219] *Privacy and Government: the Computer Marching and Privacy Protection Act* 2003.

[220] *Drivers Privacy Protection Act of 1994* (US), s 2721 (a).

[221] *Drivers Privacy Protection Act of 1994* (US), s 2725(1).

[222] *Drivers Privacy Protection Act of 1994* (US), s 2725(3).

Fair Credit Reporting Act of 1970. The Act imposes obligations on the users of consumer reports. For example, the Act requires that any consumer reporting agency should maintain reasonable procedures designed to avoid block of information resulting from identity theft.[223] The act also requires that credit reporting agencies should assure "maximum possible accuracy of the information concerning the individual about whom the report relates."[224]

Other statutes provide limited protection for certain specific interests of privacy. For example, the *Fair Credit Billing Act of* 1986 provides opportunity to the creditors to dispute errors.[225] Furthermore, § 162 (a) of the Act states that after receiving a notice from an obligor, a creditor or his or her agent may not directly or indirectly threaten to report to any person adversely on the obligor's credit rating or credit standing.

Telecommunications and Video Services The *Electronic Communications Privacy Act of 1986* sets out the provisions to regulate access, use, interception or disclosure, interception of the contents of any electronic communication, and provides privacy protections of electronic communications to individuals. Therefore, under the Act, electronic service providers are forbidden from disclosing the contents of any communications.[226] For example, in the Act, the police use a taped phone conversation with a suspect without first advising the suspect of the taping will be prohibited.[227] Moreover, a person tapes another person's conversation without his or her consent cannot be submitted as evidence.[228]

The *Video Privacy Protection Act of 1988* generally prohibits businesses, which rent or sell videotapes from knowingly disclosing "personally identifiable information" about their consumers, which includes information about the specific video materials a customer bought or rented.[229] The Act also requires the destruction of personally identifiable information not later than 1 year after the information if no longer necessary for the purpose for which it was collected.[230]

The Protection for Children The *Children's Online Privacy Protection Act of* 1998 makes it unlawful for an operator of a website or online service directed to children, or any operator that has actual knowledge that it is collecting personal information from a child, to collect personal information from a child.[231]

[223] *Fair Credit Reporting Act of* 1970 (US), 605B.

[224] *Fair Credit Reporting Act of* 1970 (US), 607 (b).

[225] *Fair Credit Billing Act of* 1986 (US), 161.

[226] Fair Credit Billing Act of 1986 (US), s 2511 (3)(a).

[227] Tricia 2011.

[228] Tricia 2011.

[229] Brief: A Handbook on Privacy Federal and State Legislation 2001.

[230] Cate (1997), p. 86.

[231] *Children's Online Privacy Protection Act of* 1998 (US), s 1303.

The Workplace Title VII of the *Civil Rights Act of 1964???* makes it unlawful for an employer to hire or discharge any individual, or otherwise to discriminate against any individual with respect to his/her compensation, terms, conditions or privileges of employment, because of an individual's race, color, religion, sex or national origin.[232] Similarly, the *Fair Housing Act of 1968* prohibits discrimination in the sale or lease of housing on the basis of "race, color, religion, sex, familial status, or national origin', but is silent on all aspects of data processing.[233]

Educational Records The *Family Educational Rights and Privacy Act of 1974* is a federal law that protects the privacy of student education records.[234] Schools may not release "directory information" relating to a student, which include names, addresses, telephone listings, dates and places of birth, major field of study, participation in officially recognized activities and sports, weight and height of members of athletic teams, dates of attendance, degrees and awards received, and so on.[235]

Tort Law

As mentioned in Chap. 1, in 1890, the Harvard Law Review published an article by Samuel D Warren and Louis D Brandeis entitled "The Right to Privacy." In this famous article, they pointed out that there was no adequate protection for privacy. They thus believed that there should be a legal right to privacy. In *Pavesich v New England Life Insurance Co.* in 1905, a newspaper published a life insurance advertisement with a photograph of the plaintiff without the plaintiff's consent.[236] The Georgia Supreme Court held that:

> One who desires to have a life of partial seclusion has a right to choose the times, places, and manner in which and at which he will submit himself to the public gaze. Subject to the limitation above referred to, the body of a person cannot be put on exhibition at any time or at any place without his consent ... It therefore follows from what has been said that a violation of the right of privacy is a direct invasion of a legal right of the individual ....[237]

This case uniquely recognized a common law tort action for invasion of privacy in the USA. Georgia was thus the first state to accept this tort.[238] In 1960, with respect to the tort of invasion of privacy, William Prosser analyzed the many cases and then pointed out that:

> What has emerged ... is no simple matter. It is not one tort, but a complex of four. The law of privacy comprises four distinct kinds of invasion of four different interests of the

232 *Civil Rights Act of 1964*, Title VII.

233 Cate (1997), pp. 86–87.

234 *Family Educational Rights and Privacy Act* 2008.

235 *Family Educational Rights and Privacy Act of* 1974 (US), 20 USC § 1232g (5)(A).

236 Solove et al. (2006), p. 24.

237 Solove et al. (2006), pp. 24–25.

238 Solove et al. (2006), p. 24.

> plaintiff, which are tied together by the common name, but otherwise have almost nothing in common except that each represents an interference with the right of the plaintiff, in the phrase coined by Judge Cooley, "to be let alone".[239]

In the words of Prosser, they are:

(1) Intrusion upon the plaintiff's seclusion or solitude, or into his or her private affairs;
(2) Public disclosure of embarrassing private facts about the plaintiff;
(3) Publicity which places the plaintiff in a false light in the public eye;
(4) Appropriation for the defendant's advantage of the plaintiff's name or likeness.[240]

This structure, finally included in the Restatement (Second) of Torts (for which Prosser served as reporter), replaced the single privacy right in the first Restatement of Torts.[241]

At present, these four tort actions are the main sources of adjudicated legal rights to privacy in the USA.[242] On the other hand, in certain degrees, Prosser's analysis also demonstrates the elusive nature of "privacy." With respect to his opinion, (3) tort of "false light" and (4) tort of appropriation do not really protect interests of privacy. Tort of false light mainly protects reputation. This tort is always covered by the tort of defamation, for example, in Australia and New Zealand. Similarly, it has been held that "the tort of appropriation only applies to the 'name or likeness' of an individual, and therefore is of limited value as a protection for privacy."[243] Moreover, it has also been held that (2) tort of public disclosure, has not proved particularly plaintiff-friendly, therefore, when it is pitted against freedom of the press, a particularly strong freedom in the USA, it usually loses.[244]

4.3.2 Countries with the Civil Law Legal System

4.3.2.1 Federal Republic of Germany

Constitutional Privacy Framework

The Federal Republic of Germany is a federal republic with a written constitution guaranteeing fundamental human rights.[245] In Germany, the Basic Law (the German Constitution) is the legal and political foundation of the country. Article 1(1) of the German Constitution emphasizes that "human dignity shall be inviolable"

[239] Prosser (1960), p. 389.
[240] Prosser (1960), p. 389; see also Solove et al. (2006), p. 25.
[241] Cate (1997), p. 89.
[242] Cate (1997), p. 90.
[243] Cate (1997), p. 89.
[244] Todd (2005), p. 751.
[245] Michael (1994), p. 92.

and all state authority have the duty to respect and protect human dignity. Article 2 (1) of the German Constitution emphasizes that "every person shall have the right to free development of his personality insofar as he does not violate the rights of others or offend against the constitutional order or the moral law." Moreover, article 10 of the German Constitution states that:

(1) The privacy of correspondence, posts and telecommunications shall be inviolable.
(2) Restrictions may be ordered only pursuant to a law. If the restriction serves to protect the free democratic basic order or the existence or security of the Federation or of a Land, the law may provide that the person affected shall not be informed of the restriction and that recourse to the courts shall be replaced by a review of the case by agencies and auxiliary agencies appointed by the legislature.

In addition, the German Federal Constitutional Court formally proposed that an individual's "right of informational self-determination," which is only limited by the "predominant public interest" in 1983.[246] It has been argued that this court decision derived the "right of informational self-determination" directly from article 1(1) and 2(1) of the German Constitution, which declare personal rights to freedom are inviolable.[247] As a consequence, the prevailing view in Germany is that the right to privacy is an essential part of a person's general personality right, and it is impossible to distinguish right to privacy from general personality right.[248]

Different Types of Privacy Protection

The Protection of Images and Photographs

In addition to the constitutional protection, the *Act on the Protection of the Copyright in Works of Art and Photographs* also provides protections for privacy. Section 22 of the Act clearly states that "an individual's image may only be disseminated or displayed publicly with his or her consent. The approval is deemed to have been granted if the person shown received a consideration for the production of the images." It should be noted that Section 22 of the Act does not prohibit the taking of an image but only its dissemination and publication.[249] Section 23 of the Act provides several exceptions, allowing disclosure and publication of images without the consent of the individual, which include that:

(1) Images having an historic context;
(2) Pictures upon which the persons appear as an accessory to a landscape or some other locality only;
(3) Pictures of assemblies, parades or similar events at which the persons shown have participated;

[246] Privacy International: Federal Republic of Germany 2007.

[247] Privacy International: Federal Republic of Germany 2007.

[248] Henry (2001), p. 157.

[249] Henry (2001), p. 166.

(4) Images, which have not been produced upon order, if their dissemination or public presentation serves a higher interest of the art.[250]

Under this Act, if an individual discloses or publishes an image in contravention of section 22 and 23, he or she will be liable on conviction to imprisonment for a term not exceeding 1 year or to a fine.[251]

In Germany, the individuals' interest in keeping their personal space, personal life, and personal information free from the public views is weighed against the need of the public to know. Therefore, the disclosure or publication of personal photographs always requires an approval of the subject. Otherwise, the disclosure or publication of photographs of an individual's personal life can only be justified if the photographs contribute to a matter of public debate.[252] In addition, the new German *Criminal Code* took effect in 2004. The new Code provides protections to personal life against the invasion of privacy by the taking of pictures of persons in their apartments or other protected areas such as changing cabins.[253] Under the Code, dissemination and publication of such photographs on the Internet will be punishable as a criminal offense.[254]

The Protection of Post, Telephone Calls and Private Conversations

As mentioned earlier, article 10 of the German Constitution protects the privacy of correspondence, posts and telecommunications. Initially, this constitutional provision mainly addresses the relationship between the individual and the state.[255] However, in 1990, the German Federal Supreme Court proposed that this principle should also be applied to individuals.[256] That is to say, both the state authority and the individuals have the duty to respect and protect other person's privacy of posts and telecommunications.

With respect to the recording and publication of private telephone conversations, the German Federal Supreme Court has proposed that recording and publication of private telephone conversations should be granted an approval of the participants in the private conversation, otherwise a violation of the general personality right will be committed.[257] It should be noted that, based on the fact that confidential meeting record has been seen as neither authentic nor objective in Germany, the minutes of a confidential meeting can thus be recorded in writing and disseminated later, and the

---

250 Henry (2001), p. 166.

251 Henry (2001), p. 165.

252 Defamation and Privacy Law and Procedure in England, Germany and France 2006.

253 Privacy International: Federal Republic of Germany 2007.

254 Privacy International: Federal Republic of Germany 2007.

255 Henry (2001), p. 171.

256 Henry (2001), p. 171.

257 Henry (2001), pp. 171–172.

publication of the minutes would not violate the personality right of the participants in Germany.[258]

In addition, the new German *Criminal Code* also prohibits the recording of spoken words. Section 201(1) of the Code clear states that any person without authorization "(1) makes an audio recording of the privately spoken words of another; or (2) uses, or makes a recording thus produced accessible to a third party, shall be punished with imprisonment for not more than three years or a fine." Section 202(1) of the Code states that any person without authorization "(1) opens a sealed letter or another sealed document that was not intended to come to his attention; or (2) obtains knowledge of the content of such a document without opening the seal by using technical means shall be punished with imprisonment for not more than 1 year or a fine."

German Tort Law

Section 823(1) of the German *Civil Code* states that "an individual who, intentionally or negligently, unlawfully injures the life, body, health, freedom, property or another right of another person is liable to make compensation to the other party for the damage arising from this." Section 824(1) of the *Civil Code* states that "an individual who untruthfully states or disseminates a fact that is qualified to endanger the credit of another person or to cause other disadvantages to his livelihood or advancement must compensate the other for the damage caused by this even if, although he does not know that the fact is untrue, he should have known." It has been held that these two sections enable the German courts to apply the tort law to protect human dignity such as the unauthorized publication of the intimate details of a person's private life.[259]

However, compared to the general principles of tort law pursuant to which any violation of an absolute right is deemed to be unlawful, the German courts have pointed out that, in the case of a violation of the general personality right, the illegality has to be established on a case-by-case basis by way of balancing the conflicting interests.[260] Thus, it has been held that a violation of the general personality right by the media does not constitute an unlawful act, if it is justified by the reasons that:

(1) An act is not considered unlawful, if the freedom of the media guaranteed in Article 5 of the Basic Law outweighs the general personality right of a person or entity.
(2) Section 193 of the Criminal Code embodies the general principle of the protection of legitimate interest in defamation cases. The information interests of the public and the exercise of the appropriate standard of journalistic care are decisive for determining whether a legitimate interest exists. The obligation to duly investigate reports increases proportionately to the weight of the likely violation of personality rights. The Federal

---

[258] Henry (2001), p. 172.

[259] Law Reform Commission of Hong Kong 2004, p. 75.

[260] Henry (2001), p. 176.

Constitutional Court has held that the freedom of the press implies duties which grow in the same manner as the relevance of the constitutional guarantee of the freedom of the media.

(3) A particular problem exists with respect to incorrect statements of fact. There is never a legitimate interest in disseminating wrong information. Therefore, the right to refrain from maintaining an incorrect statement and to request its withdrawal arises even if the wrong information was sourced with all due journalistic diligence and care. However, in such a case, a claim for damages might be excluded.[261]

Data Protection

The German state of Hessen enacted the world's first data protection Act in 1970.[262] However, the Act was not expressly linked with the protection of individual privacy, but was concerned with ensuring that new techniques of data processing conformed to overall social objectives, including data security and the accuracy of computerized records.[263] A Federal Data Protection Act (the BDSG) was enacted in 1977, which was reviewed in 1990, and amended in 1994 and 1997.[264] The final revision took place in 2002 on the basis of the EU Directive 95/46/EC.[265] The aim of this Act is to protect the individual against his right to privacy being impaired through the handling of his personal data.[266]

The BDSG applies to the collection, processing and use of personal data by (1) public bodies of the Federation; (2) public bodies of the Länder, which includes the authorities, the bodies of the judicature and other public-law institutions of a Land, of a municipality, an association of municipalities or other legal persons under public law subject to Land supervision as well as of their associations irrespective of their legal structure[267]; and (3) private bodies if they process or use data in or from data files in the normal course of business or for professional or commercial purposes.[268] Under the BDSG, personal data can be collected from the data subject only if:

(1) a legal provision prescribes or peremptorily presupposes such collection, or
(2) the nature of the administrative duty to be performed necessitates collection of the data from other persons or bodies, or
(3) collection of the data from the data subject would necessitate disproportionate effort and there are no indications that overriding legitimate interests of the data subject are impaired.[269]

---

[261] Henry (2001), pp. 176–177.

[262] Cate (1997), p. 32.

[263] Lindsay (2005), p. 156.

[264] Privacy International: Federal Republic of Germany 2007.

[265] Privacy International: Federal Republic of Germany 2007.

[266] *Federal Data Protection Act* (Germany), s 1 (1).

[267] *Federal Data Protection Act* (Germany), s 2 (2).

[268] *Federal Data Protection Act* (Germany), s 1 (2).

[269] *Federal Data Protection Act* (Germany), s 13 (2).

The storage, modification or use of personal data can be permitted only if is necessary "for the performance of the duties of the controller of the data file and if it serves the purposes for which the data were collected, if there has been no preceding collection, the data may be modified or used only for the purposes for which they were stored."[270] It is thus clear that the storage, modification or use for other purposes has been strictly limited by the Act. Under the BDSG, the data subjects have right "to be provided with information on stored data concerning him, including any reference in them to their origin or recipient, and the purpose of storage."[271] In addition, the data subject also has right to correct or block his or her personal data, and right to appeal the Federal commissioner for their personal data protection.[272]

Remedies

In Germany, the claimant is free to choose the enforcement of his or her rights under civil or criminal law or a combination of both.[273] Section 812 of the German *Civil Code* states that "a person who obtains something as a result of the performance of another person or otherwise at his expense without legal grounds for doing so is under a duty to make restitution to him." The person may thus claim compensation if his image has been unlawfully published. The amount of compensation is the fee which the person could have sought for having his or her image used.[274] In addition, section 1004 of the *Civil Code* explicitly provides protection against any interference with the general personality right and other legitimate interests.[275] Two forms of remedies exist, which are "(1) if the ownership is interfered with by removal or retention of possession, the owner may require the disturber to remove the interference; and (2) if further interferences are to be feared, the owner may seek a prohibitory injunction."[276] If the owner is obliged to tolerate the interference, the claim will be excluded.[277]

It should be noted that, if a press complaint relates to an invasion of privacy interests, the claimant is able to apply to court for an interim injunction. If the interim injunction is granted, the claimant must officially serve the court order on the defendant within 1 month; if this is not done, the order will be invalid.[278] At the interim injunction stage, no damages can be awarded.[279]

---

[270] *Federal Data Protection Act* (Germany), s 14 (1).

[271] *Federal Data Protection Act* (Germany), s 19.

[272] *Federal Data Protection Act* (Germany), ss 20, 21.

[273] Henry (2001), p. 179.

[274] Henry (2001), p. 172.

[275] Henry (2001), p. 178.

[276] *Civil Code* (Germany), s 1004 (1).

[277] *Civil Code* (Germany), s 1004 (2).

[278] Defamation and Privacy Law and Procedure in England, Germany and France 2006.

[279] Defamation and Privacy Law and Procedure in England, Germany and France 2006.

Who Enjoys the Right to Privacy?

Public Figures

In Germany, public figures' privacy interests have also been protected to some extent. German case law has divided public figures into two categories which are public figure of absolute current interest and public figure of relative current interest. Public figure of absolute current interest has been defined as those who are known because of their prominent position in public life or unique position in public life, independent from any specific context.[280] For example, most famous athletes have been deemed as absolute public figures because they achieved a certain degree of popularity and are in the full glare of publicity.[281] By contrast, public figure of relative current interest has been defined as those who are not generally recognized by the public but have achieved a certain degree of recognition in connection with a specific event.[282] German law provides some exceptions for public figures in these two categories. Firstly, there must be some public interests justification for using the image of such an individual and the commercial interests of the advertiser will be insufficient[283]; second, very private areas of their life; for example, nude pictures of them may not be published without the person's consent.[284]

The Deceased

In Germany, the deceased also has the personality right. Section 22 of the *Act on the Protection of the Copyright in Works of Art and Photographs* deals with images of dead persons. Generally, for a period of 10 years after the death of the person, approval must be sought from the next of kin.[285] Otherwise, the publication of an image may be considered as a violation of the personality right of the deceased.[286] Moreover, based on section 22 of the German Constitution Law, in 1989, the Court of Appeal of Hamburg decided that the use of voices of deceased persons is a violation of the general personality right and did not allow the use of the voice.[287]

---

[280] Defamation and Privacy Law and Procedure in England, Germany and France 2006.

[281] Blackshaw and Siekmann (2005), p. 113.

[282] Defamation and Privacy Law and Procedure in England, Germany and France 2006.

[283] Huw et al. (2005), p. 225.

[284] Privacy International: Federal Republic of Germany 2007.

[285] Henry (2001), p. 165.

[286] Henry (2001), p. 165.

[287] Henry (2001), p. 171.

Citizens of Foreign States

It has been held that the term "everyone," that contained in article 2 of the German Constitution law, clearly includes all foreign citizens.[288] Therefore, it is clear that all foreign citizens will enjoy privacy interests in Germany.

4.3.2.2 France

Constitutional Privacy Framework

Similar to Germany, France has a civil law legal system. With respect to privacy protection, there is no clear protection of right to privacy in the French Constitution. However, the French Constitutional Court held that article 2 of the *Declaration of the Rights of Man and of the Citizen of 1789* implies the respect of privacy already.[289] Based on this statement, the French Constitutional Court ruled that the right of privacy was implicit in the French Constitution in 1995.[290]

General Protection

Initially, in order to ensure the protection of privacy in France, the general principle of civil liability set out in article 1382 of the *Civil Code* was used by French courts and invoked by victims.[291] Article 1382 of the *Civil Code* states that "any act whatever of man, which causes damage to another, obliges the one by whose fault it occurred, to compensate it." The French court points out that "fault" may include the publication of confidential letters, the dissemination of facts about a person's private life, and the unauthorized use of a person's name.[292] Moreover, based on article 8 of the ECHR of 1950, article 9 of the French *Civil Code* has been used to protect right to privacy in France. Article 9 states that:

(1) Everyone has the right to respect for his private life;
(2) Without prejudice to compensation for injury suffered, the court may prescribe any measures, such as sequestration, seizure and others, appropriate to prevent or put an end to an invasion of personal privacy; in case of emergency those measures may be provided for by interim order.

---

[288] Henry (2001), p. 157.

[289] Privacy International: French Republic 2007.

[290] Privacy International: French Republic 2007.

[291] Henry (2001), p. 133.

[292] Law Reform Commission of Hong Kong 2004, p. 74.

It should be noted that the protection of privacy interests in France must yield under some circumstances, which include:

(1) When the reported fact stems from the public life of the subject (such as artist and politician) and therefore neither intimate nor private;
(2) When the subject dies, as protection then ceases in principle – '. . .the right to bar any form of disclosure of one's private life. . .belongs only to the living' – and heirs can only complain about offences to the honour or to the memory of the deceased, unless the invasion of privacy of the deceased affects by extension the privacy of the heirs;
(3) When the reported fact belongs to history, even recent history; and
(4) When the subject himself consents, expressly and specifically, to the collecting or to the disclosure of information of a private nature. Authorisation cannot be general and permanent. However, the use of information must be made strictly within the limits of the authorisation.[293]

In consequence, in order to prevent invasion of privacy, numerous specific laws then follow these general principles.

Different Types of Privacy Protection

In France, there are many specific laws on data protection, correspondence, and electronic surveillance. Moreover, French privacy protections are also incorporated in the Penal Code. Set out below is a list of different measures for the protection of privacy in France.

Data Protection

France has an *Act on Data Processing, Data Files and Individual Liberties*, which was passed on January 6, 1978. The Act covers both the public and private sectors. However, in order to make its data protection regime consistent with the EU Directive 95/46/EC, France government amended its *Data Protection Act of 1978*. This legislative process started in July 2000, and the new Act was eventually passed on August 6, 2004.

The new Act explicitly provides protections to "personal data" and its processing. Personal data means that "any information relating to a natural person who is or can be identified, directly or indirectly, by reference to an identification number or to one or more factors specific to him."[294] Processing of personal data means that:

> any operation or set of operations in relation to such data, whatever the mechanism used, especially obtaining, recording, organization, storage, adaptation or alteration, retrieval, consultation, use, disclosure by transmission, dissemination or otherwise making available, alignment or combination, blocking, deletion or destruction.[295]

---

[293] Henry (2001), p. 135.

[294] *Act on Data Processing, Data Files and Individual Liberties 1978* (France), art 2.

[295] *Act on Data Processing, Data Files and Individual Liberties 1978* (France), art 2.

Under the Act, processing of personal data may only be performed under certain conditions, which include:

(1) the data shall be obtained and processed fairly and lawfully;
(2) the data shall be obtained for specified, explicit and legitimate purpose, and shall not subsequently be processed in a manner that is incompatible with those purpose;
(3) they shall be adequate, relevant and not excessive in relation to the purposes for which they are obtained and their further processing;
(4) they shall be accurate, complete and, where necessary, kept up-to-date;
(5) they shall be stored in a form that allows the identification of the data subjects for a period no longer than is necessary for the purpose for which they are obtained and processed.[296]

Moreover, processing of personal data must have received the consent of the data subject or must meet one of the following conditions, which are:

(1) compliance with any legal obligation which the data controller is subject;
(2) the protection of the data subject's life;
(3) the performance of a public service mission entrusted to the data controller or the data recipient;
(4) the performance of either a contract to which the data subject is a party or steps taken at the request of the data subject prior to entering into a contract;
(5) the pursuit of the data controller's or the data recipient's legitimate interest, provided this is not incompatible with the interests or the fundamental rights and liberties of the data subject.[297]

The French data protection authority is an independent commission. It has two main functions: first, the data protection authority must inform all data subjects and data controllers of their rights and duties; second, it should ensure that the processing of personal data is carried out in conformity with the provisions of the Data Protection Act.[298] For example, the data protection authority should establish and publish the data protection standards and impose, when necessary, standard regulations bearing on the security of systems; moreover, it should receive claims, petitions and complaints relating to the carrying out of the processing of personal data and inform the initiators of these actions of the decisions taken regarding them; also, it shall respond to requests from public authorities and courts for an opinion and advise individuals and bodies that set up or intend to set up automatic processing of personal data; and so on.[299] In addition, the French data protection authority has been entitled to investigate, issue warnings, or impose a financial penalty if a data controller who does not comply with the obligations resulting from this Act.[300]

---

[296] *Act on Data Processing, Data Files and Individual Liberties 1978* (France), art 6.

[297] *Act on Data Processing, Data Files and Individual Liberties 1978* (France), art 7.

[298] *Act on Data Processing, Data Files and Individual Liberties 1978* (France), art 11.

[299] *Act on Data Processing, Data Files and Individual Liberties 1978* (France), art 11 (2), (b) (c) (d).

[300] *Act on Data Processing, Data Files and Individual Liberties 1978* (France), art 45.

Other Privacy Protections in Different Areas

Recording and Filming In France, a penalty of 1 years imprisonment and a fine of € 45,000 is incurred for any willful violation of the intimacy of the private life of other persons by resorting to any means of: (1) intercepting, recording or transmitting words uttered in confidential or private circumstances, without the consent of their speaker; (2) taking, recording or transmitting the picture of a person who is within a private place, without the consent of the person concerned.[301] Therefore, in France, it is unlawful to film or transmit images of an individual without his or her consent, except when the individual appears in public. Moreover, to spy on an individual's privacy and to use the product of this spying is a criminally punishable offence, and the same penalties will be applied.[302] It has been argued that this offence includes "photographing an individual on his death bed and the use of an intercom to overhear the conversations of employees."[303] Furthermore, the publication of a photograph or film of an individual's residence may constitute an invasion of privacy on the basis of article 9 of the French *Civil Code*.[304] For example, if the aerial photography of a building includes the image of its occupants, the activity of filming from the air will constitute a tortuous infringement of the right to protection of one's likeness.[305] In addition, the recording of a conversation by a party to the conversation without consent of the other party will constitute an invasion of privacy depending on the context of the conversations and recording in France.[306]

The Protection of Mail and Telephone Communications As mentioned earlier, the ECHR has been directly used in France. Article 8 (sentence 1) of the ECHR ensures that "everyone has the right to respect for his private and family life, his home and his correspondence." French government thus establishes the protection for both posts and telephone communications. In France, to intercept mail and to identify the content, sender or recipient of such mail may constitute a tortuous invasion of privacy. Likewise, interception of telephone conversations also constitutes a tortuous invasion of privacy. Today, these two principles have been recognized as a higher principle of constitutional value in France. Therefore, besides interception that is ordered by judicial authorities, the interception of posts or telephone communications will be criminally punishable under the French criminal law.

The Domicile Several laws protect rights relating to domiciles in France. Articles 675 to 680 of the French *Civil Code* prohibit making openings or spy-holes into the

[301] *New Penal Code* (France), art 226–1.

[302] *New Penal Code* (France), art 226–1.

[303] Henry (2001), p. 136.

[304] Henry (2001), p. 136.

[305] Henry (2001), p. 137.

[306] Henry (2001), p. 140.

property of one's neighbor. For example, article 675 states that "one of the neighbors may not, without the consent of the other, cut in a party wall any window or opening, in any manner whatever, even in fixed fanlights." Article 226(4) of the new French *Penal Code* prohibits the penetration or unlawful occupation of the residence of another by threats, acts of violence or constraint, and the offender will be punished by 1-year imprisonment and a fine of € 15,000. Moreover, article 432 (8) of the new *Penal Code* states that if a person entry or attempt to enter another person's residence against his will, the offender will be punished by 2-year imprisonment and a fine of € 30,000.

Based on these existing laws, the Paris Civil Trial Court decided that "the disclosure in the press of the address of domicile or of residence of an individual without the latter's consent constitutes an illicit invasion of privacy."[307] Similarly, in the case of disclosing the personal address of Monaco's Prince, the Paris Court concluded that "the domicile belongs to the domain of privacy. . .the reproduction of photographs taken in the private home of an individual without his authorisation. . .violates his privacy."[308]

Surveillance Rules In France, if security cameras are set up in personal space or place, it will be an invasion of privacy. However, if security cameras are set up in public places, and the events they monitor take place in public, it will not violate a person's privacy.[309] If the scenes that are considered as private, take place in public, these events will also be protected as matters of privacy.[310] In addition, to observe an individual's activities or private life by using a telephoto lens may also invade privacy in France. It has been argued that orders have been made preventing the use of photographs of Brigitte Bardot on her private property taken with a telephoto lens, as well as against photographs of Grimaldi and of Princess Diana and Mr Fayed on a yacht.[311]

Personal Identification In France, in the field of the arts, a pseudonym is considered a matter of privacy. Based on this principle, in 1970, the Appeal Court of Paris considered that the "right to one's name, image, voice, privacy, honour and reputation, the right to being forgotten and the right to one's own biography" should be sheltered from violation.[312]

---

[307] Henry (2001), p. 136.
[308] Henry (2001), p. 136.
[309] Henry (2001), p. 142.
[310] Henry (2001), p. 142.
[311] Henry (2001), p. 142.
[312] Henry (2001), p. 138.

Remedies

As mentioned earlier, article 9 of the French *Civil Code* clearly states that "without prejudice to compensation for injury suffered, the court may prescribe any measures, such as sequestration, seizure and others, appropriate to prevent or put an end to an invasion of personal privacy, in case of emergency those measures may be provided for by interim order." Among these measures, injunction and damage are two main remedies in France. Usually, most French judges do not provide damages to the claimant, but the following are illustrations that damages may be made:

(1) removal of an excerpt from a publication;
(2) affixing of a mask on the face of an individual in order to make him unrecognizable;
(3) publication of a warning at the beginning of a film;
(4) destruction of photographic negatives or other documents that are evidence of an invasion of privacy;
(5) publication of the decision at the expense of the perpetrator of the invasion of privacy, particularly when the violation was committed via the press;
(6) finally, criminal prosecution can be sanctioned in respect of violations of any of the laws mentioned above.[313]

It should be noted that if the application for an interim injunction failed and the publication was released, the claimant can ask that part of the judgment will be quoted on the front page of the next issue of the publication.[314]

Who Enjoys the Right to Privacy?

Public Figures

Compared to ordinary people, public figures enjoy less protection of their privacy in France. That is mainly due to the "public figure theory." According to public figure theory, public figures have to give up a certain amount of their privacy because their activities inevitably attract public attention. On the other hand, this is not to say that there is no privacy protection for public figures in France. It has been argued that French law has recognized that public figures enjoy, in principle, the same personality rights as unknown persons.[315] In order words, in France, public figures still have the right to privacy in certain aspects. First, public figures' state of health has been protected. For example, in 1996, a newspaper was taken to court for having published a photograph, which had been taken without the knowledge of his family, of the actor Gerard Philippe's young and seriously ill son.[316] Second, public

[313] Henry (2001), p. 143.
[314] Defamation and Privacy Law and Procedure in England, Germany and France 2006.
[315] Huw et al. (2005), p. 224.
[316] Henry (2001), p. 141.

figures' certain personal information has been protected. For example, disclosure of the pregnancy of the actress Isabelle Adjani was condemned on the grounds of the protection of privacy.[317]

Foreign Citizens

Article 8 of the ECHR emphasized that everyone has the right to respect for his or her privacy. In addition, article 14 of the ECHR proposes that:

> The enjoyment of the rights and freedoms set forth in this Convention shall be secured without discrimination on any ground such as sex, race, color, language, religion, political or other opinion, national or social origin, association with a national minority, property, birth or other status.

Therefore, as a member state of the ECHR, French government will provide full protection of privacy to all foreign citizens in France.

4.3.2.3 Japan

Constitutional Privacy Framework

The modern Japanese legal system is mainly based on the civil law system with English–American influences since the late nineteenth century. Japan thus has a written constitution, legal Codes and recognizable institutions of government and parliamentary democracy.[318] In Japan, the individual rights of people are guaranteed as "fundamental human rights" under the Japanese *Constitution of* 1946.[319] Although the Japanese Constitution does not explicitly provide protection for privacy, many Japanese court decisions and jurists have accepted a constitutional moral right to privacy for individuals as one of the "rights to pursue happiness" under Article 13.[320] Article 13 of the Japanese Constitution provides that "all of the people shall be respected as individuals. Their right to life, liberty, and the pursuit of happiness shall, to the extent that it does not interfere with the public welfare, be the supreme consideration in legislation and in other governmental affairs."[321] Furthermore, there is no independent privacy protection legislation in Japan. Therefore, based on Japanese Constitutional law, some particular privacy interests are mainly protected by Japanese case law. Other Japanese statutes only provide limited protection to privacy interests in some particular areas.

---

[317] Henry (2001), p. 138.

[318] Dean (1997), p. 1.

[319] Peerenboom et al. (2006), p. 121.

[320] Henry (2001), p. 270.

[321] *Constitution of Japan* (1946), art 13.

Invasion of Privacy

Elements of Invasion of Privacy

In Japan, the disclosure of certain aspects of a person's personal information constitutes a tort of invasion for privacy.[322] The elements of the tort of invasion for privacy were set out in the *Utageno Ato* case, which include:

(1) disclosure has been made of certain facts, or matters that may be viewed as facts, about a person's private life;
(2) the information disclosed must be of the type that the ordinary person would not wish to have disclosed about themselves (based on the ordinary person's level of sensitivity), in other words information, disclosure of which would cause mental suffering to the ordinary person; and
(3) the information must not yet have been disclosed to the public.[323]

In addition, if certain personal information has been collected or disclosed to the public for a special purpose, the same information should still be protected for any other purpose.[324]

Remedies

In Japan, if an individual's moral right is being infringed, the individual should be entitled to injunctive relief.[325] Therefore, theoretically, injunctive relief is main remedy for invasion of privacy in Japan. Besides injunction, damages of privacy tort are also available in Japan. However, the amount of damages awarded in privacy cases is generally very small, while compensation for legal fees is also very limited.[326]

Statutory Protection of Privacy

Similar to the common law countries mentioned earlier, other Japanese statutes prohibit various kinds of intrusive conduct in particular areas. Set out below is a list of statutory protections of privacy in Japan.

Data Protection

Initially, the *Personal Data Protection for National Agencies Act* was enacted in 1988. The object of this Act is to govern the use of personal data in computerized

[322] Henry (2001), p. 270.
[323] Henry (2001), p. 270–271.
[324] Henry (2001), p. 271.
[325] Henry (2001), p. 276.
[326] Henry (2001), p. 276.

files held by the national administrative agencies.[327] However, the loopholes of this Act are obvious: first, the Act has not brought comprehensive protection, which only applies to the public sector; second, there is no protection of certain sensitive data in the Act; third, the Act does not provide individuals with the right to access, which can help them to check and modify what personal information about him has been held. As a consequence, in order to respond to strong social concerns about massive storage, distribution and usage of personal information, in May 2003, a new *Personal Information Protection Act* was eventually enacted after a long controversy in the Diet.[328]

In order to protect individuals' rights and welfare while preserving the usefulness of personal information, the new Act sets out a policy for handling personal information, and measures for protecting personal information.[329] The new Act applies to both public and private sectors. According to the new Act, "personal Information" has been defined as "information about a living individual which can identify the specific individual by name, date of birth or other description contained in such information (including such information as will allow easy reference to other information and will thereby enable the identification of the specific individual)."[330] Although the new Act applies to private entities that handling personal information, it does not apply to persons and companies who handle the personal information of less than 5,000 individuals.[331] Moreover, this Act sets out duties of the national and local government. It also sets out duties for entities to handle personal information. According to the new Act, chapter 4 sets out 21 duties for entities, which includes specification of the purpose of use, proper acquisition, maintenance of the accuracy of data, security control measures, supervision of employees and so on.

Furthermore, in order to promote the protection of personal information in private institutions, the new Act requires that the State Minister in charge must appoint "Approved Personal Information Protection Organizations" to: (1) handle complaints about personal information by an entity; (2) give this entity information that helps it to ensure the proper handling of personal information; and (3) ensure the proper handling of personal information by this entity.[332] If the State Minister in charge finds that that the infringement on the important rights and interests of individuals is imminent, the Minister will order the entity handling personal information to consider the recommended measures.[333] If the entity violates their

[327] Horibe (2001).

[328] Privacy International: Japan 2007.

[329] *Personal Information Protection Act 2003* (Japan), art 1.

[330] *Personal Information Protection Act 2003* (Japan), art 2.

[331] Regulation Overview: Japan's Personal Information Protection Act (PIPA).

[332] *Personal Information Protection Act 2003* (Japan), art 37.

[333] *Personal Information Protection Act 2003* (Japan), art 34.

duties of handling personal information, the entity will be sentenced to imprisonment of not more than 6 months or to a fine of not more than 300,000 yen.[334]

In addition to the new Personal Data Protection Act, the Japanese Diet also adopted another four personal information protection bills in 2003. They are: (1) the *Act concerning the Protection of Personal Information Held by Administrative Organs*; (2) the *Information Disclosure and Personal Information Protection Council Establishment Act*; (3) the *Act Concerning the Protection of Personal Information Held by an Independent Administrative Agency*; (4) and the *Act concerning the Preparation of Related Laws for the Enforcement of the Act concerning the Protection of Personal Information Held by an Administrative Organ* respectively.[335] All these laws were enacted on May 30, 2005.

Compared to other developed countries' data protection law, there are still some particular areas that the Japanese law does not cover. These include:

(1) The conditions under which businesses may handle particularly sensitive personal information;
(2) The conditions under which businesses located in Japan may transfer personal information outside of Japan;
(3) The absence in the Act of legal and/or administrative mechanisms for individual redress of grievances.[336]

It thus has been held that the Japanese government will inevitably be faced with the challenge of "ensuring that its implementation measures enhance citizens" confidence in the new law while not over-burdening businesses with duplicative, contradictory or uncertain regulations'.[337] However, it is undeniable that the new Japanese Data Protection Act is still significant. As Professor Kazuo Makino states that, although the penalties set for noncompliance to the law are low, the Act is effective in making companies tighten up their security because of the damaging publicity that might arise if they are found guilty.[338] At least, the new Act takes steps to protect civil liberties, represents a significant step toward making personal data more secure, and attempts to make companies more responsible in Japan.[339]

Regulation on the Internet

Two new "anti-spam" Acts were also enacted in Japan, which are the *Law on Regulation of Transmission of Specified Electronic Mail* (the Transmission Law) and the *Law for the Partial Amendment to the Law Concerning Specified Commercial Transactions* (the Revised Transactions Law). The Transmission Law had been

---

[334] *Personal Information Protection Act 2003* (Japan), art 56.

[335] Privacy International: Japan 2007.

[336] Westin and Gelder (2003), p. 23.

[337] Westin and Gelder (2003), p. 23.

[338] Kallender (2005).

[339] Kallender (2005).

amended in 2005 and 2008, respectively. The purpose of the Transmission Law is to ensure "proper transmission of specified electronic mails, to prepare a preferable environment for the use of electronic mails, and thereby to contribute to the sound development of an advanced information and communications society."[340] The Japanese Ministry of Internal Affairs and Communication enforces the Transmission Law. According to the Transmission Law, any person who fails to comply with the Act will be imposed fines of up to JPY 1,000,000. The purpose of the Revised Transactions Law is to protect consumers. The Japanese Ministry of Economy, Trade and Industry enforces the Revised Transactions Law. Under the Act, repeat or egregious offenders can be fined up to JPY 3 million or 2 years in prison, and corporate offenders can face up to JPY 300 million fines.[341]

Medical Privacy

In 2004, the Ministry of Economy, Trade and Industry enacted Guidelines to regulate the protection of personal information in businesses that use human genetic information.[342] The Guidelines require that if businesses want to use genetic information, they must (1) give prior notification of the purpose for using, and (2) get the consent from data subjects in writing.[343]

4.3.3 Evaluation of Different Approaches

4.3.3.1 Common Law

Based on the foregoing study of certain Western developed countries' privacy protection, it is clear that the common law approach in both the UK and Australia involves primarily using some other particular legal remedies against specific privacy infringements. That is to say, in these two countries, the courts have been protecting privacy interests through the medium of other recognized heads of tortious liability.[344] Privacy interests are often protected by their courts without the input of government. For example, in the UK, the essentials of the law of confidence, which were described in the well-known case of *Prince Albert v Strange*, were cemented as a common law action by the case of *Saltman Engineering Co. v Campbell Engineering Co.* in 1948.[345] In the case of *Saltman*, the court

[340] *Law on Regulation of Transmission of Specified Electronic Mail* 2002 (Japan), art 1.
[341] Privacy International: Japan 2007.
[342] Privacy International: Japan 2007.
[343] Privacy International: Japan 2007.
[344] Todd (1997), p. 955.
[345] Richards and Solove (2007), pp. 160–161.

held that "the obligation to respect confidence is not limited to cases where the parties are in contractual relationship," and this conclusion were applied to the case of *Argyll v Argyll* for protecting personal confidences as well.[346] Since then, although the main purpose of the breach of confidence is still to safeguard commercial and governmental information, it has been applied in different ways to protect personal privacy interests. Similarly, in Australia, as mentioned earlier, the tort of trespass to land provides privacy protection against those who enter private property for the purpose of attempting to obtain an interview, or to photograph, film or otherwise record the occupants and their activities.[347] At present, the common law that indirectly protects privacy includes trespass, nuisance, defamation, copyright, breach of confidence, negligence, breach of contract, and so on. Compared to the UK and Australia, the development of common law privacy protection seems better in the USA and New Zealand. In the USA, there were three steps towards the protection of personal privacy, they are "(1) the creation of new torts of invasions of privacy; (2) the development of a constitutional doctrine; and (3) the introduction of specific legislative measures at the state and the federal level."[348] Likewise, in New Zealand, both the tort of the invasion of privacy and special privacy measures were enacted to protect privacy interests.

On the other hand, although there is no tort of invasion of privacy in the UK and Australia, it does not mean that there is no effective privacy protection in these two countries. When applying breach of confidence measures to protect privacy interests, the UK courts have focused on "the nature of the information itself rather than any relationship between the parties, or the circumstances surrounding its acquisition."[349] Also, the High Court decision in case of *ASC v Lenah Game Meats Pty Ltd* indicated the possibility of developing a tort of invasion of privacy in Australia. By contrast, the fact that the US Supreme Court has declared there is a general constitutional right to privacy does not indicate that privacy interests are always better protected in the USA than in the other common law countries.[350] For example, it has been held that the ability of a "public figure" in the USA to protect his or her reputation using the law of defamation is considerably less under the Supreme Court's ruling in *New York Times v Sullivan* than in the UK.[351]

It should be noted that the virtues of common law for privacy protection are still obvious, although the institution of civil law seems more prominent recently.[352] The most significant factor has been the significant development of particular rights by Common law judges. This development can accurately address different privacy

[346] Richards and Solove (2007), p. 161.

[347] Doyle and Bagaric (2005), p. 63.

[348] Michael (1994), p. 17.

[349] Todd (2005), p. 752.

[350] Michael (1994), p. 16.

[351] Michael (1994), p. 16.

[352] Michael (1994), p. 17.

interests in different situations. At least, this development can apply specific remedies to different victims. Therefore, it is still useful for the development of current legal system.

4.3.3.2 Civil Law

Compared to the common law approach, the civil law approach focuses on emphasizing the significance of general principle. Most civil law countries do not provide constitutional protection to right to privacy clearly. However, almost all these countries have their own data protection legislations on the basis of the requirement of the EU Directive 95/46/EC. Therefore, in these countries, personal information privacy has been protected under their own data protection legislations. Other privacy-related legislations in these countries have been extended to particular areas or industries by their legal scholars.

It should be noted that, although almost all civil law countries have their own written general principles and data protection legislation, a number of civil law countries begin to accept the common law method that is applying principles of protection through case law. For example, article 25 of the ECHR, which is the right of individual petition to the European Commission of Human Rights, has enabled the Commission and the Court to develop the right to privacy under the Convention in some cases.[353] Moreover, it is also the tradition of the civil law to establish overseeing institutions to prevent harm before it occurs. [354] Today, this method has been adopted in a number of common law jurisdictions such as the UK, Australia, and New Zealand.

Generally speaking, it is difficult to find an ideal method to protect privacy interests in all aspects. However, it is clear that personal privacy has been adequate protected by information privacy protection legislation in most Western developed countries. Moreover, with the rapid development of information technology, the transfer of information across frontiers has become easier than ever before. Therefore, today, privacy protection should not be restricted in one country, but that international standards such as the OECD and the EU Directive 95/46/EC should be implemented seriously.

4.3.4 Conclusion

With this background about privacy protections that have been afforded in Western developed countries, we are now able to consider what China can learn from these countries. The evaluation and some suggestions for improving privacy protection in China are presented in the following paragraphs.

---

[353] Michael (1994), p. 16.

[354] Michael (1994), p. 16.

4.4 What Can China Learn from Other Jurisdictions?

4.4.1 Main Models of Western Privacy Protection

Careful deliberation of the privacy protection afforded by these International Human Rights Instruments and Western laws makes it clear that there are currently four major models of privacy protection. In some countries, several models are used simultaneously.

The first model is that privacy protection standards are placed in the context of existing common law principles, such as trespass, nuisance, defamation and breach of confidence, so that these common law torts will provide remedy for victim.[355] The second model is that privacy protection standards are set in a tort of invasion of privacy.[356] Third, most often, in civil law countries, privacy protection standards are addressed in the context of the existing criminal law system, where privacy interests have been protected by a fine or imprisonment on guilt indirectly.[357] The fourth model is that privacy protection standards are set in a comprehensive personal information/data protection law (Tables 4.1 and 4.2).[358] In these countries, an information protection authority is established to implement the information/data protection law and its protection principles. The authority, usually known as a Commissioner, has general powers (1) to oversee the operation of the data protection law, (2) to monitor and promote compliance with the law, and (3) to handle complaints. In addition, it has been held that, theoretically, privacy protection also can be achieved through various forms of self-regulation, in which companies and industry bodies establish codes of practice.[359] However, the records of these efforts have proved that there is little or no evidence that the aims of the codes are regularly

Table 4.1 Checklist of adoption of international instruments

Countries	Privacy (Data) protection law	OECD guidelines adopted	Council of Europe signed	Convention ratified
The United Kingdom	Yes	Yes		
The United States	Yes	Yes		
Australia	Yes	Yes		
New Zealand	Yes	Yes		
Germany	Yes	Yes	Yes	Yes
France	Yes	Yes	Yes	Yes
Japan	Yes	Yes		

355 Australia and the United Kingdom, and Japan.

356 The United States, New Zealand, and Japan.

357 France and Germany.

358 Australia, the United Kingdom, New Zealand, the United States, Japan, France, Germany.

359 Banisar (1990).

Table 4.2 Checklist of country profiles

Countries	Generic privacy (data) protection legislation	Private/ public sector	Individuals/ companies	Manual/ automated files
The United Kingdom	Data Protection Act 1998	Public Sector	Principally Individuals	Both
The United States	Privacy Act 1974	Public Sector	Individuals	Both
Australia	Privacy Protection Act 1988	Both	Individuals	Both
New Zealand	Privacy Act 1993	Both	Individuals	Both
Germany	Federal Data Protection Act 2002 (*Bundesdatenschutzgesetz*)	Both	Individuals	Both
France	Data Processing, Data Files and Individuals Liberties 2004	Both	Principally individuals	Both
Japan	Personal Information Protection Law 2003	Public Sector	Individuals	Both

fulfilled, and the adequacy and enforcement are the major problems with these approaches.[360]

China should take note that effective privacy protection is not implemented through one legal method. Most Western developed countries have adopted different means to deal with different issues in particular areas.

4.4.2 *How the Western Laws Deal with Recognized Privacy Risks*

As mentioned in Chap. 2, in the 30 years of China's reform and opening up, the risks to privacy in China are mainly brought by: (1) the increasing official and administrative powers allowing more and more individuals or organizations to interfere with other people's private affairs, or to access to other people's personal information or data; (2) more and more commercial practices attempt to find customers in their personal place or personal space actively; and (3) with the rapid development of information technologies and information processing devices such as computers in China, it is now very easy for Chinese people to access, handle, and save personal information than ever before. In order to solve these problems, the following paragraphs examine how the Western laws deal in turn with these three Chinese social phenomena that endanger privacy.

4.4.2.1 Western Laws on Official Powers

In China, unsystematic development of legal system has produced a number of laws that authorize intrusive powers to government agencies. Therefore, today, Chinese

[360] Banisar (1990).

officials have myriad powers of intrusion. Privacy interests in China have been invaded by these official powers seriously. In 1975, the ALRC re-examined the existing branches of law controlling criminal investigative activity.[361] Several principles were established to protect privacy. The author believes that these principles should be adopted by China into the whole area of official investigative activity. These principles include:

1. Searches of the Person (including the Vehicle of the Person):
   (1) An official should not search another person except:
      (i) If the person has consented; or
      (ii) Pursuant to a warrant
      (iii) As an incident to arrest, 'frisk'-type searches being permissible where it is believed to be necessary for the purpose of discovering either dangerous weapons or evidence with respect to the particular offence for which the person is in custody
      (iv) In response to circumstances of such seriousness and urgency as to require and justify immediate action
   (2) No person other than a medical practitioner should conduct a search of body cavities or other intrusive body search. Such searches should only be allowed in the following circumstances:
      (i) With the consent of the person so to be searched
      (ii) In accordance with the order of a Magistrate
2. Principles Governing Entry and Searches of Premises:
   (1) An official should not enter private premises (this would include entry to seize property or arrest a person, as well as to ask questions or inspect documents), except:
      (i) With the consent of the occupier of the premises or
      (ii) In pursuance of a warrant
      (iii) In response to circumstances of such seriousness and urgency as to require and justify immediate action
      (iv) Pursuant to specific statutory provision which sets out the specific purposes of the entry or search
3. Principles Governing Seizure:
   (1) An official should not seize documents, articles and other property except:
      (i) With the consent of its possessor or
      (ii) With the authority of a warrant
      (iii) In response to circumstances of such seriousness and urgency as to require and justify immediate action or
      (iv) As an incident to arrest
4. Principles Governing Arrest
   (1) The power of an official, other than in "border" situations, to arrest a person for Commonwealth and Territorial offences should be brought into line with those of the Australian Federal Police (AFP), and made exercisable only when the official is satisfied that proceedings by way of summons would be ineffective or inappropriate in the circumstances. Arrest must be justified by the necessities enumerated in Principle 4.2(b) below.

---

[361] Australian Law Reform Commission 1983, p. 276.

(2) A private citizen should have the power to arrest a person for an offence only where he believes on reasonable grounds:
   (i) That the person is committing, or has just committed the offence
   (ii) That the arrest of the person is necessary in order to achieve one or more of the following purposes......
   (iii) That proceedings by summons against the person would not effectively achieve that purpose or those purposes
(3) An official who arrests another person should forthwith after the arrest, take the other person before a Magistrate to be dealt with according to law or deliver the person into the custody of a police officer, to be dealt with according to law.
(4) There should be a power to enter premises:
   (i) In order to arrest a person named in a warrant of arrest and reasonably believed to be on the premises and
   (ii) In the absence of a warrant, to accomplish the lawful arrest of a person reasonably believed to have committed a serious offence and to be on the premises. This power should not authorize officials to enter premises for arrests at night where it would be practicable to make that arrest during the day
(5) The official should inform the person arrested, at the time of the arrest of the offence for which he is arrested.

5. Use of Force
   (1) It should be unlawful to use more force, or to expose a person to more indignity, than is reasonably necessary to effect an arrest or prevent the escape of the person from lawful custody.[362]

In addition, China has signed the ICCPR in 1998. Based on the ICCPR, in 2004, the Second Session of the Tenth National People's Congress adopted an amendment of the Constitution of the PRC. The Amendment adds "Human Rights" into the Chinese Constitution and clearly states that the human right in China should be respected and protected. It is thus necessary for China to consider the requirements of the ICCPR carefully. Articles 9 and 10 (paragraph 1) of the ICCPR are essentially significant in this context. Article 9 emphasizes that:

a. Everyone has the right to liberty and security of person;
b. Anyone who is arrested shall be informed;
c. Anyone arrested or detained on a criminal charge shall be brought promptly before a judge or other officer authorized by law to exercise judicial power and shall be entitled to trial within a reasonable time or to release;
d. Anyone who is deprived of his liberty by arrest or detention shall be entitled to take proceedings before a court, in order that the court may decide without delay on the lawfulness of his detention and order his release if the detention is not lawful; and
e. Anyone who has been the victim of unlawful arrest or detention shall have an enforceable right to compensation.

---

[362] Australian Law Reform Commission 1983, pp. 276–278.

Paragraph 1 of article 10 states that "all persons deprived of their liberty shall be treated with humanity and with respect for the inherent dignity of the human person."

4.4.2.2 Western Laws on Invasive Commercial Activities

In order to prevent unfair commercial activity that endangers consumers' privacy interests, the Western developed countries have enacted a number of laws to control certain activities, such as the *Fair Credit Billing Act 1986* (US), the *Consumer Credit Act 1974* (UK), the *Law for the Partial Amendment to the Law Concerning Specified Commercial Transactions 2002* (JAP), and so on. The main aims of these laws, as the ALRC summarized, are to control:

(1) marketing techniques which intrude into his private space or private life or which use his personal history, independently of his knowledge or consent, and in circumstances where he is powerless to avoid or escape from the intrusion;
(2) loss of freedom of choice between alternative methods of transacting business according to the degree to which the various methods are potentially threatening to privacy interests;
(3) deprivation of consumer rights, including privacy rights, through unfair agreements waiving or varying the essential elements of the relationship between the consumer and the commercial institutions with which he deals; and
(4) deception as to the privacy risks involved in various alternative payment and other business systems procured by false or misleading advertising.[363]

All these are should be considered by the Chinese law-makers carefully.

4.4.2.3 Western Laws on Surveillance technology

With respect to surveillance technology, most Western developed countries' laws have proposed that, without consent of the subject, any secret surveillance of an individual's personal space, personal life, and personal information will be unlawful. That is because, under normal circumstances, an individual's interest in keeping personal information free is far more important than the need of the public to know. Therefore, usually, if information collectors want to monitor an individual's personal space, life and information, they should be permitted by the subject or this should be done openly. More specifically, in the case of interception of mail, telecommunications or recording of a conversation, public officials must prove that they are legitimately authorized to engage in such secret surveillance, provided they do so pursuant to a judicial warrant and they observe certain basic civil rights of the subject.[364] For example, as mentioned earlier, section 1(1) of the *Regulation*

[363] Australian Law Reform Commission 1983, p. 274.

[364] Australian Law Reform Commission 1983, p. 275.

of Investigatory Powers Act 2000 (UK) prohibits listening, storage or other kinds of interception or surveillance of communication system without lawful authority at any place in the UK; similarly, Australia enacted the *Telecommunications (Interception and Acess) Act 1979* (Cth) to prohibit the interception of, and other access to, telecommunications.[365] Usually, a person who is failure to comply with these Acts is guilty of an offence, and will be liable to imprisonment for a term or to a fine, or to both. All these Acts thus protect privacy interests by prohibiting the interception of communications. Otherwise, the interception is unlawful. It should be noted that Western developed countries' laws have also proposed that secret surveillance devices can be used in certain circumstances, such as for state security or law enforcement purposes.

4.5 Issues for Further Consideration

Based on the foregoing analysis of Western principles for privacy protection, it is clear that, in China, more needs to be done than mere rely on existing fragmented mechanisms concerned mainly with other aims and policies and only incidentally with privacy.[366] Some further considerations can be drawn, as shown below:

Firstly, it is necessary for China, which is moving toward greater democracy, to create the general right to privacy under the Chinese legal system. As mentioned earlier, privacy is not an independent right in China and therefore Chinese courts do not recognize an invasion of privacy as constituting an independent claim in litigation despite protection through other laws and regulations.[367] For example, as discussed in Chap. 3, most privacy cases have been heard and judged on the basis of the right to reputation in China. In fact, the right to reputation cannot provide adequate protection to privacy. The differences between invasion of privacy and other existing rights thus produce confusions and restrict the development of legal protection of privacy in China. The author believes that the establishment of the right to privacy in Chinese legal system will clarify these confusions and provides a systematic protection to privacy interests in China.

Second, it is also necessary to establish effective information privacy protection legislation in China. As mentioned earlier, the EU Directive 95/46/EC proposes that the transfer to a third country of personal data, whether are undergoing processing or are intended for processing and whether the source is public or private sector, should be permitted when the third country in question ensures an adequate level of protection.[368] It is thus clear that the lack of effective privacy protection in China

[365] *Telecommunications (Interception and Acess) Act 1979* (Cth), long title.

[366] Australian Law Reform Commission 1983, p. 299.

[367] Chao (2005), p. 660.

[368] *Directive 95/46/EC*, art 25.

will cause serious consequence. Both Chinese human rights and the relationship between China and other countries will be damaged. Therefore, if China hopes to take part in the global information community and achieve its benefits fully, China must set up an effective privacy protection regime. Moreover, a professional privacy protection authority is needed to promote implementation of privacy protection standards in China. In addition, based on the Western experiences of privacy protection, abuse and harm to privacy can happen in both public and private sectors. Therefore, the Chinese law-makers must ensure the legal privacy protection in both the public and private sectors. Also, Chinese law-makers should understand that an inquiry, and resultant laws, can never be comprehensive and exhaustive, guaranteeing a satisfactory level of privacy protection for all time.[369] The professional privacy protection authority thus must provide advice to the Chinese NPC or Chinese government for further considerations. The author believes that the general right to privacy and the adequate privacy protection regime may fill the gaps in privacy protection in China.

References

Journal Articles and Books

Blackshaw IS, Siekmann RCR (2005) A concise legal and practical overview of the creation, protection and enforcement of sports image rights in Europe. Cambridge University Press, Cambridge

Chao JC (2005) Protecting the right to privacy in China. Victoria University of Wellington Law Review 36:645

Carey P (2003) Data Protection in the UK. Blackstone, London

Cate FH (1997) Privacy in the information age. Brooking Institution Press, Washington, DC

Dean M (1997) Japanese legal system: text and materials. Cavendish Publishing, London

Doyle C, Bagaric M (2005) Privacy law in Australia. Federation Press, Syndey

Heffernan L, Kingston J, Robinson M (foreword) (1994) Human rights: a European perspective. Round Hall Press, Blackrock (in association with Irish Centre for European Law)

Hendrickx F (ed) (2002) Employment privacy law in the European union. Intersentia NV, Oxford

Henry M (ed) (2001) International privacy publicity and personality laws. Butterworths, London

Huw BS, Ansgar O, Agnès L-S (2005) Privacy, property and personality: civil law perspectives on commercial appropriation. Cambridge University Press, Cambridge

Kohel M (2002) The Privacy Amendment (Private Sector) Bill 2000: The Australian government's substandard attempt to allay privacy concerns and regulate internet privacy in the private sector. Brooklyn Journal of International Law 27:703

Lindsay D (2005) An exploration of the conceptual basis of privacy and the implications for the future of Australian privacy law. Melbourne University Law Review 29:131

Lulham S (2005) What is, and what should be, the extent of New Zealand's new tort of breach of privacy? Canterbury Law Review 11:91

Moore DJ (2003) Privacy: the press and the law. Palladian Law Publishing, Isle of Wight

[369] Australian Law Reform Commission 1983, p. 299.

Merrills JG, Robertson AH (2001) Human rights in Europe: a study of the European convention on human rights. Manchester University Press, Manchester
Michael J (1994) Privacy and human rights: an international and comparative study, with special reference to developments in information technology. Dartmouth Publishing Corporation, Aldershot
Paterson M (2005) Freedom of information and privacy in Australia: Government and Information Access in the Modern State. LexisNexis Butterworths, Australia
Peerenboom R, Petersen CJ, Chen AHY (eds) (2006) Human rights in Asia: a comparative legal study of twelve Asian jurisdictions, France and the USA. Routledge, London
Prosser WL (1960) Privacy. Calif Law Rev 48:383
Richards NM, Solove DJ (2007) Privacy's other path: recovering the law of confidentiality. Georgetown Law Journal 96:123
Robertson AH (1968) Revision of the charter of the organisation of American states. International and Comparative Law Quarterly 17:346
Sieghart P (ed) (1988) Human rights in the United Kingdom. New York Pinter, New York
Solove DJ, Rotenberg M (2003) Information privacy law. Aspen Publishers, New York
Solove DJ, Rotenberg M, Schwartz PM (2006) Privacy, information, and technology. Aspen Publishers, New York
Todd S (ed) (1997) The law of Torts in New Zealand, 2nd edn. Thomson Brookers, Wellington
Todd S (ed) (2005) The law of Torts in New Zealand, 4th edn. Thomson Brookers, Wellington
Trindade F, Cane P, Lunney M (eds) (2007) The law of Torts in Australia. Oxford University Press, Oxford
Tucker G (1992) Information privacy law in Australia. Longman Professional, London
Westin AF, Van Gelder V (eds) (2003) Special issue on consumer privacy in Japan and the new national privacy law. Privacy Am Bus 10:1

Case

A v B (QB 2001) All Eng L Rep 449.
Attorney-General v Guardian Newspaper Ltd [1990] 1 AC 109.
Australian Broadcasting Corporation v Lenah Game Meats Pty Ltd [2001] HCA 63.
Campbell v MGN Ltd [2004] UKHL 22.
Coco v A.N. Clark (Engineers) Ltd [1969] RPC 41.
Creation Records v News Group Newspaper Ltd [1997] EMLR 444.
Douglas v Hello! Ltd [2003] EWHC 2629 (CH).
Entick v Carrington [1765] 95 ER 807.
Grosse v Purvis [2003] QDC 151.
Hosking v Runting [2004] NZCA 34.
Prince Albert v Strange 41 ER 1171, 1 McN & G 2, [1849] EWHC Ch J20, (1849) 2 De Gex & Sim 652.
TV3 Network Services Ltd v Broadcasting Standards Authority [1995] 2 NZLR 720.

LEGISLATION: The Commonwealth of Australia

Health Records and Information Privacy Act 2002 (NSW)
Privacy Act 1988 (Cth)
Privacy Amendment (Private Sector) Act 2000 (Cth)
Privacy and Personal Information Protection Act 1998 (NSW)

Information Privacy Act 2000 (Vic)
Telecommunications (Interception and Acess) Act 1979 (Cth)

Federal Republic of Germany

Civil Code (Germany)
Federal Data Protection Act (Germany)

France

Act on Data Processing, Data Files and Individual Liberties 1978 (France)
Penal Code (France)

Japan

Constitution of 1946 (Japan)
Law on Regulation of Transmission of Specified Electronic Mail 2002 (Japan)
Personal Data Protection for National Agencies Act 2003 (Japan)

New Zealand

Broadcasting Act 1989 (NZ)
Privacy Act 1993 (NZ)

United Kingdom

Data Protection Act 1998 (UK)
Human Rights Act 1998 (UK)
Official Secret Act 1989 (UK)
Regulation of Investigatory Powers Act 2000 (UK)
Telecommunications (Data Protection and Privacy) Regulations 1999 (UK)

United States of America

Children's Online Privacy Protection Act of 1998 (US)
Driver's Privacy Protection Act 1994 (US)
Fair Credit Billing Act of 1986 (US)

Fair Credit Reporting Act of 1970 (US)
Family Educational Rights and Privacy Act of 1974 (US)
Federal Privacy Act 1974 (US)

International Human Rights Instruments

American Declaration of the Rights and Duties of Man, adopted by the Ninth International Conference of American States (1948), OEA/Ser LV/II 82 doc 6 rev 1 at 17 (1992)
Charter of the United Nations, opened for signature 26 June 1945 (entry into force 24 October 1945)
Guidelines on the Protection of Privacy and Transborder Flows of Personal Data, Organization for Economic Co-operation and Development, applicable on 23 September 1980
International Convention on Civil and Political Rights, opened for signature 19 December 1966, 999 UNTS 171, 6 ILM 368, art 17 (entry into force 23 March 1976)

International Data Protection Law

Asia-Pacific Economic Cooperation, APEC Privacy Framework (2005)
Directive 95/46/EC of the European Parliament and of the Council of 24 October 1995 on the protection of individuals with regard to the processing of personal data and on the free movement of such data, Official Journal of the European Communities of 23 November 1995 No L 281 (1995)

Government and Law Reform Reports

Australian Human Rights and Equal Opportunity Commission (1995) Information Paper Number Three: Community Attitudes to Privacy.
Australian Law Reform Commission (1983) Privacy. Report paper No. 22 Volume 1
Australian Law Reform Commission (2006) Review of privacy. Issue Paper 31
Law Reform Commission of Hong Kong (2004) Civil Liability for Invasion of Privacy.

Electronic Materials

About APEC (2009) Asia–Pacific economic cooperation http://www.apec.org/apec/about_apec.html. Accessed 9 April 2011
APEC Privacy Framework (2009) Asia-Pacific Economic Cooperation http://www.apec.org/apec/news___media/fact_sheets/apec_privacy_framework.html. Accessed 9 April 2011
Banisar D, privacy and human rights: an international survey of privacy laws and practice (1990) Global Internet Liberty Campaign http://gilc.org/privacy/survey/intro.html. Accessed 9 April 2011
Black G (2007) Douglas v Hello! – an OK! Result 4:2 SCRIPTed http://www.law.ed.ac.uk/ahrc/script-ed/vol4-2/editorial.asp. Accessed 9 April 2011

Brief: a handbook on privacy federal and state legislation (2001) The Texas Senate http://www.senate.state.tx.us/SRC/pdf/PRIVACYPART1.pdf. Accessed 9 April 2011

Clarke R, A history of privacy in Australia (1998) http://www.rogerclarke.com/DV/OzHistory.html. Accessed 9 April 2011

Computer Matching and Privacy Protection Act (2005) Internal revenue service http://www.irs.gov/irm/part11/ch03s42.html. Accessed 9 April 2011

Cromptom M (2000) The privacy act and the Australian federal privacy commissioner's functions http://www.cfp2000.org/papers/crompton.pdf. Accessed 9 April 2011

Defamation and Privacy Law and Procedure in England, Germany and France (2006) TaylorWessing http://www.taylorwessing.com/uploads/tx_siruplawyermanagement/IP_Defamation_and_privacy.en.pdf. Accessed 9 April 2011

Evans K (2004) Hosking v runting: balancing rights in a privacy tort. 11(2) Privacy Law and Policy Reporter 34 http://www.austlii.org/au/journals/PLPR/2004/28.html. Accessed 9 April 2011

Family Educational Rights and Privacy Act (FERPA) (2008) US Department of Education http://www.ed.gov/policy/gen/guid/fpco/ferpa/index.html. Accessed 9 April 2011

Federal Republic of Germany (2007) Privacy international http://www.privacyinternational.org/article.shtml?cmd[347]=x-347-559535. Accessed 9 April 2011

French Republic (2007) Privacy international http://www.privacyinternational.org/article.shtml?cmd[347]=x-347-559537. Accessed 9 April 2011

Fry W (2006) Developments in defamation and privacy. http://www.williamfry.ie/files/indexfile.asp?id=272. Accessed 9 April 2011

Greenleaf G (2003) District court finds privacy tort: an Australian First 10 Privacy Law and Policy Reporter 41 http://www.austlii.edu.au/au/journals/PLPR/2003/28.html. Accessed 9 April 2011

Greenleaf G (2005) APEC's privacy framework: a new low standard. 11 (5) Privacy Law and Policy Reporter 121 http://www.austlii.edu.au/au/journals/PLPR/2005/1.html. Accessed 9 April 2011

Horibe M, Privacy and personal information protection in Japan: past, present and future (2001) CNiL http://www.cnil.fr/conference2001/eng/contribution/horibe_contrib.pdf. Accessed 9 April 2011

Human Obligations Humanistic Texts http://www.humanistictexts.org/undo.htm. Accessed 9 April 2011

International Trade Administration, Development and Implementation of Cross-border Privacy Rules in the Asia Pacific Economic Cooperation Group (APEC): Comments of the Electronic Privacy Information Center (EPIC), the Consumer Federation of America, the National Consumers League, the Privacy Rights Clearinghouse, the Privacy Times, the US Public Interest Research Group and the World Privacy Forum on Behalf of US Civil Society Organizations (2006) World Privacy Forum http://www.worldprivacyforum.org/pdf/APEC_Privacy_CSO_Comments.pdf. Accessed 9 April 2011

Japan (2007) Privacy international http://www.privacyinternational.org/article.shtml?cmd[347]=x-347-559524. Accessed 9 April 2011

Kallender P, Japan tightens personal data protection (2005) InfoWorld http://www.infoworld.com/article/05/03/28/HNjapntightensdataprotection_1.html. Accessed 9 April 2011

Ken McKinnon, Privacy and the Press (2005) Australian Press Council http://www.presscouncil.org.au/pcsite/fop/cpu.html. Accessed 9 April 2011

McBride T (2000) Recent New Zealand case law on privacy: part II the broadcasting standards authority, the media and employment' 6 Privacy Law and Policy Reporter 133 http://www.austlii.com/au/journals/PLPR/2000/8.html. Accessed 9 April 2011

Mendez1 JE, Mariezcurrena J Human rights in Latin America and the Caribbean: a regional perspective (A paper submitted to the Human Development Report 2000 'Human Rights and Human Development', 1999) http://hdr.undp.org/docs/publications/background_papers/mendez2000.pdf. Accessed 9 April 2011

OECD guidelines on the protection of privacy and transborder flows of personal data OECD http://www.oecd.org/document/20/0,3343,en_2649_34255_15589524_1_1_1_1,00.html. Accessed 9 April 2011

Overview of Privacy (2007) Privacy International http://www.privacyinternational.org/article.shtml?cmd[347]=x-347-559062&als[theme]=Data%20Protection%20and%20Privacy%20Laws. Accessed 9 April 2011

Pounder C (2007) Why the APEC privacy framework is unlikely to protect privacy. Cyberspace Law and Policy Center http://www.bakercyberlawcentre.org/ipp/apec_privacy_framework/0710_pounder.pdf. Accessed 9 April 2011

Privacy and government: the computer marching and privacy protection Act (2003) Privacilla.org http://www.privacilla.org/government/cmppa.html. Accessed 9 April 2011

Privacy guide: New Zealand (2003) Caslon analytics http://www.caslon.com.au/privacyguide5.htm. Accessed 9 April 2011

Privacy principles (2006) BSA http://www.bsa.govt.nz/codesstandards-privacy.php. Accessed 9 April 2011

Regulation overview: Japan's personal information protection act (PIPA) rules and regulations http://www.zlti.com/resources/docs/Rules%20and%20Regulations/ZL.RR.Japan-PIPA.pdf. Accessed 9 April 2011

Rehabilitation of Offenders Act 1974 (2001) nacro http://www.nacro.org.uk/data/resources/nacro-2007021302.pdf. Accessed 9 April 2011

Telecommunications Interception & Access Laws: Telecommunications (Interception and Acess) Act 1979 (Cth) (2006) Electronic Frontiers Australia http://www.efa.org.au/Issues/Privacy/tia.html. Accessed 9 April 2011

Telford P (2003) Gross v purvis: its place in the common law of privacy 10 (4) Privacy Law and Policy Reporter 66 http://www.austlii.edu.au/au/journals/PLPR/2003/36.html. Accessed 9 April 2011

Tricia (2011) What is the Electronic Communications Privacy Act? WISEGEEK http://www.wisegeek.com/what-is-the-electronic-communications-privacy-act.htm. Accessed 9 April 2011

Title VII of the Civil Rights Act of 1964 Employment Law Information Network http://www.elinfonet.com/titleVIIsum.php. Accessed 9 April 2011

United Kingdom of Great Britain and Northern Ireland (2007) Privacy International http://www.privacyinternational.org/article.shtml?cmd[347]=x-347-559479. Accessed 9 April 2011

United States of America (2007) Privacy International http://www.privacyinternational.org/article.shtml?cmd[347]=x-347-559478. Accessed 9 April 2011

What is the Electronic Communications Privacy Act? WISEGEEK http://www.wisegeek.com/what-is-the-electronic-communications-privacy-act.htm. Accessed 9 April 2011

Chapter 5
Creating the Right to Privacy in the Chinese Legal System

5.1 Introduction

As discussed in Chap. 3, at present, there are no effective means to solve privacy issues in China. One of the most important reasons is that there is no general right to privacy under current Chinese law. Today, privacy has been recognized as "a fundamental social value underpins other fundamental rights and freedoms."[1] It is thus necessary for China, which is moving toward greater democracy, to create the general right to privacy in the Chinese legal system.

This chapter examines the possibility of creating the right to privacy under the Chinese legal system. This chapter has four main parts. The first part discusses the necessity of creating the right to privacy in China, in which privacy should be legally protected by Chinese law as an independent right and not merely indirectly through the protection of other rights. The second part discusses the interests in privacy and rights to its protection and attempts to identify methods to achieve the right to privacy in China. The third part examines the interests that overlap with privacy interests, but do not accurately and explicitly coincide with them, and decides whether privacy outweighs these complementary interests in China. The fourth part tries to balance privacy and interests competing with privacy in China, and examines whether privacy and its competing interests are always in conflict each other. The conclusion suggests that there is no detriment for China to enact the right to privacy. It is thus important to establish the right to privacy as an independent right under current Chinese legal system and provide protection to this significant right.

[1] Law Reform Commission of Hong Kong 2004, p. 97.

H. Wang, *Protecting Privacy in China*,
DOI 10.1007/978-3-642-21750-0_5,

5.2 Arguments for the Creation of the Right to Privacy in China

As discussed earlier, there have been a number of definitions of privacy worldwide, but none has been defined in any satisfactory manner. Moreover, in China, a number of cases have demonstrated that privacy is often confused with portrait, reputation, and personal dignity. The opponents of a general right to privacy may thus claim that a statutory right to privacy, which is defined in a unified form may introduce uncertainty into the Chinese law, and "give insufficient guidance to the public and the court."[2] In fact, it has already been argued that uncertainties in the law are usual.[3] The Hong Kong Law Reform Commission's paper on *Civil Liability for Invasion of Privacy* says that "to decline to reform the law because of the difficulty in defining the wrong is "a doctrine of despair" which could be applied to any proposed legal reform."[4] Creating the right to privacy in China predicates that Chinese legal system must acknowledge the existence of different privacy interests in China and provide remedies to victims when privacy invasions happened. In other words, China should ensure citizens have the right to claim legal protection for their privacy interests. So that the Chinese courts will have rights to determine which principles should provide to the privacy case.

In addition, someone may point out that privacy complaints in China are rare and, therefore, it is not the time for China to focus on privacy issues. The creation of the general right to privacy is an undue response to a minor social phenomenon in current China. On the other hand, the rarity of privacy complaints does not mean that the invasion of privacy is not serious in China. As mentioned in Chap. 3 of the book, such rarity can be explained by the following reasons: first, Chinese law is only a supplementary means to regulate social affairs; second, Chinese law is only a political tool; third, mediation is more preferred than litigation in China; fourth, criminal law is more important and effective than other laws in China; and finally, unique status of collective interests in socialist China. In addition to the reasons caused by socialist China itself, there are some other matters causing the rarity of privacy complaints in China. For example, at present, devices of surveillance are being widely used in China; however, we cannot speculate the precise details and levels of the use of secret surveillance in most cases.

In short, privacy is a significant value that should be legally protected by Chinese legislation as an independent right. As Godfrey Kan concludes that an explicit right to privacy would modify people's behaviour and encourage them to respect it, and at least, "liability for invasion of privacy would have a deterrent effect which would make potential intruders think twice before they act."[5]

[2] Law Reform Commission of Hong Kong 1999, p. 62.
[3] Law Reform Commission of Hong Kong 1999, p. 62.
[4] Law Reform Commission of Hong Kong 1999, p. 62.
[5] Law Reform Commission of Hong Kong 1999, p. 63.

5.3 Privacy Interests and Right to Privacy

5.3.1 Privacy Interests and Its Protection

As discussed in Chap. 1, the definition of privacy in this book is that privacy is a right, which consists of a number of individual interests that individuals have in keeping their personal information and personal affairs free from interference from others. These individual privacy interests include physical privacy, territorial privacy, and information privacy, respectively. Furthermore, it has been argued that an effective approach in analyzing privacy is "to isolate and define the interests which are commonly grouped under the heading 'privacy interests' and to explore the extent of their legal protection."[6] Therefore, in this part, the author will discuss these privacy interests in turn.

In West, physical privacy is protected by freedom of movement and expression, prohibiting physical assault, and restricting unwarranted search or seizure of the person.[7] That is because the physical person is deemed to be surrounded by legal norms and social values protecting him from physical harassment.[8] In China, some provisions of Chinese Criminal Law in crime such as "intentionally inflicts injury upon another person,"[9] "unlawfully detains another person or unlawfully deprives the personal freedom of another person,"[10] and "unlawfully subjects another person to a body search,"[11] provide protections against physical interference with the person.

With respect to territorial privacy, it has been held that "there is a physical domain within which a claim to be left in solitude and tranquillity is advanced and is recognized" in Western developed countries.[12] An individual's home has been seen as a "castle," and any one should not be disturbed by trespassers, noxious odors, loud noises, or peeping Toms when the individual at home.[13] In China, territorial privacy interests have been protected by different laws. For example, both the Chinese *Constitution Law of 1982* and the GPCL protect citizens' possession or ownership of property.[14] Article 245 (2) of the *Criminal Law of the PRC* states that

---

[6] Australian Law Reform Commission 1983, p. 21.

[7] Australian Law Reform Commission 1983, p. 21.

[8] Australian Law Reform Commission 1983, pp. 21–22.

[9] *Criminal Law of the People's Republic of China* 1996, art 234.

[10] *Criminal Law of the People's Republic of China* 1996, art 238.

[11] *Criminal Law of the People's Republic of China* 1996, art 245 (1).

[12] Australian Law Reform Commission 1983, p. 21.

[13] Australian Law Reform Commission 1983, p. 21.

[14] *Constitution of the People's Republic of China* 1982, art 13; see also *General Principles of the Civil Law of the People's Republic of China* 1986, arts 71 and 75.

"whoever unlawfully intrudes into another person's residence shall be sentenced to fixed-term imprisonment of not more than 3 years or criminal detention."[15]

Information privacy "is based essentially on a notion of the dignity and integrity of the individual, and on the relationship to information about him" in certain Western countries.[16] With respect to information privacy, the Canadian Task Force on Privacy and Computers identified and defined "Privacy in the Information Context" in the following terms:

> This notion of privacy derives from the assumption that all information about a person is in a fundamental way his own, for him to communicate or retain for himself as he sees fit. And this is so whether or not the information is subsequently communicated accurately, and whether or not it is potentially damaging to his reputation, his pocket-book, or his prospects; the context is of course the controlling factor in determining whether or not particular information will be damaging. Competing social values may require that an individual disclose certain information to particular authorities under certain circumstances (e.g., census information). He may decide to make it available in order to obtain certain benefits (e.g., credit information or information imparted to his lawyer to win a lawsuit or to his confessor to win salvation). He may also share it quite willingly with his intimates. Nevertheless, he has a basic and continuing interest in what happens to this information, and in controlling access to it.[17]

In China, restraints are imposed by the Chinese legislation on disclosure of information. For example, *Law of the PRC on Statistics* provides that data collected from investigations shall not be disclosed without the consent of data subjects[18]; and the *Postal Law of the PRC* regulates that "postal enterprises and postal staff shall not provide information to any organization or individual about users' dealings with postal services except as otherwise provided for by law."[19] However, all these provisions do not provide sufficient protection for information privacy.

Some jurists thus postulate that effective privacy protection can be achieved by identifying interests in privacy, as against a rights-based model.[20] For example, as Raymond Wacks states that:

> The long search for a definition of "privacy" has produced a continuing debate that is often sterile and, ultimately, futile. ... the premises upon which the proposed definitions are based are materially different. Thus, for example, those who assume privacy to be a "right" have not really joined issue with those who conceive it to be a "condition," "state," "area of life" and so on[21]

---

[15] *Criminal Law of the People's Republic of China* 1996, art 245 (2).

[16] Australian Law Reform Commission 1983, p. 22.

[17] Australian Law Reform Commission 1983, p. 22.

[18] *Law of the People's Republic of China on Statistics* 1983, art 15.

[19] *Postal Law of the People's Republic of China* 1990, art 6.

[20] Victoria Law Reform Commission 2002, p. 10.

[21] Wacks (1980), p. 10.

Wack's argument has been supported by the decision of Chief Justice Gleeson in the case of *Lench Game Meats*.[22] Gleeson CJ points out that "the law should be more astute than in the past to identify and protect interests of a kind which fall within the concept of privacy."[23] He believes that the lack of precision of the concept of privacy and the tension that exists between the interests in privacy and interests in free speech are the main reasons that we should be careful to deal with the privacy tort.[24]

On the other hand, this opinion is not suitable for China to adopt. First, focusing on different privacy interests may have the consequence that "privacy," as a significant concept, will be erased in China. It is undeniable that this attempt may effectively use what have existed in current China. However, as mentioned earlier, at present, there is no comprehensive and integrated set of legal rules protecting privacy interests. The reality in China is that existing privacy protections are not able to cover the relevant privacy issues. In addition, most Chinese citizens have not been aware of what privacy is. If the Chinese law-maker focuses on particular privacy interests, this approach will make current privacy protection in China more piecemeal than before, and therefore inadequate. Second, it has been argued that, although both interests and rights are able to incarnate human being's social values, interests are not seen as "fundamental to the existence of a human being."[25] That is because individual's interests can be exchanged or traded, but give up or sell individual's rights will be inconsistent with being human.[26] It is thus clear that the status of "right" cannot be substituted by the "interest." As a consequence, an interest-based model may produce gaps in future protection of privacy in China.

By contrast, the right to privacy includes the right to claim damages in respect of any interference with privacy. That is to say the right to privacy ensures individuals have right to claim legal protection for their different privacy interests. As the Victorian Law Reform Commission's paper on *Defining Privacy* states that:

> Where interests fit into already existing categories that represent particular aspects of a human subject's life, rights tend towards representing the human subject as a whole. Formulating rights is a process that tends to resist the 'cutting-up' of the human subject that is a necessary corollary of defining specific interests. Rights are claims that are more capable of addressing the whole human being.[27]

In addition, the present legal situation is that invasions of privacy have been deemed unacceptable to society worldwide, "and the development of modern human rights jurisprudence, in which the right to individual privacy is recognised,"

---

[22] Victoria Law Reform Commission 2002, p. 10.

[23] Victoria Law Reform Commission 2002, p. 10.

[24] *Australian Broadcasting Corporation v Lenah Game Meats Pty Ltd* [2001] HCA 63, [40].

[25] Victoria Law Reform Commission 2002, p. 16.

[26] Victoria Law Reform Commission 2002, p. 16.

[27] Victoria Law Reform Commission 2002, p. 17.

is preferable.[28] As a consequence, it is significant for China to create a statutory right to privacy, although particular privacy interests are legally protected in China.

5.3.2 Balancing Different Interests to Achieve the Right to Privacy in China

At present, more and more Chinese people are concerned that whether their privacy interests are protected by the current Chinese legal system. However, the Chinese peoples' requirement of privacy protection does not justify creation of a right to privacy. Balancing privacy and other privacy-related interests is the only way to achieve the right to privacy in China. For example, if a person is the offender of a serious criminal offence, most people may agree that the police should have the right of entry to arrest this person. This is because, at that time, the interests in law enforcement outweigh the individual's privacy interests. It is thus clear that we cannot presume that these competing interests of privacy are less worthy of protection. Likewise, we also cannot presume privacy interests are less worthy of protection. They must be weighed, with complementary and associated interests, against competing public and private interests.[29] As a consequence, based on the Western experiences of privacy protection, in deciding whether to accept a right to privacy in China, on the one hand, privacy interests must be weighed with any complementary interests such as in reputation and portrait which overlap with privacy interests but do not precisely coincide with them; on the other hand, in this weighing process, Chinese law makers must balance certain competing interests relevant in the context in which it is being expressed.[30] The result of this may be to draw a conclusion whether it is possible to enact the right to privacy in China.

5.4 Interests Complementary to Privacy in China

Based on the foregoing analysis, the question of whether the right to privacy can be applied in China involves balancing different interests, some complementary and some competing. The following paragraphs examine interests that are complementary to privacy in China.

---

[28] Victoria Law Reform Commission 2002, p. 11.

[29] Australian Law Reform Commission 1983, p. 20.

[30] Australian Law Reform Commission 1983, pp. 20–21.

5.4.1 Interests in Portrait

At present, there are no cases which directly discuss a right to privacy in China, other existing tort such as the right to one's portrait is used.[31] The right to portrait ensures that Chinese citizens enjoy the right of portrait, and the use of a citizen's portrait for commercial purposes without his consent should be prohibited.[32] In the case of *Two Art Models v The Organizers of the Exhibition*:

- Some teachers from the China Central Art Institution held an exhibition of life drawing without the consent of the models. Thus, the models sued these teachers for invasion of their right to portrait.[33]

With respect to this case, it has been held that it was "an invasion of privacy dealt with under the more familiar name of invasion of the right of portrait."[34] The author believes that this is not a case of invasion of right to portrait. As mentioned earlier, the right to portrait ensures that Chinese citizen's portrait for commercial purposes without their consent should be prohibited. However, as a free exhibition, the China Central Art Institution did not pursue any commercial purposes. In fact, in this case, what had been disclosed was the models' personal information that contained in this unauthorized exhibition. The author thus believes that, in this case, the essence of the plaintiffs' complaint is that their privacy has been invaded.

The limitation of the right of portrait was also tested in the case of *Qiao Yiping v Coal Products Sales Company of Fugu Country*:

- The plaintiff was Manager of Henchang Real Estate Development Company of Fugu Country in 1990. In 1991 he was photographed when receiving a gold cup and certificate of merit awarded to one of the Development Company's products on behalf of the Company. He left the Company soon afterwards. After his departure, part of the Company was taken over by the defendant company, and Henchang Real Estate Development selected a photograph showing the plaintiff accepting the gold cup and the certificate of merit in its publicity material to promote the Company. In 1994, the Postal Office of Fugu Country used the same photograph as the cover page of the local telephone directory. In June 1996, the plaintiff sued the defendant and the Postal Office for violation of his right of portrait.[35]

Although the plaintiff attempted to use the right of portrait to protect his or her personal information contained in the photos, the essence of this case is that the complainant's privacy has been invaded. However, based on the right of portrait,

[31] Chao (2005), p. 655.

[32] *General Principles of the Civil Law of the People's Republic of China* 1986, art 100.

[33] Chao (2005), p. 655.

[34] Chao (2005), p. 655.

[35] Wang and Mo (1999), p. 162.

the Chinese trial court stated that the photograph was a news photograph rather than a portrait, which is because the plaintiff was photographed when he was performing his duty as the Manager of the Henchang Real Estate Development Company.[36] Moreover, the court also stated that the occasions on which the said photograph was published did not pursue the commercial purposes.[37] In consequence, the court dismissed the plaintiff's action.

Based on these cases in China, it is clear that interests in portrait differ from privacy interests in China. If an individual uses another's portrait for a non-commercial purpose, and this non-commercial use of a person's portrait does not constitute defamation or does not cause damage to the person's reputation, the Chinese courts will usually dismiss the plaintiff's action.[38] The limitation of the right of portrait to protect privacy is thus obvious.

5.4.2 Interests in Reputation

In China, article 101 of the GPCL clearly states that "Chinese citizens and legal persons enjoy the right to reputation." Chinese citizens and legal persons have a clear interest in maintaining their personality, and any uses of insults, libel or other means to damage the reputation of citizens or legal persons have been prohibited.[39] The Chinese Supreme People's Court then issued a general judicial interpretation regarding the application of the GPCL to privacy in 1988. In *Opinions on Several Questions concerning the Implementation of the GPCL* (1988), the Chinese People's Supreme Court stated that:

> If anyone propagates the privacy of any other person in writing or orally, or fakes acts to vilify the personality of other person overtly, or damages other person's reputation by ways of insulting and slandering, which result in a certain influence, such act shall be determined as an act infringing the citizen's right of reputation.[40]

Since this general judicial interpretation has been adopted, some privacy cases have been heard and judged on the basis of the right of reputation in China.

On the other hand, the author believes that privacy interests are broader than the complementary interest in reputation. As the ALRC points out that:

> Reputation is affected only by material disclosed about an individual which is capable of disparaging him in the eyes of third parties. Privacy interests might be affected by material

---

[36] Wang and Mo (1999), p. 162.

[37] Wang and Mo (1999), p. 162.

[38] Wang and Mo (1999), p. 162.

[39] *General Principles of the Civil Law of the People's Republic of China* 1986, art 101.

[40] *Opinions of the Supreme People's Court on Several Issues concerning the Implementation of the General Principles of the Civil Law of the People's Republic of China* (For Trial Implementation), answer 140 (1).

about an individual which is perfectly true and neutral, but which he simply does not want other to know, such as personal tastes, address, income or age.[41]

The prevalent views in China are that (1) the right to reputation ensures the legal subjects to enjoy the interests brought by social appraisal, and the right to privacy ensures individual's personal information do not be obtained or disclosed illegally; (2) the information disseminated in the case of reputation is normally false and wrong, and the results of invading reputation are always negative; by contrast, the information disseminated in the case of privacy is normally truth and the release of these personal information usually cause great emotional damage.[42] Therefore, these two rights protect different interests. For example, X repeatedly insults Y by stating Y is the victim of rape will invade Y's right to reputation. That is because the statement that Y is the victim of rape, no matter it is true or false, may destroy Y's good reputation and the result will be negative. By contrast, the statement of Y has suffered serious illness may not invade her right to reputation. That is because the statement is truth and will not damage her reputation, but may cause great emotional damage to her. Therefore, clearly, the release of an individual's personal information without his consent certainly invades his right to privacy, but might not invade his right to reputation. It is thus clear that the right to reputation is insufficient to protect privacy interests.

This opinion was tested in a case involving misdiagnosis in *Yang v The No.1 Associate Hospital of No.4 Military Medical University*:

- A senior doctor of the defendant misdiagnosed the plaintiff to be an HIV carrier in 1994 and considerable negative publicity in the plaintiff's workplace and to his family was being generated because of it. The Chinese trial court held that the defendant was negligent and liable under the tort of reputation. The appeal court set aside the trial court's judgment and decided that the misdiagnosis and procedures followed by the defendant were reasonable in the circumstances and consequently dismissed the plaintiff's action.[43]

This case illustrates substantial differences between the right to privacy and the right to reputation. Reputation is a social judgment of a person, a group of people, or an organization based upon facts which are considered relevant by a community.[44] In the case of reputation, the person concerned is often harmed by such means as fabrication of fact, insult or slander, to the damage of personal dignity, reputation, and honor.[45] Therefore, as mentioned earlier, results of defamation cases are usually negative. By contrast, the right to privacy is an individual's or group's right to keep their lives and personal sphere free from interference from others.

[41] Australian Law Reform Commission 1983, p. 30.

[42] Zhu (1997), pp. 212–213.

[43] Wang and Mo (1999), pp. 161–162.

[44] McNamara (2007), p. 21.

[45] Zhu (1997), p. 213.

The results of privacy invasion are not always negative but may cause great emotional damage.

Another case also highlights this point:

- A defendant used the words "thief", "prostitute", "evil" and many other unfavorable words to describe the leading character of his story. Although the defendant did not mention the name of the plaintiff in his or her supposedly fictional story, the home address, occupation, office address, and even the experiences of the leading character of the story were the same as those of the plaintiff. Therefore, those who knew the plaintiff would realize that the story referred to her.[46]

The story not only ruined the plaintiff's reputation, but also invaded her privacy at the same time. However, careful deliberation makes it clear that, in this case, the essence of the plaintiff's complaint is that privacy interests have been invaded, and the tort of reputation incidentally protects information privacy interests. Thus, the protection of the right to privacy is narrowed by the existing system including it in the right to reputation.[47] The privacy interests are protected in many defamation cases only incidentally and in part by the protection of reputation provided by the defamation action. As a consequence, in China, using the right to reputation to protect privacy is insufficient in many cases.

5.4.3 Interests in Freedom from Discrimination

Based on certain Western developed countries' experiences, in some situations, individual's complaint of a threat of discrimination reflects his concern relates to an invasion of privacy.[48] That is because most people may fear that their personal information collected might be used as the basis for discrimination against them.[49] For example, recent scientific and technologic development has promoted researchers to identify genetic alteration that may indicate predisposition for developing diseases, such as a genetic test for inherited breast cancer that will allow women to find out whether they carry the altered gene and provide them with useful medical options.[50] However, a lot of women choose not to be tested. That is because they fear the information may cause a threat of discrimination, which will affect their employment, or be used to deny them and their families access to the health

[46] Fu and Cullen (1996), pp. 197–198.

[47] Chao (2005), p. 657.

[48] Australian Law Reform Commission 1983, p. 31.

[49] Australian Law Reform Commission 1983, p. 31.

[50] Religious Action Center of Reform Judaism.

insurance coverage they need.[51] On the other hand, "freedom from discrimination" in itself is not able to prohibit, for example, individuals or organizations from using other people's personal information. In consequence, freedom from discrimination is also insufficient to protect privacy in China.

5.4.4 Summary

The foregoing analysis of the complementary interests to privacy in China makes it clear that all these interests overlap with privacy interests, but do not accurately and explicitly coincide with them. Therefore, it is inadequate to use these complementary interests of privacy as the basis for main privacy principles in China. Clearly, the right to privacy cannot be substituted easily. Creating the right to privacy in China is thus necessary.

5.5 Interests Competing with Privacy in China

A democratic government is required to protect freedom of expression and freedom of the press. However, these two interests are capable of violating the right to privacy. Other interests identified as competing with the interest in privacy include freedom of information, the social interest in law enforcement and so on. This part of the chapter balances privacy and interests competing with privacy in China, and examines whether privacy and its competing interests always conflict with each other.

5.5.1 Freedom of Expression Versus Privacy

Freedom of expression is one of the essential foundations of a democratic society.[52] However, it has been argued that the desire to keep something private conflicts with freedom of expression, and the protection from unwanted publicity is often deemed as a derogation of the right to freedom of speech and of the press.[53] Therefore, the prevalent view is that privacy can be seriously invaded by the absolute privilege of free expression.[54] Are privacy and free expression always in conflict each other?

---

[51] Religious Action Center of Reform Judaism.

[52] Burnheim 1997.

[53] Law Reform Commission of Hong Kong 1999, p. 16.

[54] Privacy Committee of New South Wales 1980, p. 3.

In order to create the statutory right to privacy in China, it is necessary to examine the inherent conflict between privacy and free expression.

5.5.1.1 Freedom of Expression

In China, freedom of expression is one of the basic human rights protected under the Chinese Constitution. Article 35 of the *Constitution of 1982* provides that the Chinese Citizens enjoy freedom of expression. Freedom of expression is a prerequisite to the enjoyment of all human rights in China, which is very important to develop and discuss ideas in the search for truth and understanding, autonomy, and self-fulfilment of the individual, and participation in the political life of a democratic society.[55]

The traditional approach to reconciling privacy and freedom of expression is to use one of them as the starting point and then make allowances for the other.[56] At present, the prevalent approach in Western developed countries is to narrow the scope of freedom of expression. In the case of *Sunday Times v United Kingdom*, the European Court pointed out that it was "faced not with a choice between two conflicting principles, but with a principle of freedom of expression that is subject to a number of exceptions which must be narrowly interpreted."[57]

Under international law, governments are also required to restrict freedom of expression in certain aspects, such as national security or the protection of public interests. For example, paragraph 3 of article 19 of the ICCPR provides:

> The exercise of the rights provided for in paragraph 2 of this article carries with it special duties and responsibilities. It may therefore be subject to certain restrictions, but these shall only be such are provided by law and are necessary: (a) for respect of the rights or reputations of others; (b) for the protection of national security or of public order, or of public health or morals.

Likewise, article 10 of the ECHR provides:

1. Everyone has the right to freedom of expression. This right shall include freedom to hold opinions and to receive and impart information an ideas without interference by public authority and regardless of frontiers. This article shall not prevent States from requiring the licensing of broadcasting, television or cinema enterprises.
2. The exercise of these freedoms, since it carries with it duties and responsibilities, may be subject to such formalities, conditions, restrictions or penalties as are prescribed by law and are necessary in a democratic society, in the interests of national security, territorial integrity or public safety, for the prevention of disorder or crime, for the protection of health or morals, for the protection

[55] Amnesty International 2006, p. 8.

[56] Law Reform Commission of Hong Kong 1999, p. 16.

[57] Law Reform Commission of Hong Kong 1999, p. 16.

of the reputation or the rights of others, for preventing the disclosure of information received in confidence, or for maintaining the authority and impartiality of the judiciary.

With respect to these restrictions, Nowak points out that "other rights," mentioned in both article 19 of the ICCPR and article 10 of the ECHR, "whose protection might justify restrictions on freedom of expression also include the right to privacy."[58] He argues that:

> Even though the drafters of Article 19 expressly adopted the right to seek information actively, this does nothing to change the duty on States Parties flowing from Article 17 to protect the intimacy of the individual against sensational journalism. Above all, the legislature must prevent abusive access to personal data.[59]

Therefore, theoretically, if China accepts all these restrictions of freedom of expression, it appears that there is no reason to believe that creating the right to privacy in China will lead to unwanted results.

5.5.1.2 Reconciling Privacy with Freedom of Expression

Many sociologists have already pointed out that why freedom of expression is significant. Freedom of expression is a significant social value mainly due to: first, it enhances individual self-fulfilment; second, it promotes the discovery of truth; third, it promotes political participation; and fourth, it helps maintain social stability and provides a "safety valve."[60] The following paragraphs examine the relationship between privacy and freedom of expression in practice.

Individual Self-fulfillment

Emerson states that the freedom of expression, in fact, is the right of an individual purely in his capacity as an individual.[61] This is because restraining a person from expression would inhibit the growth of his or her personality, and individuals could formulate their own beliefs only through free discussion.[62] In order words, freedom of expression enhances the development of individuality. Likewise, Alan Westin points out that privacy is also significant for developing individual individuality:

> This development of individuality is particularly important in democratic societies, since qualities of independent thought, diversity of views, and non-conformity are considered desirable traits for individuals...The individual's sense that it is he who decides when to

[58] Law Reform Commission of Hong Kong 1999, p. 19.

[59] Law Reform Commission of Hong Kong 1999, p. 19.

[60] Emerson (1963), pp. 879–884; see also Fu and Cullen (1996), pp. 21–22.

[61] Emerson (1963), p. 879.

[62] Law Reform Commission of Hong Kong 1999, p. 25.

> "go public" is a crucial aspect of his feeling of autonomy. Without such time for incubation and growth, through privacy, many ideas and position would be launched into the world with dangerous prematurity.[63]

Therefore, clearly, freedom of expression and privacy serve the same goal to achieve individual self-fulfilment.

Discovery of the Truth

If an individual wants to seek knowledge and truth, he or she must hear all sides of the question, especially as presented by those who feel strongly and argue militantly for a different view.[64] It thus has been held that freedom of expression is necessary to provide a constant testing of conventional wisdom or accepted truth.[65] On the other hand, not all expression can be protected by this principle. In West, the expression that incites violence, interferes with the administration of justice, or discloses state secrets or confidential commercial information, has been prohibited.[66] As the Law Reform Commission of Hong Kong (the HKLRC) states that "the liberty to express does not extend to truth which causes private individuals annoyance or embarrassment without any corresponding benefit to the public."[67] That is to say, even though the facts are true, the expression of private facts which interferes with an individual's private realm should be prohibited.[68]

Political Participation

It has been held that it is necessary for "individuals in a society to be well informed in order for them to participate effectively in the public affairs of that society."[69] That is because freedom of expression can help an individual to participate in decision-making through a process of open discussion, and form his personal opinion on matters that may affect his lives.[70] Therefore, individuals can participate in social and political decision-making by free expression. Moreover, freedom of expression can also provide an important check on government misconduct. With respect to this function of freedom of expression, it is argued that freedom of expression is not only pivotal in ensuring the accountability of government, but

---

[63] Westin (1967), p. 34.

[64] Emerson (1963), p. 881.

[65] Fu and Cullen (1996), p. 21.

[66] Law Reform Commission of Hong Kong 1999, p. 24.

[67] Law Reform Commission of Hong Kong 1999, p. 25.

[68] Law Reform Commission of Hong Kong 1999, p. 25.

[69] Fu and Cullen (1996), p. 21.

[70] Emerson (1963), p. 882.

also ensures that a government's behavior can be openly and effectively criticized.[71]

Compared to freedom of expression, individuals' moral autonomy is also one of the important basic requirements of democracy.[72] Therefore, in certain aspects, privacy promotes autonomy and also enhances democracy. It has been held by the HKLRC that:

> Allowing free discussion in private would contribute to a pluralistic society and protect those who question mainstream thoughts and values. Protecting individuals from unwanted publicity therefore facilitates public discussion and effective participation in a democratic government. The freedom to express ideas and opinions would be undermined if individual privacy is not protected against intrusion.[73]

It is thus clear that the interests in privacy are consistent with those in freedom of expression.

The Function of Social Stability and "Safety Valve"

It has been argued that "through a free exchange of information, society's problems ... will be more quickly and accurately identified and responses can be crafted accordingly."[74] That is because if an individual has a part in the decision-making process, even when the decision goes against him, they are more ready to accept it. By contrast, privacy also contributes to social stability and security. "Emotional release" is one of the main functions of individual privacy, and one form of different emotional releases is provided by the protection privacy gives to minor non-compliance with social norms.[75] As Westin states,

> Some norms are formally adopted which society really expects many person to break. This ambivalence produces a situation in which almost everyone does break some social or institutional norms, for example, violating traffic laws, breaking sexual mores, cheating on expense accounts, overstating income-tax deductions, or smoking in rest rooms when this is prohibited. Although society will usually punish the most flagrant abuses, it tolerates the great bulk of the violations as "permissible" deviations. If there were no privacy to permit society to ignore these deviations – if all transgressions were known – most persons in society would be under organisational discipline or in jail, or could be manipulated by threats of such action.[76]

Thus freedom of expression and privacy, have the same function as security.

---

[71] Fu and Cullen (1996), p. 22.

[72] Law Reform Commission of Hong Kong 1999, p. 26.

[73] Law Reform Commission of Hong Kong 1999, p. 26.

[74] Cullen and Fu (1998), p. 158.

[75] Westin (1967), pp. 34–35.

[76] Wang and Mo (1999), p. 162.

5.5.1.3 Summary

Generally speaking, the social functions of "privacy" are difficult to distinguish from those of freedom of expression.[77] The foregoing analysis makes it clear that privacy and freedom of expression are not rights (or interests) which are mutually exclusive. There is no doubt that both the right to privacy and the freedom of expression are both significant. In fact, as the HKLRC's paper on *Civil Liability for Invasion of Privacy* says that "rather than competing with each other, privacy and freedom of expression serve the same values of a free society in certain aspects."[78] In consequence, creating the right to privacy in China will not in conflict with the existing right of freedom of expression.

5.5.2 *Freedom of the Press versus Privacy*

5.5.2.1 General

Although freedom of the press and freedom of expression are similar concepts, the better view is that there are differences between them.[79] It has been argued that the press enjoys special privileges with respect to expression which individuals do not enjoy in some certain Western countries, such as these privileges include immunity from some defamation actions in the United States.[80] By contrast, in China, the press is an instrument of the revolution. It has been argued that the masses cannot speak for themselves, and the Communist Party, as the vanguard of the working class, has to exercise democratic control and express the view of the masses.[81] As a consequence, freedom of expression and freedom of the press are sometimes different.

Freedom of the press is an institutional right rather than a set of individual free speech rights exercised by individual journalists and proprietors.[82] In capitalist society, the main purpose of the press clause is to create a "fourth estate" outside the Government as an additional check on the executive, legislature and judiciary.[83] There are several reasons why freedom of the press is an important value: first, protecting freedom of the press is significant for maintaining the market place in which ideas are exchanged; second, freedom of the press provides a forum in which

[77] Wacks (2000), p. 278.

[78] Law Reform Commission of Hong Kong 1999, p. 17.

[79] Fu and Cullen (1996), p. 20.

[80] Fu and Cullen (1996), p. 23.

[81] Fu and Cullen (1996), p. 25.

[82] Law Reform Commission of Hong Kong 1999, p. 27.

[83] Law Reform Commission of Hong Kong 1999, p. 27.

ideas for improving society can be argued; and third, the press also serves as a principal mechanism for providing commentary and criticism of government performance.[84] In consequence, it has been argued that free press can ensure "the government is accountable to the public, through not only the dissemination of information, but also the exposure of occupation and abuse of power."[85]

5.5.2.2 *Freedom of the Press in China*

The press in China receives constitutional protection under article 35 of the *Constitution of 1982*. However, direct censorship of the publication is extensive in China.[86] Both article 26 of the *Regulations of the PRC on the Administration of Publication* (2001) and article 6 of the *Rules of the PRC on the Administration of Electronic Publication* (2003) clearly state that no publication shall contain the following contents:

1. Anything that goes against the basic principles determined by the Constitution
2. Anything that endangers the unification, sovereignty and territorial integrity of the country
3. Anything that endangers state security, reputation and interests
4. Anything that instigates national separatism, infringes on the customs and habits of minority nationalities and disrupt solidarity of nationalities
5. Anything that discloses state secrets
6. Anything that publicizes pornography and superstition or plays up violence, endangers social ethics and the fine traditions of national culture
7. Anything that insults or slanders others; and
8. Any other contents prohibited by the provisions of laws and regulations.

It has been held that these restrictions are also affirmed in the standard of Ethics for Chinese Journalists.[87] Moreover, the Chinese media have also been limited by the Chinese criminal law and other laws. For example, article 250 of the *Criminal Law of the PRC* clearly states that "where a publication carries an article designed to discriminate... shall be sentenced to fixed-term imprisonment of not more than 3 years, criminal detention or public surveillance."

In China, media's right to press is not absolute. The right of freedom of express must base on a series of premises. Most importantly, media' right has been limited by many contents which are prohibited by law. Therefore, if the right to privacy is established in Chinese legal system, there will be no conflict between preventing the use of wrong means to press personal information and the media's right to press.

[84] Fu and Cullen (1996), p. 22.
[85] Law Reform Commission of Hong Kong 1999, p. 28.
[86] Fu and Cullen (1996), p. 34.
[87] Fu and Cullen (1996), p. 35.

That is because the freedom of the press is the freedom to gather news by fair and lawful means; it is not a freedom to gather news by means which are unlawful or unfair.[88] Therefore, the Chinese media is not free to investigate or publish anything they want, or anything that their readers or audiences want to know. As a consequence, there is no evidence that creating the right to privacy in China will harm the freedom of the press.

5.5.3 Other Possible Competing Interests in China

Other possible interests competing with privacy in China include freedom of information, law enforcement and so on.

Regarding freedom of information, in certain Western developed countries, the potential conflicts between freedom of information and the right to privacy are usually avoided by giving precedence to freedom of information laws.[89] At present, the reality is that there is neither freedom of information law nor privacy law in China. The protection for information privacy mainly relies on morals. As a result, in China, the moral obligation not to disclose personal information must give way to those disclosure requirements.

According to law, undue stress on the collection of adequate information on the part of law enforcement agencies may conflict with privacy interests.[90] In China, in order to "meet the needs of state security or of investigation into criminal offences, public security or procuratorial organs are permitted to censor correspondence in accordance with procedures prescribed by law."[91] Moreover, article 8 of the *State Security Law of the PRC* clearly states that: "any functionary of a State security organ may, when carrying out a task for State security... may...enter interested restricted areas, sites or units; and may have access to related files, materials and articles for examination." Therefore, it is clear that the precedence has already been given to the law enforcement in China. In fact, if Chinese law-maker deems privacy as the absolute value, an effective public function will not be carried out in China.

It is impossible to discuss all the examples of the conflicts between privacy and other competing interests in China. Based on the foregoing analysis, it is clear that excessive emphasis on the right to privacy will cause serious harms of other interests. On the other hand, this is not to say that the right to privacy should not be protected in China. The key issue of creating right to privacy in China is how to always keep the right to privacy effective when competing claims (or interests) are made against it. Sometimes, undue stress on privacy interests does little to privacy

[88] Law Reform Commission of Hong Kong 1999, p. 30.

[89] Paterson (2005), p. 22.

[90] Privacy Committee of New South Wales 1980, p. 3.

[91] *Constitution Law of the People's Republic of China 1982*, art 40.

protection. Focusing on privacy as a statutory right or public value is the best way to protect privacy effectively. If the right to privacy is created legally in China, the balance of these different values will be formulated in terms of the transgressor and the right-holder, and the right to privacy will become a collective right, and then the balance between right to privacy and its competing rights will be easily achieved.[92] As a consequence, there is no evidence that providing the right to privacy would not impinge other competing rights in China. In the contrast, what is need for China here is the creation of the right to privacy under Chinese legal system.

5.6 Conclusion

In this chapter, after weighing the complementary interests and balancing certain competing interests in China, the author submits that there is no detriment for China to enact a right of privacy. The creation of the right to privacy will be beneficial to both individual and public. It is thus wrong to put privacy against other public values. The right to portrait, the right to reputation and other existing privacy-related rights in China should only be independent personal rights parallel to the right to privacy. In fact, the prevention is far more effective than the compensation. It is thus significant for China to establish the right to privacy as an independent right and to provide effective protection to this right.

References

Journal Articles and Books

Chao JC (2005) Protecting the right to privacy in China. Vict Univ Wellin Law Rev 36:645
Cullen R, Fu HL (1998) Seeking theory from experience: media regulation in China. Democratization 5(2):155
Emerson TI (1963) Toward a general theory of the first amendment. Harvard Civil Rights – Civil Liberties Law Review 72:877
Fu HL, Cullen R (1996) Media law in the PRC. Asia Law & Practice, Hong Kong
McNamara L (2007) Reputation and defamation. Oxford University Press, Oxford
Paterson M (2005) Freedom of information and privacy in Australia: Government and information access in the modern state. LexisNexis Butterworths, Australia
Wacks R (1980) The protection of privacy. Sweet & Maxwell, London
Wacks R (2000) Law, morality, and the private domain. Hong Kong University Press, Hong Kong
Wang GG, Mo J (eds) (1999) Chinese law. Kluwer, The Hague
Westin AF (1967) Privacy and freedom. Atheneum, New York
Zhu GB (1997) The right to privacy: an emerging right in Chinese Law. Stat Law Rev 18:208

[92] Victoria Law Reform Commission 2002, p. 39.

Case

Australian Broadcasting Corporation v Lenah Game Meats Pty Ltd [2001] HCA 63

Legislation

Constitution of the People's Republic of China 1982
Criminal Law of the People's Republic of China 1996
General Principles of the Civil Law of the People's Republic of China 1986
Law of the People's Republic of China on Statistics 1983
Opinions of the Supreme People's Court on Several Issues concerning the Implementation of the General Principles of the Civil Law of the People's Republic of China (For Trial Implementation)
Postal Law of the People's Republic of China 1990

Government and Law Reform Reports

Australian Law Reform Commission (1983) Privacy. Report paper No. 22 Volume 1
Law Reform Commission of Hong Kong (1999) Consultation Paper on Civil Liability for Invasion of Privacy
Law Reform Commission of Hong Kong (2004) Civil Liability for Invasion of Privacy
Victoria Law Reform Commission (2002) Defining privacy. Occasional Paper
Privacy Committee of New South Wales (1980) Privacy protection: guidelines or legislation?

Electronic Materials

Women's health religious action center of reform Judaism http://rac.org/advocacy/issues/issuewh/. Accessed 8 April 2011
Burnheim S (1997) Freedom of expression on trial: Caselaw under European convention on human rights. Ko'aga Roñe'eta http://www.derechos.org/koaga/i/burnheim.html#N_1_. Accessed 8 April 2011
Undermining Freedom of Expression in China (2006) Amnesty International http://www.amnestyusa.org/business/Undermining_Freedom_of_Expression_in_China.pdf. Accessed 8 April 2011

Chapter 6
Establishing an Effective Personal Information Protection Regime in China

6.1 Introduction

Rapid developments of technology in China over the last 30 years have made it very easy to use personal information or data for inappropriate uses. Moreover, the laissez-faire attitude of Chinese governments to privacy issues has allowed the improper use of personal information to not only increase but also become flourish in China. Even though China has witnessed massive and rapid enactment of laws and regulations in the 1980s and 1990s,[1] the Chinese law-makers did not pay enough attention to privacy and information protection issues. For example, both the right to privacy and the privacy protection legislation have been ignored until now. Chinese law-makers merely enacted three Civil Judicial Interpretations to develop expertise in this area in 1988, 1993, and 2001, respectively.[2] However, three mere Civil Judicial Interpretations cannot protect privacy effectively. Although, in 2008, the *Amendment Seven to the Criminal Law of the PRC (Draft)* proposes to add a provision to protect privacy under the Chinese Criminal law, the loopholes of this provision are still obvious. Both the legal subjects and the scope of the protection are not sufficient. This provision only regulates the practices of the personnel of financial, telecommunications, communications, educational, and medical work units; while the objects of this provision are only to restrict the disclosure and trade of individual's information.[3] Therefore, the author believes

[1] See Sect. 2.2.1.

[2] These three Civil Judicial Interpretations are *Opinions of the Supreme People's Court on Several Issues concerning the Implementation of the General Principles of the Civil Law of the People's Republic of China 1988* (For Trial Implementation), *Reply to Several Questions on Adjudicating the Cases of the Rights of Reputation 1993*, and *Interpretation of the Supreme People's Court Regarding issues of Ascertaining the Liability of Compensation for Spiritual Damage for Tort 2001* respectively.

[3] *Standing Committee of the National People's Congress conducted the first reading of Amendment Seven to the Criminal Law of the PRC (Draft) 2007*, art 6.

H. Wang, *Protecting Privacy in China*,
DOI 10.1007/978-3-642-21750-0_6,

that some serious privacy problems still exist in China. First, individual's privacy is still placed at risk because the Chinese authorities and businesses have no standards to provide effective protection for personal information that they are keeping; second, the Chinese authorities are able to exchange personal information freely without legal supervision; third, new information technology will continue to be introduced into China; and so on. In consequence, the privacy interests of Chinese people have not been well protected so far.

In addition, as mentioned in Chap. 4, in order to encourage the constant improvement of the living conditions of people, preserve and strengthen peace and liberty, and promote democracy on the basis of the fundamental rights and establish a global strategy for information security, the Council of the European Communities enacted the EU Directive 95/46/EC concerning the protection of personal data.[4] The EU Directive 95/46/EC was implemented by the end of 1995. The European Community proposes that the transfer to a third country of personal data, whether are undergoing processing or are intended for processing and whether the source is public or private sector, should be permitted when the third country in question ensures an adequate level of protection.[5] Therefore, if China hopes to take part in the global information community and achieve its benefits fully, China must set up an effective and adequate privacy protection regime. Otherwise, both privacy protection and information transfers will be damaged in the near future. All these tell us that establishing an effective information protection regime is necessary in China.

This chapter proposes a model for effective information protection in China. This chapter sets out the basic requirements for an effective privacy and information protection regime for China. It addresses a number of issues, such as how to develop constitutional protection of privacy, how to enact a single information protection law that would cover the mainland China, how to utilize the existing privacy protection, and so on. Moreover, the role of Chinese government, the role of the Chinese Information Protection Law, and the need for the individual responsibility will be addressed briefly. In the last part of the chapter, the possible content of information privacy protection legislation for China is outlined.

6.2 Developing Constitutional Protection

The *Constitution of 1982* is the most important legislation in the PRC. It is the fundamental law in China and has the highest legal power.[6] Some Chinese scholars thus point out that the right to privacy should be ensured in the Chinese

[4] *Directive 95/46/EC*, recitals 1.

[5] *Directive 95/46/EC*, art 25.

[6] *Constitution of the People's Republic of China* 1982, art 5.

Constitution, and this will "promote and encourage its protection by increasing Chinese citizens' recognition of the right's importance."[7] Although such an approach was considered desirable, the problems still exist. Firstly, as discussed in Chap. 3 of this book, the *Constitution of 1982* only protects basic citizens' rights against private actions in practice. It is unlikely to establish a right that may conflict with other existing values of Chinese government. Secondly, it has been argued that if there is no clear definition of privacy or other supporting legislation, the right to privacy in the Chinese Constitution may not be used in the way it should be.[8] Therefore, it is not appropriate for China to add "the right to privacy" to the Chinese Constitution directly. Before the establishment of the right to privacy, the author believes that, at least, two things should be done in China. Firstly, China must clear understand that, although the aim of the Chinese Constitution is to consolidate the socialism in China, there is no inherent conflict between the China's national structure and the functions that are conducted by the right to privacy; secondly, the independent information privacy protection law must be created. The information privacy protection law, as supporting law, will give clear and adequate guidance to help Chinese people to understand what privacy and privacy protection are. Based on these two premises, the right to privacy in the Chinese Constitution will be used in an appropriate way.

In addition, it should be noted that China has signed the ICCPR in 1998. The Chinese government has indicated that China will ratify the ICCPR when the conditions are right on many occasions.[9] Moreover, based on the ICCPR, the Second Session of the Tenth National People's Congress adopted an amendment of the Constitution of the PRC in 2004. This amendment adds "Human Rights" into the Chinese Constitution and clearly states that the human right in China should be respected and protected. It is thus a good signal that, at the time of developing the economy, China has also paid attention to the human rights, and the right to privacy as one of basic human rights is no exception.

6.3 Information Privacy Protection Law

6.3.1 Guideline or Legislation?

Theoretically, at present, there are two approaches for obtaining effective privacy protection practices around the world: the guideline approach and the legislation approach.[10] The guideline approach, which includes voluntary guidelines or

[7] Chao (2005), p. 661.
[8] Chao (2005), p. 661.
[9] Lee (2007), p. 457.
[10] Privacy Committee of New South Wales 1980, p. 8.

guidelines within a framework of legislation, allows society to achieve its legitimate aims without undue intrusions into people's lives.[11] However, it has been argued that the guideline approach is a not a formal agreement, it cannot effectively prevent privacy interferences by "those who ignore all but the strict letter of the law."[12] Compared to the legislation approach, it is easy for people to ignore the guideline approach because it does not have legal force. Furthermore, the ALRC points out that "an approach that relies solely on guidelines is that it tends to concentrate on particular sectors of activity, particular areas of concern or particular problems that arise. There is the risk of a total lack of protection in areas not covered by up-to-date guidelines."[13] Therefore, if voluntary guidelines were developed in China, the level of protection to the individual's personal privacy would fall and the effective benefits would diminish.[14] As a consequence, all these tell us that the guideline approach for protecting privacy is not suitable in China.

On the other hand, nowadays, more and more international instruments require different countries to enact their own information privacy protection legislations. The most famous instruments among them are the OECD Guidelines and the EU Directive 95/46/EC, respectively. The OECD Guidelines encourage countries to adopt privacy policies, whether implemented by legal, self-regulatory, administrative or technological means.[15] The EU Directive 95/46/EC, as mentioned earlier, emphasizes that the transfer of personal data to a third country should be permitted only when the third country in question ensures an adequate level of protection.[16] According to the EU Directive 95/46/EC, once China fails to enact privacy and personal information protection legislation, the adverse economic consequences will be inevitable. In addition, certain Western developed countries experiences have shown that the legislation approach will promote "greater awareness and understanding of relative rights and duties, desired standards of practice and available remedies."[17] Based on discussed earlier, it is thus clear that a legislative approach for information privacy protection is desirable in China. The author's recommendation is that there should be information privacy protection legislation in China.

[11] Privacy Committee of New South Wales 1980, p. 8.

[12] Australian Law Reform Commission 1983, p. 84.

[13] Australian Law Reform Commission 1983, p. 84.

[14] Privacy Committee of New South Wales 1980, p. 8.

[15] OECD Minister 1998.

[16] *Directive 95/46/EC*, recitals 1.

[17] Privacy Committee of New South Wales 1991, p. 27.

6.3.2 Privacy Protection and Personal Information Protection

The definition of privacy has been discussed in Chap. 1. There are many reasons why we should provide protection to privacy. One is privacy has instrumental value.[18] The protection of privacy provides opportunity to individual to free from disturbance or intrusion. In addition, legal privacy protection will ensure Chinese government to acknowledge the existence of different privacy interests in China and to provide remedies to victims when privacy invasions happened. By contrast, personal information consists of those facts, communications, or opinions which relate to the individual and which it would be reasonable to expect him to regard as intimate or sensitive and therefore to want to withhold or at least to restrict their collection, use, or circulation.[19] In West, the prevalent view is that the personal information about individuals is collected, used and disclosed is a matter of privacy concern.[20] Indeed, the invasion of an individual's privacy can be seen as the invasion of his or her personal information. Especially, with the rapid development of information processing technology, more and more Chinese people are concerned for whether their privacy has been collected and disclosed through these information processing technologies. Therefore, in current Chinese society, the main concern of privacy protection is how to deal with the collection, disclose, use or storage of personal information. All these mentioned earlier is the reason why the author links "privacy protection" and "personal information protection" together. The author hopes that there should be independent information privacy protection legislation in China. This is an effective way to identify and address privacy problems precisely.

6.3.3 Should the Chinese Information Protection Legislation Apply to the Private Sector?

The third issue is whether the proposed Chinese information privacy protection legislation should apply to the public sector only, or be available to the private sector alike. Today, with the rapid development of economy in China, more and more Chinese people's interests and benefits depend on the use of information and data that are held by private organisations. Therefore, an attempt to avoid the issue of private sector coverage and simply to recommend legislation for the public sector is irresponsible and ill-advised.[21] Moreover, the EU Directive 95/46/EC requires that:

---

[18] See Sect. 1.2.2.

[19] Wacks (1989), p. 26.

[20] Australian Law Reform Commission 1983, p. 78.

[21] Privacy Committee of New South Wales 1991, p. 35.

> The member states and the Commission, in their respective spheres of competence, must encourage the trade associations and other representative organizations concerned to draw up codes of conduct so as to facilitate the application of the Directive, taking account of the specific characteristics of the processing carried out in certain sectors, and respecting the national provisions adopted for its implementation.[22]

In fact, this can be understood as meaning that the EU Directive requires the private sector to accept certain obligations in respect of the processing of personal information.[23] In addition, as mentioned earlier, the EU Directive 95/46/EC also emphasizes that the transfer of personal data to a third country should be permitted only when the third country in question ensures an adequate level of protection. Therefore, China's businesses that run in Europe or trade with Europe will be influenced by the EU Directive 95/46/EC inevitably. According to the EU Directive 95/46/EC, these businesses must show that their practices of exchanging personal information with Europe meet the standards of the EU Directive 95/46/EC. It will thus be significant to set up some provisions, which are able to cover the private sector in the Chinese information protection legislation, to ensure that Chinese government and business will be advantaged in practice.

6.3.4 *Effective Information Privacy Protection Legislation*

6.3.4.1 The Scope of the Proposed Information Privacy Protection Legislation

What Information Is Covered?

As discussed earlier, the proposed information privacy protection legislation should protect the personal information that relates to an identifiable individual.

Personal Information

The EU Directive 95/46/EC defines "personal data" as:

> any information relating to an identified or identifiable natural person (data subject); an identifiable person is one who can be identified, directly or indirectly, in particular by reference to an identification number or to one or more factors specific to his physical, physiological, mental, economic, cultural or social identity.[24]

---

[22] *Directive 95/46/EC*, recitals 61.

[23] Privacy Committee of New South Wales 1991, p. 35.

[24] *Directive 95/46/EC*, art 2 (a).

Similarly, "personal data" means "any information relating to an identified or identifiable individual" under the OECD Guidelines.[25] Based on these definitions, it has been argued that:

> Personal information includes written or electronic records about individuals such as social security records and doctors' records, but may also include photos or videos, where the person can be identified from the context or in other ways. A person's name appearing on a list of clients or patients may also fall within the definition of personal information because the context provides information, possibly sensitive personal information, about the individual.[26]

It should be noted that the rapid developments of technology make it very difficult to define "personal information," "processed information" and "information files" precisely. However, both the Australian and the Canadian approach have avoided the problems. That is because the Australian *Privacy Act of 1988* (Cth) applies to "personal information whether recorded in a material form or not."[27] Similarly, in Canadian *Privacy Act* (1983), personal information means "information about an identifiable individual that is recorded in any form."[28] Clearly, these two Acts focus on certain personal information in any form. In order words, these two countries adopt a broader definition of "personal information." Moreover, the EU Directive 95/46/EC states that "the protection of individuals must apply as much to automatic processing of data as to manual processing."[29] In fact, manual systems may contain sensitive information not readily stored in a computerized form.[30] If manual systems were exempted from the proposed Chinese privacy protection legislation, the possibility of evasion of lawful standards by the use of parallel manual files would arise.[31] Thus, in order to avoid problems with definitions in China, and consistent with the EU Directive, the proposed Chinese information privacy protection legislation should apply to personal information however recorded.

Sensitive Information

"Sensitive information" is a kind of personal information. Most people will be vexed if their sensitive information is collected or disclosed. Thus, a number of developed countries' information protection legislation have given a higher level of protection to sensitive personal information. For example, in the United Kingdom, sensitive personal data means personal data consisting of information as to:

---

[25] *Guidelines on the Protection of Privacy and Transborder Flows of Personal Data* (1980), art 1.

[26] Australian Law Reform Commission 2006, p. 107.

[27] *Privacy Act 1988* (Cth), s 6(1).

[28] *Privacy Act 1983* (Canada), s 3.

[29] *Directive 95/46/EC*, recitals 27.

[30] Australian Law Reform Commission 1980, p. 91.

[31] Australian Law Reform Commission 1980, p. 91.

(a) The racial or ethnic origin of the data subject
(b) His political opinions
(c) His religious beliefs or other beliefs of a similar nature
(d) Whether he is a member of a trade union (within the meaning of the [1992 c. 52.] Trade Union and Labor Relations (Consolidation) Act 1992)
(e) His physical or mental health or condition
(f) His sexual life
(g) The commission or alleged commission by him of any offence or
(h) Any proceedings for any offence committed or alleged to have been committed by the data subject, the disposal of such proceedings or the sentence of any court in such proceedings.[32]

Similarly, in Australia, sensitive information has also been protected under the NPPs.[33] As a matter of principle, in some Western countries, the sensitive personal information will be collected or disclosed only under the special protection.

On the other hand, it is not an easy task to ensure just what kind of information should be regarded as sensitive. Neither the OECD Guidelines nor the Council of Europe Convention specifically addresses sensitive information.[34] The OECD Guidelines deliberately avoid the question. As the OECD Guidelines states "it is probably not possible to identify a set of data which are universally regarded as being sensitive."[35] In fact, it has been argued in Australia that "the problem of definition of classes of information that will always be regarded as sensitive is an almost insurmountable one."[36] This conclusion based on different reasons: first, it is impossible to secure agreement on what information is to be regarded as sensitive; second, the perceptions of sensitivity vary over time; and third, cultural difference.[37] In the author's view, unless some exemptions are established in the proposed Chinese privacy protection law, it should bear in mind that any sensitive information should not be disclosed or collected by information users in China. These exemptions should grant for national security, proper administration of justice, diction of crime, collection of taxes and so on.[38] The author believes that whether to give sensitive personal information a higher level of protection under the Chinese Information Protection Legislation needs further consideration.

---

[32] *Data Protection Act 1998* (UK), s 2.

[33] *Privacy Act 1988* (Cth), s 6(1).

[34] Australian Law Reform Commission 2006, p. 109.

[35] *Guidelines on the Protection of Privacy and Transborder Flows of Personal Data* (1980), Explanatory Memorandum 19 (a); see also Australian Law Reform Commission 2006, p. 109.

[36] Australian Law Reform Commission 1983, p. 94.

[37] Australian Law Reform Commission 1983, p. 94.

[38] See Sect. 6.3.4.3.

Who Will Be Affected by the Proposed Legislation?

In the case of the proposed Chinese information privacy legislation, the activity and the persons regulated should be those who process personal information. The author specifies two groups that will be affected: information subject and information user.

Information Subject

Any person to whom personal information or data relates should be an "information subject" in China. In West, it has been held that every individual anywhere in the world will be an information subject, and "there is no minimum age limit" for an information subject.[39]

It should be noted that, whether "information subject" should include persons who are not individuals, such as "legal persons," is an issue that has been debated worldwide. At present, the prevalent approach is to exclude legal persons and to apply the privacy protection for the natural persons only, although the possibility of extending privacy protection to legal persons has already been provided for in the OECD Guidelines.[40] The reason is that a number of developed countries' experiences have demonstrated that "it is difficult to define clearly the dividing line between personal and non-personal information or between the individual entitled to protection and the small business or group claiming protection."[41] In addition, the ALRC points out that:

> This issue has political and economic implications. Fears have been expressed that, if a corporation had to disclose identifiable information about legal persons, it might be forced into disclosure of its research on a rival or competing corporation, association, firm or small business.[42]

Therefore, the author's recommendation is that, at the moment, it is not necessary to consider whether to expand privacy protection to legal persons in China. It may be better to consider the extension of the Chinese information protection legislation to protect defined legal persons in the future. Moreover, it is also an alternative way to develop the company law of the PRC as parallel legislation to protect privacy information for legal persons in China. These are matters that the Chinese law-makers should pay more attention.

---

[39] Savage and Edwards (1985), p. 24.

[40] Australian Law Reform Commission 1983, p. 198.

[41] Australian Law Reform Commission 1983, p. 198.

[42] Australian Law Reform Commission 1983, p. 198.

Information User

Any person will be "information users" if they are able to hold and control over information or data. Usually, in West, the following conditions decide whether a person is deemed to hold information or data:

1. The data forms part of a collection of data processed or intended to be processed by, or on behalf of, that person on equipment operating automatically and
2. That person controls both the contents and the use of the data in the collection and
3. The data is in a form in which it is intended to be, or has been, processed. Even if the data are not in such a form, they are covered if it is in a form into which they have been converted after being so proceed, and with a view to being further processed on a subsequent occasion.[43]

According to Chinese law, the term "information user" should encompass both Citizen (Natural Person) Legal Persons and any corporate bodies.[44] Moreover, official organ, institution and social organization as legal persons should be subject to the same obligations and liabilities under the proposed privacy protection legislation.[45] It should be comprehended that the individual or groups will be the information user if they are able to hold and control the content or use of information or data. That is to say it is not necessary to own or see a medium such as computer in order to be an information user.[46]

6.3.4.2 Basic Principles for the Information Protection

Introduction

Personal information protection principles are the basic rules governing the collection, handling, use and disclosure of personal information. The most famous statement of the privacy protection principles is stated in the OECD Guidelines. The OECD Guidelines sets out eight basic principles of national application in part two, which include: collection limitation principle, data quality principle, purpose specification principle, use limitation principle, security safeguards principle, openness principle, individual participation principle and accountability principle respectively.[47] The EU Directive 95/46/EC, in some respects, strengthens the

[43] Savage and Edwards (1985), p. 22.

[44] *General Principles of the Civil Law of the People's Republic of China* 1986, ch II and ch III s 1, s 2.

[45] *General Principles of the Civil Law of the People's Republic of China* 1986, ch II and ch III s 3.

[46] Savage and Edwards (1985), p. 22.

[47] *Guidelines on the Protection of Privacy and Transborder Flows of Personal Data* (1980), principles 7–14.

standards expressed in the OECD Guidelines, and emphasizes that the protection principles must apply to all processing of personal data by any person whose activities are governed by Community Law.[48] Today, privacy protection principles have been incorporated in privacy and information protection laws in many countries. Therefore, personal information protection principles are the standards which should be imposed on all organizations and individuals who possess or process personal information in China, and these principles also need to be adopted by the proposed Chinese information protection legislation. In order to establish effective privacy and personal information protection for China, the following paragraphs discuss the implementation of these principles.

Collection Limitation Principle

The collection limitation principle is clearly expressed in the OECD Guidelines in the following terms: "there should be limits to the collection of personal data and any such data should be obtained by lawful and fair means, and, where appropriate, which the knowledge or consent of the data subject." [49] There are two aims of this principle. The first essential aim of the collection principle, in fact, is to ensure that any person has the right to decide whether or not to provide their personal information to the information users or collectors. The second aim of this principle is to regulate the conducts of the information users, collectors, or keepers.

The proposed Chinese privacy protection legislation thus should ensure that a Chinese citizen could be "informed of the nature of the collection, the uses to which the information will be put, and whether the information will be available to third parties," before his/her personal information is collected.[50] In some cases, the purpose for which the personal information is being collected is easy to understand; for example, when a person is asked to give details of his income and assets when applying for a credit card. In some more complicated cases, at the time of collecting, a formal written statement of the details of collection should be presented to the individual.[51]

Some collections may be by legal compulsion, where the collection of personal information is authorized or required by law.[52] Therefore, under this situation, the individual has no choice to avoid the collections. However, in west, it has been held that legal compulsion is not sufficient excuse to deny the information subject's right to know the aims and purposes of the collection.[53] Therefore, the proposed Chinese

[48] *Directive 95/46/EC*, recitals 12.

[49] *Guidelines on the Protection of Privacy and Transborder Flows of Personal Data* (1980), principle 7.

[50] Australian Law Reform Commission 1980, p. 28.

[51] Australian Law Reform Commission 1980, p. 28.

[52] Australian Law Reform Commission 1983, p. 90.

[53] Australian Law Reform Commission 1983, p. 90.

information privacy protection law should ensure that the information subject will be entitled "to know not only the aims and purposes of the collection, but also the consequences prescribed for breach of the law in question."[54] By contrast, in the cases where the collections are not by legal compulsion, the co-operation between information subject and information collector should be voluntary. Moreover, based on the Western developed countries' experiences, the Chinese law-makers should take care in the way that the information subject is informed, so as to avoid damaging the relationship between the information subject and the information collector by undue emphasis on penalties prescribed for failure to cooperate.[55]

In addition, care should also be taken that not all information is collected directly from the person it concerns.[56] Sometimes, information is collected from third parties. It has been held that this is significant to ensure the relationship between the information controller and information subject is as fair as possible.[57] Therefore, if an information collector wants to collect information from the third party, he should inform the information subject that the information will be collected.

Data Quality Principle

Both the OECD Guidelines and the EU Directive 95/46/EC emphasize the significance of data quality. The principle 8 of the OECD Guidelines states that "personal data should be relevant to the purposes for which they are to be used, and, to the extent necessary for those purposes, should be accurate, complete and kept up to date." Similarly, article 6(d) of the EU Directive 95/46/EC stresses that the "personal data must be accurate and, where necessary, kept up to date; every reasonable step must be taken to ensure that data which are inaccurate or incomplete, having regard to the purposes for which they were collected or for which they are further processed, are erased or rectified." Based on these explanations, it is clear that this principle requires that not only the collection of the information should be fair and lawful, but also the information itself should be accurate, complete and kept up to date.

The proposed Chinese privacy protection legislation thus should require that personal information held by information controllers be accurate, relevant and uptodate. In order to achieve this aim, some reasonable steps must be taken: first, the information subject should have right to confirm whether an information controller maintains his or her personal information; second, the information subject should have right to access the maintained information; and third, the information subject should have right to challenge the qualities (such as accuracy,

[54] Australian Law Reform Commission 1980, p. 29.

[55] Australian Law Reform Commission 1980, p. 29.

[56] Australian Law Reform Commission 1983, p. 90.

[57] Australian Law Reform Commission 1983, p. 90.

relevant and timeliness) of that information and the right to modify the maintained information. The basic reason for allowing information subjects to access and amend the records of personal information kept about them is to ensure that, when decisions are made on the basis of that information, it is as accurate and complete as possible.[58]

Purpose Specification Principle

The "purpose specification" principle is also one of the fundamental principles of privacy protection. This principle requires that the purposes to collect personal information "should be specified not later than at the time of information collection and the subsequent use limited to the fulfillment of those purposes or such others as are not incompatible with those purposes and as are specified on each occasion of change of purpose."[59] In order words, this principle requires the information collectors who are going to collect other people's personal information to present a purpose in good faith.

On the other hand, it should be understood that the necessity to present a purpose for seeking access cannot always prevent some individuals from seeking access inappropriately. Therefore, in order to ensure that the offender can be identified and appropriate action can be taken in the case of inappropriate access, there is a need for adequate audit trails in China.[60] An essential component of this audit trail is to check the identity of the applicant or user of the information.[61] This procedure will reduce the possibility of misusing personal information in China.

Security Safeguards Principle

Principle 11 of the OECD Guidelines states that "personal data should be protected by reasonable security safeguards against such risks as loss or unauthorized access, destruction, use, modification or disclosure of data." Without information and data security there can be no prospect of privacy protection.[62] Therefore, the proposed Chinese information privacy protection legislation should provide some appropriate security means to insure the protection of information privacy from improper collection, disclosure, and use.

---

[58] Australian Law Reform Commission 1983, p. 107.

[59] *Guidelines on the Protection of Privacy and Transborder Flows of Personal Data*, principle 9.

[60] Privacy Committee of New South Wales 1991, p. 24.

[61] Privacy Committee of New South Wales 1991, p. 24.

[62] Privacy Committee of New South Wales 1991, p. 23.

In principle, as the Privacy Committee of New South Wales states that:

> regard should be had to physical safeguards (such as locked filing cabinets and doors, identification cards and so on), organizational safeguards (such as graded access to data so that only those with a need to know and sufficient authority can obtain access) and informational safeguards (such as passwords, PIN codes, encryption of data, monitoring of unusual access patterns, logging of access, and so on).[63]

In practice, according to the principles of the EU Directive 95/46/EC, the proposed Chinese privacy law must ensure that: first, the information controller must implement appropriate means to protect personal information against "accidental or unlawful destruction or accidental loss, alteration, unauthorized disclosure or access, in particular where the processing involves the transmission of data over a network, and against all other unlawful forms of processing"[64]; second, the information controller also needs to "choose a processor providing sufficient guarantees in respect of technical security measures and organizational measures governing the processing to be carried out, and must ensure compliance with those measures."[65] In addition, different practical means, such as appropriately maintain data or information in different copies, can also minimize the possibility of misuse of data in China.

Openness Principle

Principle 12 of the OECD Guideline states that:

> There should be a general policy of openness about developments, practices and policies with respect to personal data. Means should be readily available of establish the existence and nature of personal data, and the main purposes of their use, as well as the identity and usual residence of the data controller.

Based on this principle, it is clear that openness about developments, practices and policies with respect to personal information or data is one of the main aims of privacy protection law worldwide. In order to achieve this aim, it has been recommended in advanced Western countries that, at the time personal information is collected from an individual that individual should be informed of "(1) the purposes for which the information is collected; and (2) the categories of individuals and organizations to whom that information may lawfully be disclosed (e.g. taxation and welfare authorities)."[66]

In addition, article 18(1) of the EU Directive 95/46/EC clearly states that information controller or user "must notify the supervisory authority ... before carrying out any ... operation or set of such operations intended to serve a single

---

[63] Privacy Committee of New South Wales 1991, p. 23.

[64] *Directive 95/46/EC*, art 17 (1).

[65] *Directive 95/46/EC*, art 17 (2).

[66] Privacy Committee of New South Wales 1991, p. 24.

purpose or several related purposes." In fact, this is also an effective way to achieve "openness." The type of information which must be registered includes "the name and address of the information controller and of his representative, the purpose or purposes of the processing, a description of the category or categories of data subject and of the data or categories of data relating to them description of the type of information it contains, the third parties to whom it might be communicated, and information security measures" respectively.[67] In West, a number of countries already implemented procedures for the notification or registration of information or data holdings, which include Australia, the United Kingdom, Germany, France, Denmark, Ireland, the Netherlands, Norway, Sweden and Canada.[68] Therefore, the proposed Chinese information privacy protection legislation should provide for the notification of both public and private sectors holdings of personal information or data.

Evaluation

At present, the existing models of privacy principles are different in the level of detail and guidance that they provide around the world.[69] For example, the privacy principles in the OECD Guidelines are considered as high level, while the health privacy principles in Victoria are considerably more detailed.[70] A significant question thus emerges in China as to whether the proposed information privacy protection principles should be more detailed, or they should provide high level guidance in China only. With respect to these two models, the author believes that unduly detailed obligations are not flexible. By contrast, the advantage of adopting high level principles is obvious. It has been held that high level principles are more flexible to accommodate unforeseen circumstances and to change technological environment.[71] As the APEC Privacy Framework (2005) points out that "the 1980 OECD Guidelines were drafted at a high level that makes them still relevant today. In many ways, the OECD Guidelines represent the international consensus on what constitutes honest and trustworthy treatment of personal information."[72] Therefore, high level privacy principles will be more beneficial to China. The author's recommendation is therefore that the Chinese privacy legislation should adopt personal information protection principles in broad terms.

[67] *Directive 95/46/EC*, art 19 (1).

[68] Privacy Committee of New South Wales 1991, p. 37.

[69] Australian Law Reform Commission 2006, p. 201.

[70] Australian Law Reform Commission 2006, p. 201.

[71] Australian Law Reform Commission 2006, p. 201.

[72] APEC Privacy Framework 2005; see Sect. 2.2.1 of this book.

6.3.4.3 Exemptions

Generally

The information privacy protection and the right to privacy are not absolute. Therefore, the privacy protection principles must be formulated and applied in practice with care. Usually, exemptions in a privacy or information privacy protection law are granted for national security, proper administration of justice and diction of crime or the collection of taxes.[73] For example, article 13 of the EU Directive 95/46/EC contains a number of exemptions from the protection principles. These exemptions include national security, defense, public security, criminal law enforcement, economic development and so on.[74] Based on the standard of the EU Directive 95/46/EC, the author believes that the proposed Chinese privacy legislation should also allow certain exemptions from privacy protection principles' requirements. Under these exemptions, other existing values in China can be protected.

First, personal information held for the purpose of national security, public security, criminal law enforcement and tax information should be exempted from the proposed information privacy protection law. In China, the state security, public security, criminal law enforcement and taxes are the bases for protecting the State power of the people's democratic dictatorship and the socialist system. They are foundation to achieve the socialist modernization in China. All these have been emphasized in the Chinese Constitution. Therefore, China must protect state security and society security effectively.

Second, personal information held for the purpose of statistical, research, education, social work, and other purposes that 'do not pose a particular threat to the privacy of information subjects' should be exempted from the proposed information protection law.[75] Normally, in the area of research and education, much information and knowledge are kept or processed is anonymized, and personal identifier have been stripped out and providing individuals and their associated information cannot be reconstructed.[76] Therefore, in these areas, the information used is not for recognizing any particular person. That is to say, if there is no risk of endangering the privacy of information subject, the assessment or collection of information or data should be exempted.

On the other hand, it has been argued that national and local authorities with license to infinitely restrict privacy rights in any case may lead to citizens are defenseless against governmental intrusions into their private place and space.[77] As

[73] Savage and Edwards (1985), p. 31.

[74] *Directive 95/46/EC*, art 13.

[75] Savage and Edwards (1985), p. 31.

[76] Bainbridge (2001), pp. 180–181.

[77] Oxman (2000–2001), p. 196.

Professor Roger Clarke points out that "when a general statement of principle is used, and a class of organization or activity is exempted from it, the protections are entirely lost: there remains no segment of the Principle to which the organization or activity is subject."[78] Therefore, it should be clearly understood that the Chinese proposed information privacy legislation should also have appreciate limitation on any proposed exemptions. In order to help Chinese law-makers to consider reasonable exemptions in the proposed legislation, the exemptions in this book are drafted broadly. However, it is important that the Chinese law-makers use this room not to further expand the exemptions, but rather to strictly define their scope.[79]

The Number of Exemptions

The OECD Guidelines states that, in order to limit the application of the Guidelines, there should be a provision dealing with exceptions, the number of exceptions to the privacy principles, however, should be as few as possible.[80] Likewise, APEC Privacy Framework states that exceptions contained in this Framework should be limited and proportional to meeting the objectives to which the exceptions relate.[81] Therefore, "keeping exemptions to a minimum and limiting them to particular provisions" will be significant to ensure that privacy protection in China applies as widely as possible.[82]

Location of the Exemption Provisions

Based on other countries' successful privacy or information protection legislation, the Chinese law-makers should set out exceptions together in one part of the proposed information privacy protection legislation, which will make the exemption provisions more accessible and clear.[83] For example, the main exemptions under the *Data Protection Act of 1998* (UK) appear in the Part IV. Various miscellaneous exemptions and transitional exemptions are listed in Schedules 7 and 8, respectively.

---

[78] Clarke (1998), p. 2.

[79] Oxman (2000–2001), p. 203.

[80] *Guidelines on the Protection of Privacy and Transborder Flows of Personal Data*, Explanatory Memorandum, para 4, 46.

[81] *APEC Privacy Framework* 2005, 13 (a).

[82] Australian Law Reform Commission 2006, p. 207.

[83] Australian Law Reform Commission 2006, p. 207.

6.3.4.4 Personal Information Protection Authority

Today, independent information privacy protection authority has been deemed as one of the key elements in effective privacy protection. The EU Directive 95/46/EC requires member states to establish an independent qualified authority to monitor the data protection within its territory of the provisions adopted by the member states pursuant to this Directive.[84] According to the EU Directive 95/46/EC, the authority should be invested with (1) investigative powers "to collect all the information necessary for the performance of its supervisory duties"; (2) effective powers of invention to ensure that data protection principles will be carried out appropriately; and (3) the power to "engage in legal proceedings."[85] The functions and powers of the privacy protection authority are examined in detail in the following paragraphs.

The Functions of the Privacy Protection Authority

The privacy protection authority's functions have been set out in a number of advanced Western countries' privacy acts. After summarizing these functions, the author concludes that the general functions of the proposed Chinese information privacy protection authority should include: (1) promoting and perfecting general privacy protection principles; (2) researching and investigating acts, practices or developments in information processing and computer technology to ensure the adverse influences are minimized in China; (3) ensuring agencies, which may handle personal information, to comply with the proposed privacy protection principles; (4) considering the Chinese information privacy protection legislation in all reasonable areas and ensuring that any adverse conflicts between privacy and other competing interests are minimized; and (5) providing advice to the Chinese NPC, Chinese government, and others. In addition, China's international obligations and relevant international guidelines on privacy should also be considered carefully.

The Powers of the Privacy Protection Authority

Based on Western developed countries' experiences, powers of the Chinese information protection authority should be considered in three groups, which are oversight powers, compliance powers, and complaint handling powers respectively.

First, the Chinese privacy protection authority should have general powers to oversee the operation of the proposed Chinese information privacy protection

[84] *Directive 95/46/EC*, art 28 (1).

[85] *Directive 95/46/EC*, art 28 (3).

legislation. Usually, the general oversight powers should "relate to the giving of advice, research and monitoring of technological developments and education."[86] Second, the privacy authority should have general powers to monitor and promote compliance with the proposed Chinese information privacy protection legislation, such as powers to monitor whether the proposed legislation has been complied and to investigate privacy issues. Finally, the effective privacy authority should also have complaint-handling powers. For instance, after conducting investigations into a complaint, the privacy authority needs to make a decision to judge whether the complainant's rights under the proposed Chinese information privacy protection legislation have or have not been invaded. The decision of the privacy authority may also include whether compensation should be paid to the complainant. The decisions of the privacy authority should be enforced in the Chinese basic people's court.

6.3.4.5 The New Rights for Chinese Information Subjects

As mentioned earlier, in the personal information regime, Chinese law-makers should pay attention to fair information practices between information subject and information user. It is thus to be expected that the proposed Chinese information privacy protection legislation should give individuals the right to protect themselves when their personal information is being collected or used by others. In this book, the new rights that may be granted for Chinese information subjects include: the right to access; the right to amendment; the right to compensation; and the right to be informed respectively. The following paragraphs discuss these possible new rights.

The Right to Access

In West, recognition of the right of the individuals in receiving access to information held about them has been seen as fundamental to the protection of their interest in information privacy.[87] This right is the right to access. The subject of this right is the information subject himself. The right to access can help an individual to check what personal information about him has been held by the information collector or user. In addition, the right to access can also protect the information subject from use by the information controller of inaccurate, out of date or misleading personal information when the information controller makes decisions about the information subject.[88]

---

[86] Australian Law Reform Commission 2006, p. 282.

[87] Australian Law Reform Commission 1980, p. 37.

[88] Australian Law Reform Commission 1983, p. 140.

At present, the right to access has been recognized in many Western developed countries such as the United States[89] and the United Kingdom.[90] A 1974 Report to the United States Senate on the subject of criminal records offered the main reasons for adopting right to access, which are:

> First, an important cause of fear and distrust of computerized data systems has been the feelings of powerlessness they provoke in many citizens. The computer has come to symbolize the unresponsiveness and insensitivity of modern life. Whatever may be thought of these reactions, unresponsiveness and insensitivity of modern life. Whatever may be much to disarm this hostility.
>
> Second, such rights promise to be the most viable of all the possible methods to guarantee the accuracy of data system. Unlike more complex internal mechanisms, they are triggered by the most powerful and consistent of motives, individual self-interest.
>
> Finally, it should now be plain that if any future system is to win public acceptance, it must offer persuasive evidence that it is quite seriously concerned with the rights and interests of those whose lives it will record. The committee can imagine no more effective evidence than authentic rights of access and challenge.[91]

To some extent, these reasons are also relevant to the Chinese debate.

The right to access, on the other hand, is not absolute. That is because the information is the property of the information controller rather than of the information subject.[92] For example, under the Chinese law, the information, no matter how intimate, is the property of the person who compiled it.[93] Therefore, the Chinese lawmakers should pay attention to balance the right to access and other existing rights in this area.

The Right to Amendment

In the information privacy protection regime, the right to amendment of personal information or data is a necessary adjunct to the right to access.[94] It has been argued that if the reason for the right to access is that the information subject can insure himself that the information controller's perception of him is correct, the right to ensure that the records are amended will naturally follow from this.[95] In addition, if the information consists of suggestions, comments, opinions and evaluations, the right to amendment will be more significant.

---

[89] *Privacy Act of 1974* (US) 5 USC 552 (a) d.

[90] *Data Protection Act 1998* (UK), s 7.

[91] Australian Law Reform Commission 1980, p. 38.

[92] Australian Law Reform Commission 1980, p. 42.

[93] *Copyright Law of the People's Republic of China* 1990, art 10.

[94] Australian Law Reform Commission 1983, p. 124.

[95] Australian Law Reform Commission 1983, p. 124.

The Right to Compensation

If the Chinese information privacy protection principles are adopted, the effect should be to entitle an individual who is the subject of personal information held by an information user, and who suffers damage by reason of the inaccuracy and unauthorized access of the information, to get compensation from the information user for such damage.

Based on the Western countries' experience, the right to compensation should not arise if the inaccurate information is received from the information subject or from a third party and that fact is indicated by the information, and, if the information subject has objected to the alleged inaccuracy, this objection has been noted in the information or data.[96] If damage is proved to have resulted from the unauthorized access, the information subject should be able to claim compensation from the information user. Under this situation, the right to compensation only exists where the information is disclosed without the authority of the user or where, as a result of his negligence, an outsider gains access to the information.[97]

The Right to be Informed

In the proposed information privacy protection legislation, the right to be informed should also be created. Usually, the aim of this right is to inform information subject any decisions that have been made against them on the basis of their personal information.[98] The notification should include information about their legal entitlement to exercise certain rights.[99] It has been held that the right to be informed is "thoroughly desirable as a good administrative practice."[100] The author believes that, at least, it will inform an individual that he has been entitled some legal rights.

6.3.4.6 Remedies

The EU Directive 95/46/EC emphasizes that "if the information controller fails to respect the rights of information subjects, national legislation must provide for a judicial remedy."[101] Therefore, if the proposed Chinese information privacy protection legislation creates privacy protection principles and rights for Chinese people, then remedies for breach of these standards should also be created by the

[96] Savage and Edwards (1985), pp. 97–98.
[97] Savage and Edwards (1985), p. 99.
[98] Australian Law Reform Commission 1983, p. 193.
[99] Australian Law Reform Commission 1983, p. 193.
[100] Australian Law Reform Commission 1983, p. 194.
[101] *Directive 95/46/EC*, recitals 55.

legislation. The following paragraphs discuss the remedies that should be created under the proposed Chinese personal information protection legislation.

Civil Compensation

As mentioned earlier, article 6 of the *Amendment Seven to the Criminal Law of the PRC (Draft)* proposes to add a provision on protection of privacy. This is the only law that protects privacy in China directly. However, with respect to civil compensation, this amendment only states that unlawful invasion of others citizens' individual information will be fined "if the circumstances are serious."[102] Therefore, in fact, there is no explicit recommendation of civil remedy has been made for interference with privacy under the Chinese law so far. It is thus necessary that, under the proposed Chinese information privacy protection legislation, damages for interference with privacy should be created. That means, under the proposed legislation, financial damages can be recoverable if it can be proved that the defendant has violated an individual's privacy interests. The Chinese privacy authority should investigate privacy issues and make a decision to judge whether the information protection principles under the proposed legislation have been invaded. Based on this decision, the privacy authority should decide whether the civil compensation should be paid to the complainant.

Criminal Penalties

It is also necessary that some activities that seriously invade other people's privacy should be punished criminally. With respect to the criminal penalties, article 6 of the *Amendment Seven to the Criminal Law of the PRC (Draft)* states that if the circumstances are serious where personnel of financial, telecommunications, communications, educational, and medical work units and the like who sell or unlawfully provide to others citizens' individual information that was obtained in carrying out their duties or in the course of providing services, they will be penalized with up to 3 years of fixed-term imprisonment or criminal detention. Other activities that have already been the subject of Chinese criminal law should be continued. After establishing the proposed information privacy protection legislation, Chinese basic people's count should have duties to enforce these standards through criminal sanction.

[102] *Standing Committee of the National People's Congress Conducted the First Reading of Amendment Seven to the Criminal Law of the PRC (Draft) 2007*, art 6.

6.4 Existing Laws and Structures

China should also pay more attention to existing privacy protection.

6.4.1 International Context

International privacy instruments have provided useful guiding principles. For example, the most famous of these, as discussed earlier, have been the OECD Guidelines and the EU Directive 95/46/EC. The ICCPR, which China has ratified, also clear states that "no one shall be subjected to arbitrary or unlawful interference with his privacy."[103] Since China entered the World Trade Organization (WTO), Chinese laws for privacy or personal information protection will be affected by these international instruments inevitably. Therefore, it is necessary to develop an expert privacy body to study foreign countries' advanced experiences of privacy protection, and also examine how China can learn from these countries.

6.4.2 Existing Laws and Structures

Western experiences of privacy protection also demonstrate that the development of privacy protection must consider the existing legal background and institutions of China.[104] That is because of using existing laws can avoid establishing an entire new law in different areas, which may produce uncertainties to Chinese legal system. Therefore, it is still appropriate to use or amend existing legislations that have privacy functions to protect privacy. Chapter 3 of this book has analyzed the laws that already exist in China and how they protect privacy interests. The following sections cover some examples, which need to be considered and reinforced in China.

6.4.2.1 Consumer Protection

The *Law of the PRC on the Protection of the Rights and Interests of Consumers* was enacted on 31 October 1993. The Act was designed to protect consumers' legal rights. However, this law does not pay enough attention to the protection of privacy and personal information. The provisions that are most protective of privacy only requires that "a business operator should not insult or slander consumers, search the

[103] *International Covenant on Civil and Political Rights*, art 17.

[104] Australian Law Reform Commission 1983, p. 183.

body of a consumer or articles carried by a consumer, and infringe upon the personal freedom of a consumer."[105] Obviously, the protection is not enough. Chinese law-makers should extend the framework of consumer protection to providing: (1) controls on advertising; and (2) specific controls on commercial practices which involve harassment or offence, particularly in the areas of door-to-door selling, inertia selling, mock auctions, pyramid and multi-level selling schemes, and referral selling.[106]

In addition, article 32 of the Law on Consumer states that China Consumers' Association should exercise the following duties and functions:

1. Provide information and advice services for consumers; participate in the supervision and inspection of commodities and services by the relevant administrative departments
2. Report to, inquire of or make suggestions to relevant administrative departments on issues concerning the legal rights and interests of consumers
3. Accept complaints by consumers and conduct investigation into and mediation of such complaints
4. Where a complaint involves issues concerning the quality of commodities and services, it may require an appraisal department to appraise the quality. Such appraisal department shall advise the appraisal findings
5. Assist aggrieved consumers in instituting legal proceedings against acts which harm the legal rights and interests of consumers and
6. Reveal and criticize acts harmful to the legal rights and interests of consumers through the mass media

Obviously, China Consumers' Association cannot deal with privacy issues effectively. In order to legally respond to the issues concerning privacy, the author believes that China Consumers' Association should also be empowered to deal with privacy issues. Ideally, the Association should be entitled to receive complaints of privacy invasion in any areas of commercial activity. Its duties should include: (1) investigating complaints; (2) informing general privacy principles; (3) notifying the resources of any government or industry bodies for whom such complaints should be of immediate concern; (4) aggregating experience of complaints; (5) making recommendations for new and specific laws in areas where they are shown to be needed and providing them to the Chinese NPC, Chinese government and others.[107]

---

[105] *Law of the PRC on the Protection of the Rights and Interests of Consumers*, art 25.

[106] Australian Law Reform Commission 1983, p. 285.

[107] Australian Law Reform Commission 1983, p. 286.

6.4.2.2 Workers' Rights

The *Labor Law of the PRC* prohibits discrimination in hiring, firing, or the terms of employment on the basis of someone's "race, colour, religion, sex, or national origin."[108] However, based on Western developed countries' experiences, the protection of workers' rights to privacy should be strengthened in the following two respects in China.

First, monitoring the electronic communications of employees should be legislatively prohibited. With the development of computer technology, Chinese workers produce a huge number of phone calls and e-mails every working day. In order to prevent employees from misusing of company's resources, in some private companies in China, more and more Chinese employers monitor their employee communications. Obviously, these employers seriously invade their employees' right to privacy. In fact, it has been held that such practices will alienate workers, increase their stress levels and destroy company loyalty, all of which are detrimental to overall company performance and customer service.[109] Thus, the Labor Law should be extended to prohibit electronic monitoring of workers.

Second, sexual harassment at work and other misconduct offenses should be legislatively prohibited. At present, sexual harassment has been seen as a privacy concern worldwide, involving psychological and sometimes physical harassment and intimidation.[110] How to prohibit sexual harassment at work and other offensive misconduct should be considered by China. The author believes that there should be guidelines in relation to sexual harassment at work in China. Developed countries' experiences show that it is the responsibility of management to ensure that proper standards of conduct are maintained at all times in the workplace and to make clear that sexual harassment in any form is regarded as completely unacceptable behavior, although management has no right to intrude into the personal relationships of staff.[111]

6.4.2.3 New Technology

As discussed in Chap. 2 of the book, with the rapid development of information technologies and information processing devices such as computers in China, it is now very easy for Chinese people to access, handle, and save personal information than ever before. Moreover, new technology has also increased the effectiveness of surveillance devices. Most importantly, most of them are readily available in China today. For example, the wide popularity of computers and the Internet in China has

---

[108] Labour *Law of the People's Republic of China* 1995, art 12.

[109] Knowles (2000).

[110] Australian Law Reform Commission 1983, p. 297.

[111] Australian Law Reform Commission 1983, p. 297.

permitted Chinese people to gain and save information more conveniently and easily. Traditional protection, such as Constitutional protection for the privacy of correspondence of Chinese citizens is no more adequate than ever before. Therefore, if Chinese law-makers plan to design effective laws or use existing laws for privacy protection, they must pay more attention to some particular areas of new technology in China: first, there is no legislation to regulate the use of surveillance devices in China; second, how to effectively prohibit "Chinese style internet manhunt"; and so on.

6.4.3 *Uniformity of Standards*

Given that the development of the proposed information privacy protection law in other legal areas is uneven and the areas they cover are different. Therefore, after ensuring the possibility of creating the right to privacy in the Chinese legal system, it is the time to define a uniform standard in Chinese legal system. The following paragraphs discuss the possibility of unifying privacy standards in China.

6.4.3.1 Uniformity within China

As motioned earlier, there are other laws and regulations protecting privacy. With respect to the protection of personal information, *Amendment Seven to the Criminal Law of the PRC (Draft)* suggests to add a provision to article 253 of the Chinese criminal law on protection of privacy. This provision will penalize Chinese servants who sell or unlawfully provide to others citizens' individual information that was obtained in carrying out their duties or in the course of providing services.[112] The Commercial Bank Law requires that the Commercial banks should "ensure confidentiality for depositors in handling individual savings deposits and protect their personal privacy".[113] The *Announcement of the Securities Association of China on Issuing the Interim Measures for the Management of Bona Fide Information of the Members of the Securities Association of China* states that the Securities Association of China should not disclose information about state secrets, commercial secrets and personal privacy.[114] The *Insurance Law of the PRC* requires that "the insurer or re-insurance underwriter should be obliged to keep confidential

[112] *Standing Committee of the National People's Congress Conducted the First Reading of Amendment Seven to the Criminal Law of the PRC (Draft) 2007*, art 6.

[113] *Law of the People's Republic of China on Commercial Banks* 1995, art 29.

[114] *Announcement of the Securities Association of China on Issuing the Interim Measures for the Management of Bona Fide Information of the Members of the Securities Association of China*, art 16.

information about the operations and property of the insured".[115] With respect to general trespass offences, article 245 of the *Criminal Law of the PRC* penalizes individuals "who unlawfully subjects another person to a body search or a search of his residence or unlawfully intrudes into another person's residence." With respect to theft of information, article 252 of the *Criminal Law of the PRC* penalizes who infringing upon the citizens' right of communication freedom. With respect to Computer crime laws, article 9 of *Administration of Internet Electronic Mail Services* states that:

> An Internet e-mail service provider shall have the obligations of keeping confidential the users' personal registered information and Internet e-mail addresses. An Internet e-mail service provider or any of its employees shall not illegally use any user's personal registered information or Internet e-mail address; and shall not, without consent of the user, divulge the user's personal registered information or Internet e-mail address, unless otherwise prescribed by any law or administrative regulation.

NPC's Decision on Safeguarding Internet Security protects the "legitimate physical and property rights of legal persons, social organizations and individuals, those who fall into one of the following cases that constitute a crime shall assume criminal responsibility in accordance with criminal law stipulations: (1) insulting other people or fabricating stories to slander others via the Internet; (2) illegally, intercepting, changing, or deleting other people's e-mail or other data information, thus infringing upon other people's freedom of communication; (3) engaging in theft, fraud and burglary via the Internet."[116]

In fact, careful deliberation of these provisions makes it clear that some of these provisions are protecting personal privacy information in China, but others are not. Therefore, the recommendation of this book is, for those aim to protect personal information privacy directly, the standards of protection should comply with the proposed information privacy protection law. That is because all these existing provisions have the same aim to protect information privacy. That is also the reason why I link the terms "privacy" and "personal information" together in the Proposed Chinese personal information protection law. Otherwise, different standards of information privacy protection will cause confusion in Chinese legal practice. What is needed is a clear definition of what personal information is and what the relationship between personal information and privacy in the proposed privacy legislation is, otherwise both proposed information privacy protection law and other existing provisions may not be used to protect privacy in the way it should be. On the other hand, this is not to say we should leave other intrusive conducts behind. Chinese law-maker should accept legislative responsibility to deal with other kinds of intrusive conducts that endanger privacy, such as the use of surveillance devices. As a consequence, in current China, the most important thing is that the

---

[115] *Insurance Law of the People's Republic of China* 1995, art 31.

[116] *National People's Congress Standing Committee Decision on Safeguarding Internet Security 2000*, s 4.

government, the legislative authority and proposed Privacy Protection Authority must have regard to proposals for uniformity.

6.4.3.2 Uniformity with International Standards

Unifying Chinese standards and international requirements is also significant. As mentioned earlier, article 25 of the EU Directive 95/46/EC states that the transfer to a third country of personal data should be permitted only when the third country in question ensures an adequate level of protection. In addition, China entered the WTO in 2001. Therefore, more and more trades between China and other countries will lead to increased information flows inevitably. If China hopes to take part in the global information community and achieve its benefits fully, China must set up an effective information privacy protection regime. Therefore, proposed Chinese information privacy protection law should not be substantially different from these international standards.

6.5 The Role of Chinese Government

As discussed earlier, the significance of the statutory protection for privacy is self-evident. However, statutory protection alone is unlikely to be adequate to protect privacy. Governmental action and attitude are also important to the protection of privacy in China in the future. Although the Chinese government has paid more attention to privacy protection recently, the functions of the Chinese government in privacy protection regimes are still very limited. This may be because of constitutional constraints, privacy's competing interests, and the limited legal protection of privacy in China. It is thus time for the Chinese government to play a greater role. There are two roles that the Chinese government must pursue in the near future.

First, the Chinese government should play an important role in securing protection for information privacy in the future. This can be achieved by facilitating the expending debate about privacy protection.[117] That is because the expanding discussion of privacy protection can help Chinese law-makers to aggregate different opinions and experiences, which will perfect legal protections of privacy. Moreover, the Chinese government can educate or inform information users and information collectors about the significance of protecting privacy and how to protect privacy.

Second, Chinese government must pay more attention to privacy protection across national boundaries. As mentioned elsewhere in this book, article 25 (1) of the EU Directive 95/46/EC clearly emphasized that the transfer to a third country of

[117] Cate (1997), p. 125.

personal data should be permitted only when the third country in question ensures an adequate level of protection. Article 25 (2) of the EU Directive 95/46/EC also provides that:

> the adequacy of the level of protection afforded by a third country shall be assessed in the light of all the circumstances surrounding a data transfer operation or set of data transfer operations; particular consideration shall be given to the nature of the data, the purpose and duration of the proposed processing operation or operations, the country of origin and country of final destination, the rules of law, both general and sectoral, in force in the third country in question and the professional rules and security measures which are complied with in that country.

In fact, the aim of the EU is easy to understand. All these are an effort by the EU to establish European protection for information privacy as a global standard.[118] However, the reality is that there is no adequate level of privacy protection in China. As a result, at present, it is very difficult for Chinese businesses to move personal data from Europe to China legally. If China hopes to take part in the global information community and achieve its benefits fully, Chinese government must pay more attention to privacy protection and set up an effective privacy protection regime actively. Moreover, today, discussion between Europe and other non-European countries is about how articles 25 and 26 will be interpreted and enforced.[119] The author thus suggests that the Chinese government should also negotiate the policies and other arrangements for satisfying the requirements of article 25 of the EU Directive 95/46/EC and other significant international instruments. This will be the best way to avoid trade disputes between China and the EU.

6.6 The Role of The Chinese Privacy Protection Law

6.6.1 Principles for Statutory Protection

Statutory protection is necessary to protecting privacy. It is impossible that there is an effective privacy protection regime without statutory protection. If the proposed Chinese Information Privacy Protection Act is finally enacted, it will guarantee that Chinese citizens have resource to protect their basic privacy rights. However, the premises of achieving these goals are that the Chinese personal information law must be clear and consistent. That is to say, just as important as privacy interests being protected by the proposed information privacy protection law, the personal information protection law itself should be explicit as to the clarity, consistency of its protection. In order words, Chinese citizens should be served by a deliberate and specific privacy law. With those goals in mind, at least two principles for the

---

[118] Cate (1997), p. 126.

[119] Cate (1997), p. 127.

statutory protection should be considered carefully, which are clarity and consistency.

First, the Chinese privacy protection law must be clear. That is because if the proposed information privacy protection legislation cannot be clearly and easily understood by Chinese citizens, it will harm Chinese legal practice. In addition, unclear information privacy protection law may also cause that the measures that are designed for privacy protection may conflict with other existing legal rights in China.

Second, the Chinese privacy law must be consistent. At present, privacy protection in China is only secondary purpose of some existing laws. Although *Amendment Seven to the Criminal Law of the PRC* (Draft) proposes to add a provision on protection of privacy, as mentioned earlier, the loopholes of this provision are obvious. Both the legal subjects and the objects of this provision are not sufficient. This provision only regulates the practices of the personnel of financial, telecommunications, communications, educational, and medical work units; while the objects of this provision are only to restrict the disclosure and trade of individual's information.[120] All these result that there is no effective privacy protection in China. Furthermore, this point has been emphasized by the EU Directive. EU Directive 95/46/EC clearly requires that the national laws on the processing of personal data "must not result in any lessening of the protection they afford but must, on the contrary, seek to ensure a high level of protection in the Community."[121] Therefore, Chinese privacy protection legislation should provide "a basic level of privacy protection" that is able to "yield more rational and consistent protection."[122]

6.6.2 The Need for Extending the Scope of Statutory Protection

It has been held that independent privacy protection legislation is able to promote more uniform protection, to avoid definitional problems in legislating statutes, and to eliminate the potential for conflicting interpretations of overlapping laws.[123] On the other hand, the disadvantage of a single law is also obvious. As Cate states that "an omnibus law runs the risk of imposing a one-size-fits-all legislative solution on diverse issues that occur in a wide variety of distinct contexts, thereby creating too little or too much protection in specific situations."[124] Therefore, it must be clearly understood that even if the Chinese Information Privacy Protection Act is finally

[120] *Standing Committee of the National People's Congress Conducted the First Reading of Amendment Seven to the Criminal Law of the PRC (Draft) 2007*, art 6.

[121] *Directive 95/46/EC*, recitals 10.

[122] Cate (1997), p. 110.

[123] Cate (1997), p. 120.

[124] Cate (1997), p. 120.

enacted, privacy issues will still exist in China. For example, business and industry may be particularly concerned at the prospect of privacy protection in different industrial sectors.[125] That is because most industrial sectors have already been regulated by different Chinese legislations, and the different approaches of protection for privacy may result in incompatibility in these sectors. Once the incompatibility of privacy protection exists, it will result in inconvenience and, possibly, commercial disadvantage.

On the other hand, China should not give up the efforts. In fact, based on the Western experiences of protecting privacy, a single basic law is still preferable to facilitate "the development of private mechanisms for protecting privacy and the exercise of individual choice."[126] Therefore, after considering Western experiences of privacy legislation, the author's recommendation is that, in the future, the Chinese Privacy Protection Law should be a single information privacy protection legislation, supplemented by specific legal measures for different industrial sectors. That is to say the proposed privacy protection law must tie with existing relevant laws and administrative regulations. Chinese law-makers should also pay attention to some Chinese industrial sectors that are already regulated by the Chinese legislations. For example, insurance is an area of extensive personal information in China. At present, the Chinese insurance industry has already been regulated by Chinese legislation. However, information privacy protection in the Chinese insurance industry is only a by-product of its legislative efforts. Therefore, in the future, the Chinese law-reformers and law-makers should consider if the Chinese privacy protection law should cover the insurance industry in China.

6.7 Need for the Individual Responsibility

6.7.1 Generally

At present, not only is the definition of privacy difficult to pin down, but also the application of the privacy principles is becoming more difficult than ever before. That is because, based on some particular privacy cases, the privacy principles may not be sufficient to determine what the answer will be. Individual responsibility for privacy protection means that there should be awareness among individuals of the privacy implications of their activities. Therefore, individual responsibility is also important for privacy protection in China. For example, in the computer and Internet field, individual responsibility may require the use of technological or other forms of self-help, such as encryption software; in the personal information protection regime, individual responsibility may require that the information

[125] Australian Law Reform Commission 1983, p. 187.

[126] Cate (1997), p. 121.

subject must find out why information or data is being collected and how the information collector intends to process the personal information; other individual responsibilities may include refusing to provide unnecessary personal information to product and service suppliers, changing companies, or paying with cash rather than check or credit card.[127] All these are effective means of protecting individual privacy.

6.7.2 *Self-regulation*

6.7.2.1 Significance of Self-regulation

All those mentioned above are different forms of individual responsibility. In the author's opinion, however, the most effective form of individual responsibility is self-regulation. Initially, self-regulation means an approach that stresses the value of voluntary action by members of the academic community to respond to those pressures.[128] In this book, the term of self-regulation means the individual's need to regulate his self for privacy protection. Simply, for example, one must learn about the often invisible actions of software and hardware by reading instruction manuals and help screens, finding resources about privacy in print or on the Internet, and perusing the fine print in credit and other consumer transactions.[129]

Compared to the statutory protection for privacy, self-regulation is more flexible. Based on current knowledge of privacy, even in developed countries, neither government nor privacy protection legislation can protect privacy interests in almost every aspect. However, self-regulation might promote the reputation of a community as a whole, and it might facilitate the creation of more objective standards for protecting privacy, which will benefit the community itself and society more generally.[130] Moreover, the advantages of self-regulation also include efficiency, increased incentives for compliance, and reduced cost.[131] Sometimes, it will be more effective than simple punishment, and deliver more for ordinary people than a formal legal system.[132] Therefore, once the Chinese government imposes legal duties to reinforce self-regulation, it will be beneficial both to society and to individuals, and privacy in China may be protected to the maximum level.

---

[127] Cate (1997), pp. 103–104.
[128] El-Khawas (1981), p. 56.
[129] Cate (1997), p. 103.
[130] Swire (1997).
[131] Lievrouw and Livingstone (2002), p. 441.
[132] Wakeham (1998).

6.7.2.2 How to Achieve and Improve Self-regulation?

As mentioned earlier, self-regulation is very important in the privacy domain. Therefore, any discussion of how to achieve effective self-regulation seems significant. The prerequisite to achieving effective self-regulation is that there should be impetus and expertise to perform the self-regulation in China. In order words, Chinese citizens must be voluntary to self-regulate in the first. In addition, the knowledge of how to self-regulate is also necessary. It has been held that high self-regulation reflects abstract principles and values, and appears among only a few highly educated individuals.[133] Therefore, first, education is necessary to achieve effective self-regulation in China. Education can help Chinese citizens to understand the social value of privacy, how privacy can be protected effectively, and the substantial significance of self-regulation. Moreover, education reinforces to those involved in the collection, storage and use of such information, such as journalists, what is considered acceptable.[134] At least, education leads to more widespread support of protection of privacy rights. Second, the staff of the Chinese governmental agency should be able to audit privacy self-regulation. This is because auditing self-regulation is another effective means to enforce privacy principles against the noncompliant.

Although self-regulation is significant, it should be noted that self-regulation cannot provide accurate standards of privacy protection to Chinese people. The standards of self-regulation are still indistinct. Self-regulation cannot cover every issue that will arise in the privacy domain. Moreover, under different circumstances, our experiences of self-regulation are not exactly the same. Therefore, review of self-regulation is the only way to explain different circumstances. That experience is the source of effective self-regulation.

6.7.2.3 Summary

Based on the earlier discussions, it is clear that, at the same time as being pursuant to the impartial society, self-regulation is one of the most effective ways to protect privacy. Self-regulation makes the world more fair, free, and secure. Reasonable protection of privacy, such as effective self-regulation, will benefit China. Moreover, it should bear in mind that the legislative controls in the world cannot find and regulate all immoral behavior. Therefore, an effective self-regulation mechanism is significant and necessary for China.

[133] Moral Development Milestones.

[134] Merold (1997).

6.7.3 *Evaluation*

Individual responsibility is significant, but it is not a panacea.[135] The private nature of individual responsibility may fail to give adequate attention to the needs of the public; for example: the lack of public disclosure of, and scrutiny over, corporate privacy policies; the unwillingness of companies and industrial organizations to take privacy protection seriously; and the failure of many of these groups to act consistently with their public pronouncements on privacy or to live up to the promises they make.[136] In fact, individual responsibility in the privacy domain can be seen as a game that depending on collaboration between two parties. Therefore, the possibility that individual responsibility of practice can offer a sustainable, effective and comprehensive alternative to statutory regulation depends on a range of factors including the Privacy Act, individual's awareness, public policy objectives and a host of other variables.[137]

6.8 Consideration of the Reform Draft

It should be noted that Chinese government also proposes to enact a privacy protection law in recent years. The initial aim of enacting privacy protection law is "to promote confidence in financial systems to encourage individuals to trust banks as guardians of their wealth and providers of liquidity to finance the economy."[138] Based on the current situation, it has been held that there are several possible routes that the Chinese privacy protection law might be enacted, which are:

1. Regulations that the regulatory authority issues over the financial services sector – these would be limited in scope and focus on credit reporting, but could be implemented quickly.
2. "Administrative" regulations – these would be preliminary but could be enacted quickly and would pave the way for a more comprehensive law to be enacted at a future point.
3. A national law that governs personal data that the Standing Committee or the National People's Congress pass. This is a longer-term prospect, but would result in a more comprehensive, more permanent, law or
4. A provincial law, as in California, with the passing of the first US data breach law.[139]

---

[135] Cate (1997), p. 108.

[136] Cate (1997), p. 108.

[137] Internet Self-Regulation: An Overview 2000.

[138] Treacy and Abrams (2008).

[139] Treacy and Abrams (2008).

In fact, it is clear that the Chinese government's approach of reforming is not on the basis of the demand of Chinese people and the fundamental human rights issues, as the most Western developed countries are. Privacy protection law is only the Chinese leaders' desirability of establishing a more modern economy. Therefore, it is inevitable that the draft of this legislation would face difficulties. At present, there are no real signs that this draft privacy law will be enacted in China in the near future.[140] Due to the limitation of the materials and information about the Chinese reform draft, the author of the book cannot discuss the draft law adequately and accurately.

6.9 The Recommended Legislative Scheme

This Law affirms the protection for information privacy of the Chinese Citizens in legal form.

Scope and Application

1. The Legislation must be clarity and consistency.
2. The Legislation's goal is the protection of personal information in the PRC.
3. The Legislation should apply to both the public sector and the private sector. There should not be any discrimination in legislative controls as between the public and private sector, and the controls should be uniform in PRC.
4. The Legislation should apply to personal information, however, recorded.
5. The Legislation should be applicable to particular types of data, organizations, and sectors in the PRC.
6. The Legislation should be consistent with the global trend of privacy and personal information protection law.

Definitions

1. The Legislation should define "personal information" in the first. The recommendation is that the definition contained in *Directive 95/46/EC on the protection of individuals with regard to the processing of personal data and on the free movement of such data* should be adopted.
2. In the case of this Legislation, the activity and the persons regulated should be those who process personal information. The Legislation should define "information user" and "information subject",respectively.
3. Another term which should be defined carefully is "data." The Legislation must ensure the definition is adequate enough to cover personal information, however, recorded.

[140] Treacy and Abrams (2008).

Information Privacy Protection Principles

Information privacy protection principles are the basic rules governing the collection, handling, use and disclosure of personal information. Therefore, information privacy protection principles are the standards, which should be imposed on all organizations and individuals who possess or process personal information in the PRC.

1. The Information Privacy Protection Principles will be the core of the Legislation. Whether the Legislation is effective will depend on how these principles are constructed.
2. The Information Privacy Protection Principles should be expressed in broad terms.
3. The Information Privacy Protection Principles should be minimum standards for general application in the PRC;
4. Possible exemptions for particular cases should be addressed in other part of the Legislation.
5. The standards set out in the Information Privacy Protection Principles should meet the standards required by *OECD Guidelines on the Protection of Privacy and Transborder Flows of Personal Data* and *Directive 95/46/EC on the protection of individuals with regard to the processing of personal data and on the free movement of such data.*
6. The Information Privacy Protection Principles in the PRC should include:

   (a) Manner and Purpose of collection of personal information
   (b) Data quality
   (c) Security of data containing personal information
   (d) Storage of data containing personal information
   (e) Openness of data containing personal information
   (f) Access to data containing personal information
   (g) Alteration of data containing personal information
   (h) Requirements to check accuracy of personal information
   (i) Use and disposal of data containing personal information

Exemptions

Based on the standards in *Directive 95/46/EC on the protection of individuals with regard to the processing of personal data and on the free movement of such data*, the Legislation must allow certain information processing applications exemption from requirements of proposed Information Privacy Protection Principles.

1. The possible exemptions should be kept to a minimum. That is because it is important to ensure that privacy protection applies as widely as possible.
2. The possible exemptions should be set out together in one part of the Legislation, which would make the exemption provisions more accessible.
3. The possible exemption provisions in the Legislation should not be overly complicated.

Offences and Remedies

The Legislation should entitle an individual who is the subject of personal information held by an information user, and who suffers damage by reason of the inaccuracy and unauthorized access of the information, to get compensation from the information user for such damage.

Establishment of the Personal Information Protection Commissioner

The Legislation should establish the constitution of Chinese Personal Information Protection Commission.

Appointment and Dismissal of Personal Information Protection Commissioner

The Commissioner should be nominated by the Chinese Government, but dismissed only on the approval of the NPC.

Commissioner's Functions and Powers

1. The types of functions performed by the Commissioner should include:
    (a) Promoting and perfecting proposed information privacy protection principles;
    (b) Researching and investigating acts, practices or developments in information processing and computer technology to ensure the adverse influences are minimized in China;
    (c) Ensuring agencies, which may handle personal information, to comply with the proposed privacy protection principles;
    (d) Considering the Chinese information privacy protection legislation in all reasonable areas and ensuring that any adverse conflicts between privacy and other competing interests are minimized;
    (e) Considering China's international obligations and relevant international guidelines on privacy;
    (f) Providing advice to the Chinese NPC, Chinese government and others.
2. The Commissioner's powers should include:
    (a) The power to oversee the operation of the Legislation. The general oversight power relate to the giving of advice, research and monitoring of technological developments, and education
    (b) The power to monitor and promote compliance with the Legislation, such as power to monitor whether the proposed legislation has been complied and to investigate privacy issues
    (c) The Commissioner should also have complaint handling powers, such as power to conduct investigations into a complaint, power to decide whether compensation should be paid to the complainant
    (d) The power to make public statements
    (e) The power to make special reports to the NPC
    (f) The power for enforcement and review of determinations.

The Provision of Expert Assistance

There should be a provision in the Legislation, which will entitle the Information Privacy Protection Commission to obtain assistance from experts for the purpose of protecting personal information. These experts may include people, who are expertise in information processing technology, Internet, system and so on.

Staff

1. Staff should be impetus and expertise to perform the personal information protection.
2. Staff should be employed by the China's Information Privacy Protection Authority, and be under the control and direction of the Authority.

References

Journal Articles and Books

Bainbridge D (2001) Data protection. CLT Professional, Welwyn Garden City

Chao JC (2005) Protecting the right to privacy in China. Vict Univ Wellin Law Rev 36:645

Cate FH (1997) Privacy in the information age. Brooking Institution Press, Washington, DC

El-Khawas E (1981) Self-regulation: an approach to ethical standards new. Directions for Higher Education 33:55

Lee K (2007) China and the International covenant on civil and political rights: prospects and challenges. Chinese J Int Law 6:445

Lievrouw LA, Livingstone SM (eds) (2002) Handbook of new media. SAGE, London

SA Oxman (2000–2001) Exemptions to the European Union personal date privacy directive: will they swallow the directive? Boston College International and Comparative Law Review 24:191

Savage N, Edwards C (1985) A guide to the data protection act: implementing the act. Blackstone Press, London

Wacks R (1989) Personal Information: Privacy and the Law. Oxford University Press, Oxford

Legislation

Announcement of the Securities Association of China on Issuing the Interim Measures for the Management of Bona Fide Information of the Members of the Securities Association of China

Asia–Pacific Economic Cooperation, APEC Privacy Framework (2005)

Constitution of the People's Republic of China 1982

Copyright Law of the People's Republic of China 1990

Data Protection Act 1998 (UK)

Directive 95/46/EC of the European Parliament and of the Council of 24 October 1995 on the protection of individuals with regard to the processing of personal data and on the free movement of such data, Official Journal of the European Communities of 23 November 1995 No L 281 (1995)

General Principles of the Civil Law of the People's Republic of China 1986

Insurance Law of the People's Republic of China 1995

International Covenant on Civil and Political Rights, opened for signature 16 December 1966, 999 UNTS 171, 6 ILM 368 (entered into force 23 March 1976)
Labour Law of the People's Republic of China 1995
Law of the People's Republic of China on Commercial Banks 1995
Law of the People's Republic of China on the Protection of the Rights and Interests of Consumers
National People's Congress Standing Committee Decision on Safeguarding Internet Security 2000
Organization for Economic Co-operation and Development, Guidelines on the Protection of Privacy and Transborder Flows of Personal Data (1980)
Privacy Act 1983 (Canada)
Privacy Act of 1974 (US)
Privacy Act 1988 (Cth)
Standing Committee of the National People's Congress conducted the first reading of Amendment Seven to the Criminal Law of the PRC (Draft) 2007

Government and Law Reform Reports

Australian Law Reform Commission (1980) Privacy and Personal Information. Discussion Paper 14
Australian Law Reform Commission (1983) Privacy. Report paper No. 22 Volume 1
Australian Law Reform Commission (1983) Privacy. Report paper No. 22 Volume 2
Australian Law Reform Commission (2006) Review of privacy. Issue Paper 31
Privacy Committee of New South Wales (1980) Privacy Protection: Guidelines or Legislation?
Privacy Committee of New South Wales (1991) Privacy and Data Protection in New South Wales.

Electronic Materials

Clarke R (1998) Exemptions from general principles versus balanced implementation of universal principles http://www.privacy.gov.au/act/review/Att3-Except.pdf. Accessed 8 April 2011
Internet Self-Regulation: An Overview (2000) Selfregulation.info http://pcmlp.socleg.ox.ac.uk/selfregulation/iapcoda/030329-selfreg-global-report.htm. Accessed 8 April 2011
Knowles B (2000) Are employers violating worker's privacy with electronic monitoring? http://www.speakout.com/activism/issue_briefs/1300b-1.html. Accessed 8 April 2011
Moral Development http://www.abacon.com/berk/cd/cdmile510.pdf. Accessed 8 April 2011
Merold RN The necessary elements of self-regulatory privacy regimes and the role of consumer education in a self-regulatory privacy regime National Telecommunications and Information Administration (NTIA) http://www.ntia.doc.gov/reports/privacy/selfreg4.htm. Accessed 8 April 2011
OECD Minister (1998) Ministerial declaration on the protection on privacy on global networks http://www.austlii.edu.au/au/journals/PLPR/1998/73.html. Accessed 8 April 2011
Swire PP (1997) Markets, self-regulation, and government enforcement in the protection of personal information. Social science research networks http://papers.ssrn.com/sol3/papers.cfm?abstract_id=11472. Accessed 8 April 2011
Treacy B, Abrams M (2008) A privacy law for china. Hunton & Williams http://www.hunton.com/files/tbl_s47Details%5CFileUpload265%5C2269%5Cprivacy_law_for_China.pdf. Accessed 8 April 2011
Wakeham L (1998) Can self-regulation achieve more than law? http://www.pcc.org.uk/news/index.html?article=NjY=. Accessed 8 April 2011

Chapter 7
Conclusion: Chinese Privacy in the Twenty-First Century

7.1 Introduction

Privacy is a necessary element of quality life in modern society.[1] Although rapid development of technology has made it impossible to foresee the development trend of privacy with certainty, it is significant for Chinese lawmakers to consider the future. This chapter thus looks ahead to possible developments, which might affect privacy in China. In this chapter, the significance of the privacy balance will be restated briefly. Moreover, a number of other possible future developments, which could affect the direction of Chinese privacy legislation, will be briefly discussed.

7.2 The Significance of the Privacy Balance

As discussed in this book, privacy interests vary significantly and often conflict with other existing values in China, such as interest in freedom of expression, freedom of the press, freedom of information, law enforcement, and so on. Western developed countries' experiences demonstrate that privacy interests "even conflict with what may seem to be more mundane interests such as the desire for instant credit, better targeted mass mailings, lower insurance rates, faster services when ordering merchandize by telephone, qualified employees, or special recognition for frequent travelers."[2] It is thus clear that privacy interests are not absolute. Privacy is significant and necessary, but it is not all. As Cate states,

[1] Cate (1997), p. 101.
[2] Cate (1997), p. 102.

H. Wang, *Protecting Privacy in China*,

DOI 10.1007/978-3-642-21750-0_7,

> Privacy is only one of the elements essential to modern life . . . It is therefore only one tool, which must be used in coordination with other tools, to achieve the ends we desire, such as self-fulfillment and self-determination, societal productivity, and higher quality of life. As a result, individuals and institutions as a whole share an interest in identifying and facilitating those means – including privacy – that are necessary to achieve desired ends. What is needed is a balance, of which privacy is part.[3]

Likewise, what is needed for China is also a balance. As discussed in Chap. 5 of this book, privacy must be weighed, with complementary and associated interests, against competing public and private interests.[4] That is to say, on the one hand, privacy interests must be weighed with any complementary interests such as in reputation and portrait, which overlap with privacy interests but do not precisely coincide with them; on the other hand, in this weighing process, Chinese lawmakers must balance certain competing interests relevant in the context such as freedom of expression and freedom of the press in which it is being expressed.[5] If China fails to consider the importance of the existence of different values, the Chinese protection for privacy will not be workable or desirable.

7.3 Other Possible Developments in China

It is also the time to discuss some possible developments which will influence the future developments for privacy protection in China. Based on the Western developed countries' experiences of protecting privacy, main developments in China may include: the new information technology; the need for social education to ensure privacy protection principles are adequately recognized; and the regulation of trans-border data flows, respectively.[6]

7.3.1 Development of New Technology

If possible, the Chinese law-reformers and lawmakers should regularly review the development of new information technologies in China. It is indisputable that the rapid development of new information technology in Chinese contemporary society provides many advantages to Chinese people. However, sometimes, some of these new information technologies also invade ordinary people's privacy interests. Therefore, in order to avoid this social phenomenon, Chinese lawmakers or reformers should regularly review the development of new information

[3] Cate (1997), pp. 101–102.

[4] Australian Law Reform Commission 1983, p. 20.

[5] Australian Law Reform Commission 1983, pp. 20–21.

[6] Australian Law Reform Commission 1983, p. 201.

technologies that may be relevant to Chinese privacy protection. With this goal in mind, there is a need for the Chinese government to appoint specialist personnel, who are able to comprehend and recognize the privacy implications of new technology in the future China.[7]

7.3.2 *Society Education*

Society education is one of effective ways to ensure that the privacy protection and self-regulation are adequately recognized in China. It will promote the self-regulation and complaints mechanisms. In West, it has been held that these two mechanisms are more likely to be used by the educated and articulate than the poor, disadvantaged, and inarticulate, and so society education will assume a special importance as an effective way of assuring the privacy of disadvantaged groups in a society.[8] Therefore, if the proposed Chinese information privacy protection legislation is finally enacted, the Chinese government should attach the highest importance to informing the current society about privacy protection principles with information concerning the way in which any concerned Chinese people can pursue his rights.[9]

7.3.3 *Trans-border Flows of Personal Information*

Finally, it will be significant for China to consider trans-border flows of information. With the development of information technology, trans-border flows of information are increasing promptly. The basic philosophy for implementing domestically the privacy protection rights granted to individual data subjects is expressed in the OECD Guideline:

1. Provide the reasonable means for individuals to exercise their privacy rights
2. Encourage and support self-regulation, whether in the form of codes of conduct or otherwise
3. Provide for adequate sanctions and remedies in case of failures to comply with privacy protection requirements
4. Establish legal, administrative, or other procedures or institutions for the protection of privacy and individual liberties in respect of personal data and
5. Ensure that there is no unfair discrimination against data subjects.[10]

---

[7] Australian Law Reform Commission 1983, p. 202.

[8] Australian Law Reform Commission 1983, p. 202.

[9] Australian Law Reform Commission 1983, p. 203.

[10] Turn (1979), pp. 91–92.

Based on the Australia's experiences, the Chinese government should provide that Chinese residents have the right of access and amendment of personal information, data and records, even if held outside China.[11] In addition, the information subject should also have right to access the information that is held in overseas about Chinese residents, but available to companies and others in China.[12] It is a legitimate future concern of the Chinese government, not only to protect the interests of China, but also to ensure that information can move in and out of China under conditions that ensure appropriate respect for individual privacy.[13]

7.4 Conclusion

The rapid development of technology in modern society has increased concern about privacy in China. As Cate states that:

> How those concerns have been and should be addressed depends on many factors: how privacy is defined; what values privacy is perceived to serve; which values conflict or are affected by the protection of privacy; the societal, legal, and cultural setting in which the issues are raised; and the services, products, and benefits associated with the activities that impinge on personal privacy.[14]

The author acknowledges that absolute right to privacy would mean a total withdrawal from contact with others, and for most people this is clearly undesirable. Privacy, therefore, involves establishing a balance between different values. That is to say, China must clearly realize that the protection of privacy is always balanced with competing rights. Therefore, the legal protection of privacy in China should serve as a gap-filler, facilitating individual action in those situations in which consent and other forms of self-help are unworkable or inapplicable.[15]

The Chinese lawmakers should not only pay attention to privacy protection in theory, they should also ensure some real protection for privacy rights in practice. At least, the Chinese government should create the right to privacy and establish an effective privacy protection regime under the Chinese legal system. At the same time, the Chinese government should play a significant role to popularize the privacy protection principles in Chinese society, to enact or reform any laws when it is necessary to protect Chinese people's privacy interests, to solve the problems when privacy interests in conflict with other existing values, to negotiate with other countries when problems of Trans-border flows of information emerges. In addition, the long-term goal of Chinese privacy protection should enact basic

---

[11] Australian Law Reform Commission 1983, p. 206.

[12] Australian Law Reform Commission 1983, p. 206.

[13] Australian Law Reform Commission 1983, p. 206.

[14] Cate (1997), pp. 129–130.

[15] Cate (1997), p. 131.

principles of privacy protection to facilitate the activities of information users and the valuable services and products they offer, ensure consistent international privacy protection for personal information, and reduce the cost of administering and complying with inconsistent national legal regimes.[16] Moreover, it should be noted that the protection of privacy requires not only national legal protections but also individual responsibility, such as self-regulation. Also, prohibiting unlawful statutory power to the maximum level and studying other developed countries' successful experiences of how to deal with privacy issues are also necessary. China needs to have an honest discussion about the pain of adjustment.

Today, China's status on the international stage and Chinese jurists' efforts, have confirmed the Chinese government's confidence in protecting privacy. The reality that the protection of privacy delivers real and sustainable results to Chinese people's lives cannot be easily changed. The protection of privacy expands opportunities in people's normal lives. It creates equality, freedom, and fairness for human beings. Although barriers to the protection of privacy still exist, the author believes, through government's efforts, that these barriers will decrease steadily and Chinese people will accept the concept of privacy rights absolutely. China is a volunteer, not a conscript, in achieving the protection of privacy and building on more open and fair jurisdiction.

The question of how to reasonably deal with privacy issues will be the most significant debate in the Chinese juristic domain in the near future. Therefore, it is hoped that this book will provide an inspiration, or a precedent, for further studies in relation to the protection of privacy in China.

References

Books

Cate FH (1997) Privacy in the information age. Brooking Institution Press, London

Turn R (ed) (1979) Transborder data flows: concerns in privacy protection and free flow of information. American Federation of Information Processing Societies, Washington, DC

Government and Law Reform Reports

Australian Law Reform Commission (1983) Privacy. Report paper No. 22 Volume 1

Australian Law Reform Commission (1983) Privacy. Report paper No. 22 Volume 2

[16] Cate (1997), p. 132.

MIX
Papier aus verantwortungsvollen Quellen
Paper from responsible sources
FSC® C105338

If you have any concerns about our products,
you can contact us on
ProductSafety@springernature.com

In case Publisher is established outside the EU,
the EU authorized representative is:
Springer Nature Customer Service Center GmbH
Europaplatz 3, 69115 Heidelberg, Germany

Printed by Libri Plureos GmbH
in Hamburg, Germany